Quick Guide to Financial Formulas
For 1-2-3 Users

Steve Adams

Brady

New York London Toronto Sydney Tokyo Singapore

LOTUS BOOKS

Published by Brady Computer Books
A Divison of Simon & Schuster, Inc.
15 Columbus Circle
New York, NY 10023

Manufactured in the United States of America

10 9 8 7 6 5 4 3 2 1

Library of Congress Cataloging-in-Publication Data

Adams, Steve. 1948-
   Quick guide to financial formulas for 1-2-3 users / Steve Adams.
      p.   cm.
   Includes index.
   1. Business mathematics—Data processing. 2. Lotus 1-2-3
(computer program) I. Title. II. Title: Quick guide to financial
formulas for one-two-three users.
HF5691.A28   1990
332'.0285'5369--dc20   90-39565
                                                    CIP

ISBN 0-13-745134-2

For information about our audio products, write us at:
Newbridge Book Clubs, 3000 Cindel Drive, Delran, NJ   08370

Quick Guide to Financial Formulas for 1-2-3 Users

LOTUS BOOKS Business Solutions Series

Who This Book Is For

Business-oriented users of 1-2-3 at all levels—managers, small business owners, entrepreneurs, business students, and those planning their personal finances.

What's Inside

- Hands-on introduction to industry standard financial formulas—explains key financial concepts and shows how to implement them quickly in 1-2-3.

- Practical methods for calculating loans, leases, effective interest rates, stocks and bonds, return on investment, depreciation, personal income tax, and more—all topics are illustrated with real-life examples and complete 1-2-3 models.

- Bonus guide to all 1-2-3 @functions at the back of the book.

About *LOTUS BOOKS*

LOTUS BOOKS, written in collaboration with Lotus Development Corporation, help you derive the most from Lotus software. These books comprise four series:

Start Here books introduce first-time users to Lotus software with simple step-by-step instructions.

Complete Guides provide indispensable references and tutorials for users at all levels.

Business Solutions address specific business problems and provide tools to help make better business decisions.

Technical Reference provide advanced material for power users, programmers, and application developers.

Table of Contents

Limits of Liability and Disclaimer of Warranty

Trademarks

Introduction

If a house appreciates at 10% per year, how much will it be worth in seven years? If you deposit $10,000 in a three-year certificate of deposit, how much will you have when it matures? If a college education costs $20,000 today and expenses increase by 5% per year, how much will college cost when Mary enters college in 12 years? If sales increase 1% per month, what will the sales volume be in three years?

The same formula will solve all of these problems. However, Lotus 1-2-3 has no built-in function for it. The formula is fairly simple. Do you know it? Look around your office. Is there a convenient place to look it up?

Here it is:

$$FV = PV(1+i)^n$$

where FV is the future value; PV is the present value; i is the periodic interest rate; and n is the number of periods.

Quick Guide to Financial Formulas for 1-2-3 Users explains this formula (see Chapter 1) along with dozens of other mathematical calculations and @Function applications that are used in business, financial management, statistics, and other fields. *Quick Guide to Financial Formulas for 1-2-3 Users* will help any 1-2-3 user build more powerful worksheets—executives, managers, small-business owners, students, and home users. Even professional financial managers who are well versed in financial calculations will find it a helpful reference for applications that are not committed to memory. Beginning spreadsheet users will find that it unlocks the power of 1-2-3 in ways they may not have even considered.

All of the models and examples in this book can be created with 1-2-3 Release 2 or later; none requires Release 2.2 or 3.0. Nearly all of the models can be set up with any release. In a few cases, however, you will have to adapt the models slightly for earlier releases. This is explained when the need arises.

Quick Guide to Financial Formulas for 1-2-3 Users Is Different

There is no mystery why 1-2-3 is the standard by which other programs are judged. It is extremely powerful and versatile. And—up to a point, at least—it is easy to learn and to use. All this power and versatility, however, can get in the way of putting 1-2-3 to work to solve real-life problems. The trick is to get 1-2-3 to do exactly what you want it to do, without having to wade through long explanations of extraneous information.

A reader browsing through this introduction in a book store has a wide range of choices. There may be any number of books about 1-2-3. Some are primers, intended to get you started. Some are encyclopedic, explaining everything 1-2-3 can do. A few of the latter are better, at least in some respects, than the Lotus manuals; many are not. Even the best do not provide much help with building your own worksheets.

Other books (and computer programs) contain massive 1-2-3 worksheets designed for specific purposes. They may tell you exactly what to do if your assumptions happen to be the same as the author's. But the assumptions often don't match. You can, for example, enter equivalent values over five years into two well-known, commercially available programs that include lease-purchase models and get results for present value that differ by more than $10,000 on a $100,000 asset. Both are right on their own terms, but their assumptions are different. (One assumes that all payments are at the beginning of the year, calculates payments and interest on an annual basis, and uses the Modified Accelerated Cost Recovery System (MACRS) for depreciation. The other assumes all payments occur at the end of the year, calculates payments and interest on a monthly basis, and uses straight-line depreciation.) Either could—and probably would—get you into trouble on tax calculations.

In a university bookstore, you will also find excellent texts on finance, economics, portfolio management, statistics, and many other topics. These books are long on theory, and their examples are deliberately generalized and simplified for the sake of illustration. It will take some work to adapt them to your own practical situation.

In the end, you have to build your own 1-2-3 models, and the beauty of the program is that it lets you do that. That's what *Quick Guide to Financial Formulas for 1-2-3 Users* is about. There are no grand models or theories, only nuts and bolts. For each application, there are brief and practical explanations. Simple worksheet models break the calculations down into steps. Sample problems and solutions *show* (rather than tell) you how to use the formula. When you get the right answer, you'll know you're using the formula properly. In short, this book gives hands-on explanations of the formulas, @Functions, and techniques you need to build your own models with 1-2-3.

What You Need to Know

Quick Guide to Financial Formulas for 1-2-3 Users makes no assumptions about your knowledge of mathematics or finance. The book also makes few assumptions about your knowledge of 1-2-3. However, it is not a primer. Even a novice can begin to take advantage of 1-2-3's potential using this book, but if you're just beginning to use the program, you may want to refer to the manual or another basic text. When in doubt, you can usually get the information you need on the screen simply by pressing F1 for Help. Anyone who has completed a simple introductory tutorial, either from the Lotus manual or another source, should not have any difficulty.

Nevertheless, the emphasis of this book is on solving problems with 1-2-3, not simply on running the program. You should know, for example, how 1-2-3's basic slash (/) commands and their menus work. Generally, when / commands are used, a brief explanation is provided in the text. However, it is assumed that you know how to use the basic commands. For example, you should already know how to save a worksheet with /**F**ile **S**ave and retrieve one with /**F**ile **R**etrieve. You will also need a rudimentary understanding of entering and editing formulas, how @Functions work (specific @Functions are explained where they are used), defining and formatting ranges, setting column widths, inserting and deleting columns and rows, the /Copy command, and absolute and relative cell references. A very brief explanation of these features is provided here.

Saving and Retrieving Files

When you first start up 1-2-3, you see a blank worksheet. You simply begin entering labels, values, and formulas to create a worksheet. A new worksheet has no name until the first time you save it. Particularly when you are building a complex worksheet, it is a good idea to save the new version every time you make a significant change or addition. That way, if you make a mistake, you can simply retrieve the last version rather than erasing your latest entries or repeating steps you have already completed.

You cannot save a completely blank worksheet. You must do something—it could be anything—first. It could be entering something into a cell, entering a range format, or setting a new column width. When you enter the /File Save command, 1-2-3 asks you, "Enter name of file to save:" The program automatically enters the path name of the current directory. If you are saving a new file in Release 2, for example, and you are using a subdirectory named 123, you would see, "Enter name of file to save: C:\123*.WK1". (With Release 1A, the extension will be .WKS; with release 3, it will be .WK3.)

When you execute /File Save, a list of the existing worksheet files in the current directory will appear in the control panel at the top of the screen, with the first one highlighted. If you want to overwrite an existing file, simply select the name you want to use with the arrow keys and press Enter. In most cases, however, you will want to assign a new name to the file when you are creating a new worksheet. To save the worksheet in the current directory, simply type the new name and press Enter. In most cases, you don't need to worry about an extension (.WKS, .WK1, or .WK3) because 1-2-3 will supply it automatically. Thus, you can simply type P&L to save a profit-and-loss statement under that name.

Note: With Releases 2 and 3 you can save a file in the format of the next earlier release. Thus, to save a Release 2 worksheet as a .WKS file, you might enter P&L.WKS. With Release 3, you could save the file as P&L.WK1. However, you cannot create a .WKS file with Release 3. Note also that if you have a Release 3 file with multiple worksheets or a file that is sealed, you must use the Translate utility to convert the file to the .WK1 format. See your manual for details.

If you are saving a worksheet that you have saved before or if you want to save a file in a different subdirectory or different disk, there are several possible routes to saving the file. When you save a file that you have saved before, 1-2-3 automatically enters the old path and file name. For example, if you have already saved a file named C:\123\P&L.WK1, you will see, "Enter name of file to save: C:\123\P&L.WK1." You have these options:

1. To save the file under the old name, simply press Enter. With all releases, you can select Cancel to avoid overwriting the old file or Replace to save the new version in its place. Beginning with Release 2, you also can select Backup. In this case, the new worksheet is saved as P&L.WK1, and the older version is preserved as P&L.BAK.

2. To save the file under a new name, type the new name and press Enter. You might, for example, rename your file P&LQTR1 to create a first-quarter P&L statement. The old file will remain intact.

3. To save the file in a new directory or on a different disk, press Esc until the old path and file names are erased. For example, to save P&L on a disk in drive A, you would press Esc until the path is erased, type A:P&L, and then press Enter. Similarly, if you have a subdirectory named \123\STATEMENTS, you could press Esc to erase the default entry and then type C:\123\STATEMENTS\P&L to save the file in that subdirectory. (Actually, you need to include only the lowest level of the path you are changing. If the new subdirectory is on the same disk as the old one, you don't have to include C: to designate the current disk. If the current subdirectory

is C:\123\DATA, then simply entering \STATEMENTS\P&L will do the job.)

Again, 1-2-3 automatically provides the correct extensions when you use any of these options. With Releases 2 and 3, you can use any of these methods to save a file in the format for the previous release by adding the appropriate extension, .WKS or .WK1.

Once a file is saved, you can retrieve it with the /File Retrieve command. When you execute the command, 1-2-3 asks "Name of file to retrieve." Initially, the current path name is entered (C:\123\STATEMENTS*.wk?, for example). A list of the worksheet files in the current directory appears in the control panel, with the first one highlighted. To retrieve a file, you can use the arrow keys and press Enter to select a worksheet from the list or type the name of the file you want to retrieve. If you want to retrieve the worksheet named P&L from the current directory, for example, you can simply type P&L. 1-2-3 automatically supplies the path and extension (such as .WK1).

To retrieve a file from a different directory, press Esc until you have erased the path name from the prompt and then type the name of the file, including the full path name. To retrieve a file named P&L from drive A, for example, you would press Esc until the current path name is erased from the prompt and then type A:P&L. If the P&L file were in C:\123\DATA, you would type C:\123\DATA\P&L. (Again, you need to type only the lowest level of the path name. Thus, if the current directory is C:\123, you could retrieve P&L from C:\123\DATA simply by typing \DATA\P&L.)

Remember that anything currently on the screen is erased when you retrieve a file. Thus, you should be careful to save any worksheet you are working on before you retrieve another.

Using Formulas and @Functions

You can make three types of entries in a cell on your worksheet. The first is a simple value—that is, any number. The second is a label. 1-2-3 will treat any entry that begins with a letter (or any other character other than a number, +, -, or @ in an entry designating one of the program's built-in functions) as a label. You can convert value to a label by preceding the entry with one of three special characters: '10 creates the label 10, aligned flush left; ^10 creates the label 10, centered; and "10 creates the label 10, aligned flush right. You can also use ^ or " to align any label that starts with a letter or another character other than +, -, or @. Labels always have the numerical value of 0 when you perform mathematical operations. The third type of entry is a formula, the most basic way to tap the power of 1-2-3, as we are about to see.

Entering Simple Math Formulas

The simplest type of 1-2-3 formula is a simple mathematical calculation, using the basic mathematical operators + (addition), - (subtraction), * (multiplication), / (division), and ^ (exponentiation). For example, the formula 4+2 returns a value of 6, 4-2 returns 2, 4*2 returns 8, 4/2 yields 2, and 4^2 yields 16 (4 to the second power, or 4 squared).

Generally, 1-2-3 performs exponentiation first, then multiplication and division, and then addition and subtraction, regardless of the order in which the operators are entered. Thus, 2+2*2^2=10 because 2^2=4, 2*4=8, and 2+8=10. However, you can use parentheses to override the natural order of calculation. Any calculation enclosed in parentheses is performed before the natural order takes effect. Thus, 2+(2*2)^2=18 because 2*2=4, 4^2=16, and 2+16=18. On the other hand, (2+2*2)^2=36 because 2*2=4, 2+4=6, and 6^2=36. You can perform other variations: ((2+2)*2)^2=64; (2+2)*2^2=16; and so on. Just remember that 1-2-3 performs the calculations within each set of parentheses first and then follows the natural order of calculation.

Many simple mathematical formulas are used throughout the book. There are two limitations, however. First, if one of the variables in the formula changes, you have to change the basic formula. Second, simple mathematical formulas do not take advantage of 1-2-3's powerful @Functions, which can reduce complex mathematical formulas to a simple entry.

You can use cell references to overcome the first obstacle. In a formula, a cell reference refers to the value in a designated cell. When a cell reference appears at the beginning of a formula, it must be preceded by +, -, or ((opening parenthesis). Suppose, for example, that you enter the value 2 in A1. In A2, you can enter +A1+2. The result is 4. If you enter -A1+2 or +A1-2, the result is 0 because -2+2 and 2-2 both equal 0. The formulas will recalculate automatically if you change the value in A1. Suppose, for example, that you change the value in A1 from 2 to 4. Now, +A1+2 = 6, -A1+2 = -2, and +A1-2 = 2. You can use a reference to a cell any time a value is called for in a formula. Remember that a cell reference at the beginning of a formula must be preceded by +, -, or (. Otherwise, 1-2-3 will interpret the entry as a label.

Expanding Your Calculations with @Functions

@Functions allow you to reduce complex mathematical calculations to simple forms. You can use them to add columns or rows of numbers, to perform complex calculations involving the time value of money, to extract specific information from your worksheet, or to perform a wide variety of other specialized tasks. All of the @Functions used in this book are explained as they appear. In addition, Chapter 9 provides a complete guide to all of 1-2-3's built-in functions. At this point, all you need is a general understanding of how @Functions work.

All @Functions begin with an @ sign. 1-2-3 will accept this in any formula, whether the @ sign appears at the beginning of the formula or somewhere within it. They always require this format:

```
@FUNCTION(argument)
```

where @FUNCTION is the name of the function (preceded by the @ sign), and the argument is a set of values on which the function calculation is based. The argument is enclosed in parentheses. The components of an argument are separated by commas; there are generally no spaces included. Thus, the general format is

```
@FUNCTION(argument1,argument2,argument3,...)
```

The most basic @Function is @SUM(range). This function adds up the values in the range designated in the argument. Range can be a series of values, a range of cells, or the name of a range you have designated with the /Range Name Create command. (Ranges are explained further below). For example, the formula @SUM(2,3,4) = 9. If you enter 2 in A1, 3 in A2, and 4 in A3, you can get the same result with @SUM(A1,A2,A3) or with @SUM(A1..A3), where A1..A3 defines the range of cells that contain the values you want to total.

The arguments for @Functions vary considerably. Again, @Functions are explained as they are used, and Chapter 9 provides a guide to all 1-2-3 @Functions, including those for Releases 2.2 and 3.0.

Editing Formulas

The F2 function key is one of the most important on your keyboard when you use 1-2-3. It allows you to edit cell entries, rather than entering an entire new formula. This is particularly useful when you want to modify a complicated formula. To edit a formula, simply position the pointer in the cell you want to revise and press F2. The contents of the cell will be displayed in the control panel.

Initially, the cursor will be at the end of the entry. You can now use the left and right arrow keys to move around within the formula. You can also press Home to move to the beginning of the formula or End to move to the end. Normally, 1-2-3 is in the Insert mode. This means that any characters to the right of the cursor will be pushed to the right as you type. You can switch to the overwrite mode (OVR) by pressing Ins once, and back to insert by pressing the key again. To record a change, simply press Enter or move the pointer up or down with the cursor keys. (The right and left arrow keys move the cursor within the cell entry.)

Suppose, for example, that you have accidentally entered Profets instead of Profits as a label in A1. Just move the pointer to A1 and press F2 to edit the entry. Now move the cursor to the e, press Del to erase it, type i to replace it, and then press Enter to record the change. Or, suppose you have entered the value 1-2-3 in a cell when you meant to enter a label referring to the program. (As a value, the display will be -4 because the entry looks like the formula 1 minus 2 minus 3.) To correct the error, press F2 to edit, Home to move to the beginning of the entry, and then ' to convert the formula to a label. When you press Enter to record the change, the label 1-2-3 is displayed.

The Edit key (F2) is often useful in building complex formulas a step at a time. Breaking a complex formula down into its components has two important advantages. First, you can check your work for accuracy as you go. Second, building a formula in stages makes it much easier to arrange parentheses correctly. Just build the formula in the order 1-2-3 will make the calculations, as explained in the last section. Start with the innermost set of parentheses, then move to the next inner pair, and so on. Mathematical calculations can also be arranged in the order of calculation (exponentiation, multiplication and division, and then addition and subtraction).

The compound interest formula is not really complicated enough to require this approach, but it provides a simple example. The basic formula for future value is $PV(1+i)^n$, where PV is present value, i is the *periodic* interest rate, and n is the number of periods. As explained in more detail in Chapter 1, the period for the interest rate and the periods for n must be expressed in the same terms. Thus, if interest is compounded monthly, i is the annual percentage rate divided by 12, and n must be expressed in months. Suppose you want to know the future value of $10,000 at 12% APR, compounded monthly for five years. The formula becomes 10000*(1+0.12/12)^(5*12). This formula has two sets of parentheses of equal status (i.e., neither pair encloses the other). Within each pair, 1-2-3 will perform calculations in the natural order.

You can break down the formula this way:

1. Type (1+0.12/12) and press Enter. The display is now 1.01.

2. Press F2 to edit. The cursor will be at the end of the formula. Now type ^(5*12), to make the formula read (1+0.12/12)^(5*12). When you press Enter, the display will be 1.816696. This is the factor by which any deposit will increase over five years at 12% APR compounded monthly.

3. Press F2 to edit again, press Home to move to the beginning of the formula, and type 10000*. The formula now reads

10000*(1+0.12/12)^(5*12). When you press Enter, the display will be 18166.96. So the future value of $10,000 at the stated terms is $18,166.96.

The Edit key is useful both for correcting mistakes and for building elaborate formulas. You may want to use it frequently as you work your way through this book. You will also need to use some of 1-2-3's /Range commands, as we will see in the next section.

Working with Ranges

In 1-2-3 a range is any rectangle of cells, defined by the cells at two opposite corners, usually top left and bottom right. For example, A1..C10 defines a range of three columns by ten rows. C1..A10 defines the same range. Ranges have many uses in 1-2-3. For example, you can copy or move a range of cell entries to a new location with the /Copy and /Move commands. Some @Functions call for ranges in their arguments. You can also format ranges so that the display will be shown as dollars and cents, percentages, text, or several other options.

Whenever you use a /Range command, or any other command, such as /Copy or /Move, that requires you to identify a range, 1-2-3 automatically takes you through a series of steps to complete the command. At some point (usually at the end) in the sequence you will be asked to define the range, with the current cell defined as the starting point. If the pointer is in C10, for example, the prompt will be, "Enter range:C10..C10." If you simply press Enter, the range will consist of the single cell C10. However, you can expand the range by pressing period (.) and using the cursor keys to move the pointer to any other cell. The cells in the range will be highlighted as you move the pointer.

It is not always necessary to enter the period, because most commands assume that the range begins with the current cell. Even if the period is not needed, entering one will not disrupt the procedure for defining a range. You are always free to experiment. If you don't enter the period and the highlighted range expands when you move the pointer, then you are successfully defining a range. If the pointer simply moves to a new cell, go back to the original cell, type a period, and repeat the procedure. You always press Enter to complete a range definition. When you are working with a predefined range, pressing Esc will usually allow you to start over.

In general, to define a range, you position the pointer in the top left corner, type a period (if necessary), move the pointer to the bottom right corner, and press Enter.

Formatting Ranges

Range formatting allows you to display values in a form that is easy to understand. For example, $10,000.00 is easier to read than 10000, even though the underlying values are the same. Similarly, the meaning of 10% is clearer than 0.1, even though, again, the values are the same.

The /Range Format command allows you to format a range (or a single cell) almost any way you want. Formats define whether the display of a cell is expressed, for example, as currency with a $ sign ($10,000.25 vs 10000.25), as a percentage (10% vs. 0.1), with commas (10,000.25 vs. 10000.25), or in several other ways. When you format a range, you also can set the number of decimal places displayed.

If you do not format a range, the display will be in the General format, which displays up to as many decimal places as will fit in the column, but does not display commas or trailing zeroes to the right of the decimal. We will not explore all of the possible range formats here. You can consult your manual; however, the only real way to get a solid grip on formats is to experiment. Always remember that only the *display* is affected by formatting; the underlying values are not. Suppose, for example, you format a range to display zero decimal places. If you enter 2.4 in A1 and 2.3 in B1, 2 will be displayed in each cell. However, if you add the two in C1, the display will be 5, because the underlying value is 4.7.

In the models and figures of this book, range formatting is used extensively to illustrate the point being discussed more clearly. The most commonly used formats are Currency, which adds a dollar sign and commas, rounded to zero or two decimal places; Percent, which displays a decimal as a percentage; Commas, which adds commas but no $ sign; and Fixed, which allows you to set the number of decimal places without adding anything else. The figures that display formulas are taken directly from worksheets showing numerical calculations, using /Range Format Text. Thus, what you see are the actual formulas underlying the calculations.

Naming Ranges

Naming ranges with /Range Name Create command is another way to simplify your formulas. Once you have assigned a range name, you can use it in formulas as you would an ordinary cell reference or range reference. For example, if you assign the name INCOME to D24, the formulas +D24 and +INCOME both retrieve the value from that cell. Similarly, if you assign the range name REVENUES to the range C10..C20, @SUM(C10..C20) and @SUM(REVENUES) both add up the total of the values in the range.

When you enter /Range Name Create, 1-2-3 asks you to "Enter name." When you type the name, you are asked to "Enter range:" Just define the range as usual and press Enter. When you enter the command, previously named ranges are listed in the control panel. If you select one of these, the name will be reassigned to the range you designate in the next step. You can eliminate a range name with /Range Name Delete or eliminate all range names with /Range Name Reset. If you assign many range names, you can set up a directory with /Range Name Table. Just be sure to put the table in a blank area of your worksheet because any entries in the way will be overwritten.

Other Basic Techniques

In general, using this book requires you to know only the most basic 1-2-3 procedures. Anything beyond that is explained as it is used. Three more basic techniques are worth mentioning here: copying, setting column widths, and inserting and deleting columns and rows.

The /Copy command allows you to copy values, labels, or formulas from one range to another. For example, if you need the same set of labels in two parts of your worksheet, you can avoid retyping with /Copy. /Copy is particularly useful for copying complex formulas to set up tables, like the loan models in Chapter 6 and the tax model in Chapter 8. This requires some practice, however. When you copy formulas, it is *critical* that you understand absolute and relative cell references. This is explained in detail in Chapter 3.

Otherwise, copying is very straightforward. When you enter /Copy, 1-2-3 asks you to "Enter range to copy FROM:" Initially, the range will be the current cell (e.g., E5..E5). You can either type the range (e.g., A1..B12) or define it with the pointer. When you press Enter, 1-2-3 asks "Enter range to copy TO:" Again, you can either type the answer or identify the TO range with the pointer. If you are copying a single cell, the TO range may be another single cell. However, as is sometimes the case when building tables, you may want to copy the same formula into a range of cells. In this case, you simply select the range to copy TO. When you copy a range of cells to another range, the TO range is simply the top left corner of the new range. However, you can copy a row or column of formulas across a larger range. See the loan tables in Chapter 6 for an example. Again, it is absolutely critical to understand absolute and relative references when copying formulas.

In the standard 1-2-3 display, columns are nine spaces wide. Often, you will want to expand column widths so that more information is displayed or shrink them so that more information appears on the screen or in a printed report. This is simply accomplished with /Worksheet Column Set. You will see this prompt: "Enter column width (1..240):9." You can either type a new number or adjust the column width with the right and left arrow keys. Press Enter when you are finished.

When adjusting columns, remember that, like formatting, column widths affect only the display, not the underlying values. This is particularly important in the case of decimal places. Unlike formatting, a column width merely displays as many decimal places as will fit, without rounding. Thus, in a column three spaces wide, 1.19999999 will be displayed as 1.1. By comparison, a cell formatted to display one decimal place would show 1.2.

We close this review of basic techniques with a mention of inserting and deleting columns and rows. This is easily accomplished with the /Worksheet Insert and /Worksheet Delete commands. After entering the command, you can select Column or Row to insert and delete, define a range that includes at least one cell in each column or row, and press Enter. Note that columns are always inserted to the left of the starting point, and rows are inserted above. (Otherwise, you could not insert a column to the left of column A or a row above row 1.)

When you insert or delete, 1-2-3 automatically relabels columns and rows accordingly. In most cases, the program also correctly adjusts formulas containing cell references or range references throughout the worksheet. For example, if C1 contains the formula +B1 and you delete column A, column C becomes column B and the formula is adjusted to +A1. However, if you delete a cell actually referred to in a formula, the formula returns an ERR message. This would occur in the above example if you deleted column B instead of column A. Inserting and deleting at the edges of ranges referred to in formulas requires special attention. This is discussed in detail in Chapter 8.

A final note about inserting and deleting: Remember that inserting or deleting an entire column or row can be risky, especially in large worksheets, because you may disrupt a distant part of the worksheet without realizing it. The standard solution is to set up large worksheets in a "diamondback" pattern. That is, you put your first block of calculations at the top left, the next below and to the right, and so on. This allows you to work with each block independently of the others. You can not only insert and delete but also adjust column widths in any of the blocks without affecting the others. The only drawback is that this method spreads the worksheet over a large area, and moving around can be a bit awkward. You can overcome this by assigning a range name to the first cell of each block and maneuvering with the F5 (GOTO) function key. You may also want to use the /Range /Name /Table to set up an index.

With the worksheet basics explained here, any 1-2-3 user should be able to work any of the problems and examples in this book. Where additional skills are needed, they are explained in the text. The next section provides a brief overview of the book.

Overview

Quick Guide to Financial Formulas for 1-2-3 Users assumes a basic understanding of 1-2-3, including how formulas and @Functions work. 1-2-3's @Functions will make a wide range of financial calculations, but they cannot cover every possibility. The power of 1-2-3, combined with a little basic math, is impressive. Following is a brief summary of the calculations covered in each chapter.

Chapter 1 covers basic compound interest calculations. Topics include calculating rates, present value, future value, and term, given a variety of variables.

In Chapter 2, annuities are introduced. An annuity is a series of even payments at a fixed interest rate. 1-2-3's annuity @Functions assume that payments are at the end of each period, as is the case with most loans and other ordinary annuities. Leases, and other annuities where payments come at the beginning of the period, are annuities due. For almost any annuity, 1-2-3's @Functions and a few simple formulas allow you to solve for payments, future value, present value, term, and balance.

Data tables, another powerful 1-2-3 feature, are explained in Chapter 3. Data tables allow you to make many separate calculations using one or more formulas and to compare the results in one area of your worksheet. Both compound interest and annuities are discussed.

Chapter 4 addresses return on investment, using 1-2-3's @NPV (net present value) and @IRR (internal rate of return) functions. Here, you will learn how to apply these two functions to a variety of different calculations, including end-of-period payment, beginning-of-period payments, and cash flows that occur at varying intervals.

Depreciation is the topic of Chapter 5. First, the Modified Cost Recovery System (MACRS) is discussed. You will learn to adapt 1-2-3 features—including Release 3.0's @VDB function (variable declining balance)—to the IRS rules for the midyear and midquarter depreciation. Also covered are 1-2-3's @Functions for double-declining balance (@DDB), straight line depreciation (@SL), and sum of the years' digits (@SYD). A general discussion of the IRS rules is included.

Chapter 6 provides more complex examples of calculations involving the time value of money. These include loan amortization, balloon payments, salvage value, annual loan totals, and savings with a beginning balance. You also get a solid introduction to the database @Functions, which allow you to extract statistical information from any 1-2-3 database.

More sophisticated examples of business finance calculations appear in Chapter 7. Here, you will find methods for evaluating securities, examining cash flow, and assessing investments on the basis of risk. Chapter 6 also provides practical applications for 1-2-3's statistical functions, including calculations of variance and standard deviation, as well as regression analysis.

Chapter 8 shows how to build a complete worksheet from the building blocks suggested in the earlier chapters. The example is a personal income tax model that can easily be updated every year. This model can calculate your tax *exactly*, even if your tax is determined by the IRS tables for taxpayers with taxable incomes of less than $50,000. The model is also an excellent example of how you can combine @Functions and 1-2-3 formulas to get exactly the result you want.

Finally, Chapter 9 is the quintessential guide to 1-2-3's @Functions. @Functions for all releases, including Release 3.0, are covered. This is more than a bare-bones description of each function. There are more than 100 examples of how to put the power of 1-2-3 to work.

Conclusion

Lotus 1-2-3 puts the power of the microchip at your fingertips. *Quick Guide to Financial Formulas for 1-2-3 Users* is about how to make the most of the opportunity. It doesn't cover every aspect of 1-2-3. Instead, it provides some suggestions for using a wide range of the program's capabilities. If you try a few of the examples, you will quickly find ways to adapt 1-2-3's flexibility to your own needs. If you understand the problem, 1-2-3 will usually provide a solution.

1

Working with Compound Interest on a Lump Sum

Interest, appreciation, inflation, loan payments, return on investment, IRAs, annuities, saving to reach a goal.... Many business and personal financial decisions require calculations involving time and money. The formulas for computing the time value of money range from simple to relatively complicated. 1-2-3 makes it easy to perform calculations that would be difficult even on a sophisticated business calculator.

Simple interest is the simplest form of interest. If you invest $100 at 12% annual interest, you receive $12 each year. The interest is calculated by multiplying the principal, or original amount, by the interest rate in decimal form. Simple interest of 12% per year on $100, for example, is $12 ($100 $\times$ .12). The interest remains the same, year after year, until the arrangement is terminated.

Simple interest rarely applies to real life. Interest is usually compounded. That is, you earn or pay interest on interest, with monthly or daily compounding. This chapter covers compound interest on lump sums. Interest problems involving regular payments, such as loans and leases, are dealt with in the following chapters.

Lump-sum interest calculations apply, for example, to certificates of deposit, but there is a broad range of other applications. The same formulas allow you to calculate the appreciation on real estate, to gauge the effect of inflation, or to project the decline of the tropical rain forest or of farmland in a once-rural county. If you know the rate of increase or decrease, you can also determine how long it will take for a deposit to reach a goal, the rain forests to be reduced by half, or the world population to double. If you know the amounts at the beginning and end of a given period, you can calculate the rate of change. You might, for example, want to determine the appreciation rate on a piece of real estate if you sell it for a profit after five years.

We start out by calculating the future value of a lump sum, such as a certificate of deposit. You can easily adapt the basic model for calculating the time required to reach a goal, the rate of change, or the present value of a future amount.

Measuring Growth: Future Value

Most financial institutions advertise an annual percentage rate (APR) for loans, deposits, and investments. The APR is the *periodic interest rate* multiplied by the number of periods a year. If the APR is 12% and interest is compounded monthly, you receive (or pay) 1% of your balance each month, and the balance shifts with each compounding. If you deposit $100 at 12% APR compounded monthly, you receive $1 interest the first month (1% of $100), $1.10 the second month (1% of $101), and so on. If compounding is daily, the interest accumulates at a rate of 1/365 of the APR each day. (Some banks and other institutions calculate interest based on a 360-day year, with 30-day months. In this case, the daily interest rate is 1/360 of the APR.) You can even compound interest continuously—at a steady rate with no interval at all—as explained under *Continuous Compounding* at the end of this chapter.

Unless interest is compounded annually, the APR will be lower than the *effective annual rate*. The effective annual rate is the rate of growth each year *after compounding*, as will be explained shortly.

1-2-3 does not offer an @Function for calculating compound interest on a lump sum. (@FV works only for annuities, or regular series of payments, which are discussed in Chapter 2.) However, you can use a relatively simple formula to figure compound interest on any amount, for any compounding period. In addition, you can set up a model worksheet that allows you to calculate the growth of any amount, given the interest rate, compounding period, and term.

This formula is not limited to financial calculations. You can calculate the future value for any constant growth rate, such as population, inflation, or the weight of a feeder calf.

The Equation

If you deposit $10,000 at 12% interest today, how much will you have in 10 years? The same formula works, regardless of the compounding period. However, the compounding period and the terms must match. For example, if the return is 12% compounded monthly, the monthly rate is 1%, and the period must be expressed in months. Calculating compound interest (or growth) on a lump-sum investment is not too difficult. Here's the equation:

$$FV = PV(1+i)^n$$

where FV is the future value; PV is the present value, or original sum; i is the periodic interest rate in decimal form; and n is the number of periods.

The future value and present value need not be in dollars. You can use the same formula to calculate the result of any constant or average rate of growth, such as the population of a city, or any other value.

If the present value is declining—if you are withdrawing funds from an annuity, for example—simply enter the rate as a negative value:

$$FV = PV(1-i)^n$$

The future value formula can be used to calculate compound interest annually, monthly, daily, or for any other period. Periodic interest and the number of periods are adjusted to the compounding period.

For monthly compounding there are 12 periods per year, and the periodic interest rate is 1/12 the annual rate. For daily compounding, there are 365 periods per year, and the periodic rate is the annual rate divided by 365. If you wanted to compound 100 times a year, the calculation would be the same—100 periods per year at 1/100 the annual rate.

This reflects the way compound interest is actually paid. The formula merely reduces the repetitious calculation for each compounding period to a simple, workable form.

To calculate the future value of $100 in one year at 12% APR, compuunded monthly, you can simply enter the compound interest formula directly into a 1-2-3 cell:

```
100*(1+.12/12)^12
```

Answer: $112.68.

To calculate the future value in two years, simply multiply the exponent by 2:

```
100*(1+.12/12)^(12*2)
```

Answer: $126.97.

> **Note:** The second pair of parentheses is necessary because 1-2-3 exponentiates before it multiplies.

To figure the future value with daily compounding, substitute 365 for 12 as the number of periods:

```
100*(1+.12/365)^(365*2)
```

Answer: $127.12.

As you will see in the examples below, there is a considerable difference between compounding annually and compounding monthly or daily. For making projections and planning, the difference between monthly and daily compounding may be insignificant.

Inflation and appreciation (on real estate, for example) work exactly the same way as compound interest. Since inflation and appreciation are usually given on a yearly basis, compounding is typically annual.

Determining What You Really Pay: Effective Interest Rate

It is important to distinguish between the effective interest rate and the annual percentage rate (APR), which often is the most prominent figure in advertisements for financial services. The advertised APR is the periodic interest rate multiplied by the number of periods per year. The *effective* annual rate is the periodic rate, compounded. For example, if the

APR is 12%, compounded monthly, the *monthly* interest rate is 1%. The *effective* annual rate is the monthly rate compounded for 12 periods.

The formula for calculating an effective annual rate is similar to the one for computing compound interest:

$(1+i)^n-1$

Thus, to calculate the future value of $1 at 12% APR, compounded monthly, enter:

```
(1+.12/12)^12-1
```

Answer: 12.68%.

For daily compounding substitute 365 for the period:

```
(1+.12/365)^365-1
```

Answer: 12.75%.

If your calculation is for a single year, you can treat the effective rate as simple interest. If you deposit $1,000 at 12% APR, the effective rate is 12.68%, and your interest for the first year will be about $126.80 (12.68% of $1,000). For longer periods, you can use the effective interest rate as the periodic interest rate, compound annually.

Building a Model

Let's apply the future value formula to some practical examples. Suppose you want to compute the future value of $10,000 at 10% interest, compounded monthly for 10 years. You could enter this formula:

```
10000*(1+.10/12)^(10*12)
```

Taking that approach, however, you have to repeat the entire formula for every new calculation. Building a model that uses cell references will make the job much easier.

The model shown in Figure 1.1 allows you to solve for future value for any combination of present value, annual interest, number of years, and compounding period. Just fill in the blanks in cells B1 to B4, and the spreadsheet will do the rest.

	A	B
1	Present Value	
2	Annual Interest (QPR)	
3	Years	
4	Periods/Year	
5	Future Value	+B1*(1+B7)^B8
6		
7	Periodic Interest	+B2/B4
8	Number of Periods	+B3*B4

Figure 1.1. Calculating the future value of a lump sum.

Let's take a quick look at the formulas:

Periodic Interest = Annual Interest(APR) / Periods/Year

Number of Periods = Years   X   Periods/Year

In row 5, we've plugged these values, as cell references, into the future value formula:

$PV(1+i)^n$

You can format the cells in the formula (or change the labels in column A) as appropriate for your calculation.

Note: This model returns ERR messages until you fill in a value for Periods/Year in B4 because of division by zero.

Examples

Comparing Annual, Monthly, and Daily Compound Interest

Compute the future value of $10,000 at 10% interest for 10 years com-
pounded annually, monthly, and daily.

We can solve this problem by filling in the blanks in our model. Figure
1.2 shows the calculation for monthly compounding.

	A	B
1	Present Value	$10,000.00
2	Annual Interest (APR)	10.00%
3	Years	10
4	Periods/Year	12
5	Future Value	$27,070.41
6		
7	Periodic Interest	0.83%
8	Number of Periods	120

Figure 1.2. Monthly compound interest for 10 years at 10% APR.

To figure daily compounding, change Periods/Year to 365; for annual
compounding, enter 1. The model does the rest.

Answers: $27,070.41 for monthly compounding; $27,179.10 for daily
compounding; and $25,937.42 for annual compounding.

Analyzing Real Estate Appreciation

If a house is worth $100,000 today, how much will it be worth in 10 years
if it appreciates at 6% a year, compounded annually?

This is simply the future value of $100,000 in 10 years at 6% interest
(APR), compounded annually. With the model, you can make the calculation in seconds, as shown in Figure 1.3.

	A	B
1	Present Value	$100,000.00
2	Annual Interest (APR)	6.00%
3	Years	10
4	Periods/Year	1
5	Future Value	$179,084.77
6		
7	Periodic Interest	6.00%
8	Number of Periods	10

Figure 1.3. The future value of a house that appreciates 6% a year for 10 years.

Finding the Effective Percentage Rate

What is the effective annual rate if the annual percentage rate (APR) is 12%, compounded daily?

There are a variety of ways to make this calculation. Figure 1.4 shows a horseback solution, using the basic model. Here, you can see that the effective rate is about 13% since $1 will be worth $1.13 after one year at 12% APR compounded daily. However, the answer is not exactly accurate because of rounding, and you have to make a mental calculation to derive the rate from the model.

	A	B
1	Present Value	$1.00
2	Annual Interest (APR)	12.00%
3	Years	1
4	Periods/Year	365
5	Future Value	$1.13
6		
7	Periodic Interest	0.03%
8	Number of Periods	365

Figure 1.4. The effective rate for 12% APR, compounded daily.

To make the model more presentable for calculating the effective interest rate:

1. Change the format of cell B1 to General (/Range Format General Enter).

2. Change the label in A5 to Effective Rate.

3. Change the format of B5 to percent with two decimal places (/**R**ange Format **P**ercent **2** Enter).

4. Change the formula in B5 to +B1*(1+B7)^B8-1.

5. Save the worksheet under a new name, such as EFFECTPR.

The solution is shown in Figure 1.5.

	A	B
1	Present Value	1
2	Annual Interest (APR)	12.00%
3	Years	1
4	Periods/Year	365
5	Efffective Rate	12.75%
6		
7	Periodic Interest	0.03%
8	Number of Periods	365

Figure 1.5. Calculating the effective interest rate for 12% APR, compounded daily.

Calculating the Growth of a Certificate of Deposit

The bank advertises a three-year certificate of deposit with an annual percentage rate of 11.2%, compounded daily. If you deposit $5,000, how much will the CD be worth when it matures? The solution is shown in Figure 1.6.

	A	B
1	Present Value	$5,000.00
2	Annual Interest (APR)	11.20%
3	Years	1
4	Periods/Year	365
5	Future Value	$6,996.33
6		
7	Periodic Interest	0.03%
8	Number of Periods	1095

Figure 1.6. A $5,000 CD at 11.2% APR, compounded daily, will mature to $6,996.33 in three years.

Compensating for Inflation

You need a retirement fund of $250,000, in today's dollars, when you retire in 23 years. If inflation averages 7% per year, how much must you actually accumulate?

Inflation works exactly the same as compound interest. The solution to this problem is simply the future value of $250,000 in 23 years at 7% interest, compounded annually, as shown in Figure 1.7.

	A	B
1	Present Value	$250,000.00
2	Annual Interest (APR)	7.00%
3	Years	23
4	Periods/Year	1
5	Future Value	$1,185,132.47
6		
7	Periodic Interest	7.00%
8	Number of Periods	23

Figure 1.7. If inflation averages 7% a year, for 23 years, it will take well over $1 million to do the job $250,000 could do today.

If your current income is $250,000 and you want to figure how much you'll have to earn 23 years from now to break even, assuming a constant tax rate, the calculation is the same.

Farmland in Retreat: Projecting a Declining Value

Suppose there are 873,000 acres of farmland in Yoknapatawpha County. If that amount declines by 1.7% per year, as family farms fail and farmers sell their land to developers, how much will there be in 10 years?

Simply enter -0.017 in the model for Annual Interest Rate (APR) and 1 for Periods/Year, since compounding is annual. Since the example does not involve currency, you may also want to change the label in A2 to Rate of Change (%) and the format of cells B1 and B5. (Use the /Range Format , command sequence to format the values to commas and no decimal places.) The result is shown in Figure 1.8.

	A	B
1	Present Value	873,000
2	Rate of Change (%)	-1.70%
3	Years	10
4	Periods/Year	1
5	Future Value	735,444
6		
7	Periodic Interest	-1.70%
8	Number of Periods	10

Figure 1.8. Calculating a declining value.

Finding the Time Required to Reach a Goal: Term

In the last section, we solved several problems involving compound interest on a lump sum, using a fairly simple formula:

$$FV = PV(1+i)^n$$

Suppose you want to know how long it would take a deposit of $1,000 to grow to $10,000, assuming an interest rate of 10% compounded monthly. You cannot solve the basic equation for term with simple arithmetic, because n—the number of periods—is an exponent. The @CTERM function provides an easy solution.

The Equation

Because @CTERM yields the value of an exponent, the function uses natural logarithms to calculate to calculate the number of periods required for a lump sum to grow to a given future value:

$$Term = \frac{\ln{(FV/PV)}}{\ln{(1+i)}}$$

where ln is the natural logarithm; *FV* is the future value; *PV* is the present value; and *i* is the periodic interest rate.

Thus, you could achieve the same result by using the @LN function (natural logarithm) to enter this formula:

```
@LN(FV/PV)/@LN(1+i)
```

This, formula, in fact, is directly derived from the basic compound interest formula. You can make the derivation as follows:

$$FV = PV(1+i)^n$$

$$FV/PV = (1+i)^n$$

Since the natural log (ln) of x^n is

$$x^n = n \times ln(x)$$

we can say the following:

$$ln(FV/PV) = n \times ln(1+i)$$

$$ln(FV/PV)/ln(1+i) = n$$

Using @CTERM

The @CTERM function makes this somewhat elaborate calculation automatically. To make the calculation, enter:

```
@CTERM(i,FV,PV)
```

where *i* is the periodic interest rate; *FV* is the anticipated future value; and *PV* is the present value or original amount.

Remember that the interest rate must be calculated for each period. Thus, to compound monthly, you must divide the annual interest rate by

12. To determine how long it will take for $1,000 to grow to $10,000 at 10% interest, compounded monthly, enter:

```
@CTERM(.10/12,10000,1000)
```

Answer: 277.5 months, or 23.1 years.

To calculate term for a declining value, enter the interest rate as negative value. In this case, the future value will be smaller than the present value.

For example, suppose your company produces 100,000 tool cases a month but expects to reduce production by 5% per month because of declining demand. How long will it be before production falls to 75,000 per month? Future value still comes first in the formula, even though it is smaller than present value. Enter:

```
@CTERM(-.05,75000,100000)
```

Answer: 5.61 months.

Doubling Your Money: The "Rule of 72"

Incidentally, you can quickly estimate the number of periods required to double a lump sum by using what is known as "The Rule of 72." To get the number of periods, just divide 72 by the periodic interest rate, expressed as a whole number (not a decimal).

For example, if the annual interest rate is 10% it will take about 7.2 years (72/10) to double a lump sum. The precise answer (using @CTERM) is 7.27 years if compounding is annual, or 6.96 years with monthly compounding, but the rule is accurate enough for many projections.

You can also calculate the interest rate required to double your money in a given period by dividing 72 by the term. Thus, to double your money in 10 years, you need to earn about 7.2% annual interest (72/10 = 7.2%).

Building a Model

You can build a simple worksheet model that allows you to experiment with different values for interest, future value, present value, and compounding period without having to reenter the entire formula. The model is shown in Figure 1.9.

	A	B
1	Annual Interest (APR)	
2	Future Value	
3	Present Value	
4	Periods/Year	
5	Total Periods (Term)	@CTERM(B8,B2,B3)
6	Years	+B5/B4
7		
8	Periodic Interest	+B1/B4

Figure 1.9. Calculating the time required to reach a goal for a lump-sum investment.

Here are the calculations:

Periodic Interest = Annual Interest/(Periods/Year)

Total Periods (Term) = @CTERM(Periodic Interest,Future Value,Present Value)

Years = Total Periods (Term)/(Periods/Year)

You can format the cells in column B and change the labels in A as appropriate for the type of calculation you are making. Again, you can calculate the term for a declining value by entering a negative interest rate and a present value that is larger than the future value.

> **Note:** This model returns ERR messages until you fill in values in B1..B4 because of division by zero.

Examples

Finding the Period to Double an Investment with @CTERM

How long will it take an investment to double in value, from $10,000 to $20,000, at 10% annual interest, compounded daily, monthly, and annually?

You can solve this problem by entering .10 for Annual Interest Rate (APR), 20000 for Future Value, and 10000 for Present Value. For Periods/Year, enter 1 for annual compounding, 12 for monthly compounding, or 365 for daily compounding. Figure 1.10 shows the solution for daily compounding.

	A	B
1	Annual Interest (APR)	10.00%
2	Future Value	$20,000.00
3	Present Value	$10,000.00
4	Periods/Year	365
5	Total Periods (Term)	2,530
6	Years	6.93
7		
8	Periodic Interest	0.03%

Figure 1.10. Doubling an investment at 10% APR, compounded daily.

Answers: 6.93 years with daily compounding, 6.96 years with monthly compounding, and 7.27 years with annual compounding.

Car Depreciation: Term for a Declining Value

Suppose you buy a new car for $30,000 and expect to trade it in when it is worth half that amount. If it depreciates at a rate of 20% per year, how long should you plan to keep the car? Enter -0.20 for APR, 15000 for Future Value, 30000 for Present Value, and 1 for Periods/Year, as shown in Figure 1.11.

	A	B
1	Annual Interest (APR)	-20.00%
2	Future Value	$15,000.00
3	Present Value	$30,000.00
4	Periods/Year	1
5	Total Periods (Term)	3.11
6	Years	3.11
7		
8	Periodic Interest	-20.00%

Figure 1.11. It will take a car 3.11 years to depreciate by half at 20% per year.

Calculating the Interest Rate on a Lump-sum Investment

Suppose a $10,000 investment grows to $15,000 over five years. What is the average return? You can compute the average interest rate with a formula derived from the basic compound interest formula. The @RATE function makes the task much easier. You can use the same methods to calculate any constant or average rate of change, such as appreciation on a house, sales growth, or population change.

The Equation

@RATE uses this formula to calculate the compound interest (or percentage increase) from a present amount to a future amount over a given period:

$$(FV/PV)^{(1/n)} - 1$$

where FV is the future value; PV is the present value; and n is the number of periods.

To calculate the return when $10,000 grows to $15,000 over five years, enter:

```
(15000/10000)^(1/5)-1
```

Raising an amount to 1/n yields the nth root of the amount. For example, $4^{(1/2)}$ yields 2, the square root of 4. The formula $8^{(1/3)}$ also yields 2, the cube root of 8. Or, $2^5 = 32$; $32^{(1/5)} = 2$, the 5th root of 32.

The formula is a simple derivation of the basic compound interest formula:

$$FV = PV(1+i)^n$$

$$FV/PV = (1+i)^n$$

Taking the nth root,

$$(FV/PV)^{(1/n)} = 1+i$$

$$(FV/PV)^{(1/n)} - 1 = i$$

Using @RATE

To use @Rate to calculate the interest rate or rate of change on a lump sum, enter:

```
@RATE(FV,PV,term)
```

where *FV* is the future value; *PV* is the present value; and *term* is the number of periods.

Remember that the interest rate will be annual if the term is expressed in years, monthly if the term is in months, and daily if the term is in days. For example, if a $10,000 deposit has grown to $15,000 in five years, you can compute the effective annual interest rate by entering:

```
@RATE(15000,10000,5)
```

Answer: 8.45%.

To determine the monthly interest rate, change the term to 60:

```
@RATE(15000,10000,60)
```

Answer: 0.68%.

Note that because of compounding, the second answer is *not* 1/12 of the first (0.68%*12 = 8.14%). To reconcile the answers, you can use the conversion described under *Finding the Effective Percentage Rate* earlier in this chapter. The formula for converting periodic interest to an effective annual rate is $(1+i)^n-1$. Thus, to calculate the effective rate of .68%, compounded monthly, enter:

```
(1+.68%)^12-1
```

Answer: 8.45% (which is the same answer we got for the annual rate).

You can build this calculation into your model, so that you always get the effective annual rate as well as the periodic rate.

Building a Model

Since the formula @RATE uses for calculating interest on a lump sum derives from the basic compound interest formula, the worksheet model is also similar, as shown in Figure 1.12.

You will enter the future value in B1, the present value in B2, the number of years in B3, and the number of periods per year (12 for monthly compounding, 365 for daily compounding) in B4. You change the labels in column A and format the cells in column B to suit your calculation.

The model makes the rest of the calculations:

```
Term = Years(Periods/Year)

Periodic Rate = @RATE(Future Value,Present Value,Term)
```

	A	B
1	Future Value	
2	Present Value	
3	Years	
4	Periods/Year	
5	Term	+B3*B4
6		
7	Periodic Rate	@RATE(B1,B2,B5)
8	Annual Percentage Rate (APR)	+B4*B7
9	Effective Annual Rate	(1+B7)^B4-1

Figure 1.12. A model for calculating the periodic rate, APR, and effective annual rate, given future value, present value, and term.

$$APR = Periodic\ Rate(Periods/Year)$$

$$Effective\ Rate = (1 + Periodic\ Rate)^{\wedge}(Periods/Year) - 1$$

Note: The model returns ERR messages until you enter values in B2..B4 because of division by zero.

Examples

Finding the Rate Required to Reach a Goal

You have $25,000 in term life insurance. If you died, what interest rate, compounded monthly, would your daughter have to earn on the benefit to generate $50,000 for her college education in 12 years?

To solve the problem, enter the values in the model as shown in Figure 1.13.

	A	B
1	Future Value	$50,000.00
2	Present Value	$25,000.00
3	Years	12
4	Periods/Year	12
5	Term	144
6		
7	Periodic Rate	0.48%
8	Annual Percentage Rate (APR)	5.79%
9	Effective Annual Rate	5.95%

Figure 1.13. Calculating the required interest rate for $25,000 to grow to $50,000 in 12 years.

Tracking a Stock Market Gain

On January 1, 1995, the Dow Jones Industrial Average is 3,239. On July 1 of the same year, it is 3,432. (This is a hypothetical example, of course.) What is the rate of increase, compounded daily?

As it happens, there are 181 days in the first six months of the year. You can calculate the number of days between July 1, 1995, and January 1, 1995, by entering:

```
@DATE(95,7,1)-@DATE(95,1,1)
```

The @DATE function assigns a number between 1 and 73050 to any date between January 1, 1900, and December 31, 2099. July 1, 1995, for example, is 34881. The argument is in the form (year,month,day). For years in the 20th century, the date is entered as a two digit number. Starting with the year 2000, the year number is preceded by a 1. Thus July 1, 1995 is (95,7,1); July 1, 2005 is (105,7,1). Date functions are explained in more detail in Chapter 9.

To solve the problem, enter 3432 in the Future Value Cell of the model and 3239 for the present value.

There are two ways to enter the term into the model:

1. Enter 181 directly in the Term cell (B5). This will overwrite the formula entered in B6, so be sure to save your worksheet under a new name, so your template will remain intact.

2. Enter 181/365 in the Years cell (B3). This calculates the fraction of a year represented by 181 days.

Either way, the APR is 11.67%, and the Effective Annual Rate is 12.38%, as shown in Figure 1.14. (You may want to change the cell formats in column B.)

	A	B
1	Future Value	3432
2	Present Value	3239
3	Years	0.496
4	Periods/Year	365
5	Term	181
6		
7	Periodic Rate	0.03%
8	Annual Percentage Rate (APR)	11.67%
9	Effective Annual Rate	12.38%

Figure 1.14. Calculating the daily compound rate of increase for the stock market.

Figuring an Inflation Rate

At the end of 1980, just before the Reagan administration began, the Consumer Price Index was 247.0 (1967 = 100). At the end of 1984, the CPI stood at 311.1. What was the approximate average inflation rate during Reagan's first term?

This is an annual compounding question. Just fill in the blanks in the model as shown in Figure 1.15.

	A	B
1	Future Value	311.10
2	Present Value	247.00
3	Years	4
4	Periods/Year	1
5	Term	4
6		
7	Periodic Rate	5.94%
8	Annual Percentage Rate (APR)	5.94%
9	Effective Annual Rate	5.94%

Figure 1.15. Calculating an average inflation rate.

Because the compounding period is annual, the periodic rate, the APR, and the effective annual rate are all 5.94%.

How Much Is It Worth Now?: Present Value of a Future Amount

So far, the present value or beginning amount has been given in all of the examples. You can just as easily calculate the present value of a future amount if you know the future amount, interest rate, and number of periods. The present value is the future amount discounted at the percentage rate for each period back to the present. You are simply calculating in reverse.

Suppose, for example, that you have invested in a retirement program that will pay $10,000 a month, beginning in 20 years. That figure doesn't mean much unless you take inflation into account. To determine the present value, you can discount the monthly payment at a predicted inflation rate to determine its value in today's dollars.

Or you might be considering an investment in a real estate partnership that promises to return $25,000 on a $10,000 investment in seven years. You don't know the rate of return, but you do know that you can earn 10% APR, compounded monthly, in an alternative investment. If the present value of $25,000, discounted at 10%, is more than $10,000, the partnership yields a higher return.

The present value calculation is not limited to finance. It applies to any situation where you know the future amount and the rate of growth.

The Equation

1-2-3 does not provide an @Function for determining the present value of a future amount. (The present value function, @PV, yields the present value of a series of even cash flows at a given percentage rate.) However, you can easily calculate the present value of a future amount by inverting the basic Future Value formula this way:

$$PV = FV/(1+i)^n$$

where PV is the present value; FV is the future value; i is the periodic interest rate in decimal form; and n is the number of periods.

As always, the periodic interest rate and the number of periods must match. If interest is compounded monthly, i is the APR/12, and n must be expressed in months. If interest is annual, use annual interest and enter the term in years.

You can enter the formula directly into a cell. For example, to calculate the present value of $10,000 a month in 20 years if inflation averages 5%, you would enter:

```
10000/(1+.05)^20
```

Answer: $3,768.89. Thus, the monthly payment is worth only a little more than a third of what $10,000 a month would be worth today.

When compounding is monthly, you must convert APR to a monthly rate and express term in months. To figure the present value of $25,000 due in seven years at 10% APR, divide APR by 12 and multiply the number of years by 12:

```
25000/(1+.10/12)^(7*12)
```

Answer: $12,450.69. This is the amount you must invest today to have $25,000 in seven years, at an APR of 10%, compounded monthly. The real estate partnership described earlier yields a higher return, since it requires an initial investment of only $10,000.

Note: Additional parentheses are not needed in the middle part of the formula, because 1-2-3 performs calculations in the following order: exponentiation, multiplication and division, and, finally, addition and subtraction. However, you do need extra parentheses in the exponent because the program exponentiates before it multiplies.

For daily compounding, divide the APR by 365 and multiply the term in years by 365:

```
25000/(1+.10/365)^(7*365)
```

Answer: $12,415.82. This is the amount you must invest now to reach a goal of $25,000 in seven years.

Building a Model

The model for calculating present value of a future amount is similar to the one for calculating future value, because the Future Value formula is simply inverted. If you have already made a future value model, you may want to adapt it. The model is shown in Figure 1.16.

	A	B
1	Future Value	
2	Annual Interest (APR)	
3	Years	
4	Periods/Year	
5	Present Value	+B1/(1+B7)^B8
6		
7	Periodic Interest	+B2/B4
8	Number of Periods	+B3*B4

Figure 1.16. Calculating the present value of a future amount.

Here are the formulas:

Periodic Interest = Annual Interest (APR) / (Periods/Year)

Number of Periods = Years X (Periods/Year)

In row 5, these values are plugged in as cell references into the present value formula:

$$FV/(1+i)^n$$

You can format the cells in the formulas (or change the labels in column A) as appropriate for your calculation.

> **Note:** This model returns ERR messages until you fill in a value for Periods/Year in B4 because of division by zero. (To adapt the future value model, change the labels in A1 and A5. Then change the second operator in B5 from * to /:+B1/(1+B7)^B8. Otherwise, the model is identical.)

Examples

Pricing an Investment

You have an opportunity to invest in a project that promises to return $125,000 in four years. If you require a return of 15% APR, compounded monthly, what should you be willing to pay? The solution is shown in Figure 1-17.

	A	B
1	Future Value	$125,000.00
2	Annual Interest (APR)	15.00%
3	Years	4
4	Periods/Year	12
5	Present Value	$68,857.06
6		
7	Periodic Interest	1.25%
8	Number of Periods	48

Figure 1.17. The present value of a future return.

Answer: If you require a return of at least 15%, compounded monthly, you should pay no more than $68,857 for the investment.

Planning for Retirement

Your investment counselor projects that your retirement fund will be worth $2,365,123 in 15 years. What is that worth in today's dollars if inflation averages 4% per year? What if inflation averages 7.5%? In this case, compounding is annual, as shown in Figure 1.18.

	A	B
1	Future Value	$2,365,123.00
2	Annual Interest (APR)	4.00%
3	Years	15
4	Periods/Year	1
5	Present Value	$1,313,268.85
6		
7	Periodic Interest	4.00%
8	Number of Periods	15

Figure 1.18. Calculating the present value of an amount to be received in 15 years if inflation averages 4%.

To determine the present value if inflation averages 7.5%, enter .075 for Annual Interest (APR) in B2.

Answer: $799,331.21.

Adapting Models for Continuous Compounding

Sometimes, financial institutions compound interest continuously, like algae growing in a petri dish, rather than daily or monthly. To calculate continuous compound interest, first convert the continuous rate to an effective rate for a day, month, or year. Once you have made the conversion, you can use the effective rate in any of the examples in this chapter. Here's the equation:

$$E = e^r - 1$$

where E is the effective rate for a given period; e is a constant, the base used for natural logarithms; and r is the stated rate for the period.

For example, if the APR is 10%, the effective annual rate is $e^{0.10} - 1$. Fortunately, the @EXP function will calculate e^r for you.

Using @EXP to Determine an Effective Rate

The @EXP function makes it easy to calculate e^r in the formula. @EXP(x) returns the value of e^x, where x is a number and e is the constant (approximately 2.7182818) used as the base for natural logarithms. (See Chapter 9 for an explanation of @EXP and logarithms.) Thus, to calculate the effective annual interest rate at 10% APR, compounded continuously, enter:

```
@EXP(0.10)-1
```

Answer: 10.52%.

To avoid rounding errors, calculate effective periodic rate on your worksheet and include the entire calculation in your formula. You can do this either by using @EXP within the formula itself or by making the @EXP calculation in a separate cell and incorporating it in the formula as a cell reference.

For example, as we saw at the beginning of the chapter, the equation for calculating the future value of a lump sum is:

$$FV = PV(1+i)^n$$

where FV is the future value; PV is the present value, or original sum; i is the periodic interest rate in decimal form; and n is the number of periods.

To calculate the future value of a $1,000 three-year certificate of deposit at 10% APR, compounded continuously, you can adapt the future value formula this way:

```
1000*(1+(@EXP(0.10)-1))^3
```

Or, more simply, since the 1+ and the -1 in the formula are a wash:

```
1000*@EXP(0.10)^3
```

Answer: $1,349.86.

Conclusion

This chapter provides the basic tools for calculating simple compound interest on a lump sum. These techniques apply to many common financial problems, such as calculating the future value of a certificate of deposit. They can also be applied to any situation where you have a certain value—present, past, or future—that increases or decreases at a constant rate. Examples included compensating for inflation and the shrinkage of farmland in a rural county.

Remember that you must calculate the interest and term on the same basis. That is, if the term is calculated in months, then you must determine the effective monthly interest rate. In some cases, this requires you to reconcile periods. For example, banks often compound interest daily but compute the results on a monthly basis. With the models and examples in this chapter, you can reconcile periods for any combination of periods, even using continuous compounding.

These techniques, however, do not apply to many common financial calculations. For loans, leases, and regular savings, for example, you must take into account both compound interest and the added value of each payment. A series of regular payments at a constant interest rate is called an annuity. Annuities are the topic of the next chapter.

2

Analyzing Loans, Leases, and Savings (Annuities)

Originally, the word "annuity" referred to regular annual income payments. Now, however, the term applies to any series of even payments at a fixed interest rate for a given term. In a standard mortgage, for example, you pay off the original amount plus interest with a series of even payments, and the interest rate remains the same for the life of the loan. Periodic savings at a fixed interest rate is also an annuity, as is a lease or a retirement plan that pays out a fixed amount each month, quarter, or year.

Annuity cash flows are usually called payments, but they can be either inflows or outflows. For example, the formulas are the same for a loan and a retirement annuity derived from a lump sum investment. If you think about it, when you purchase an annuity for a lump sum, the seller agrees to pay a certain amount each period. The transaction is, in effect, a loan in reverse.

There are two basic types of annuity. In an *ordinary annuity*, payments are made *at the end of each payment period*. A series of payments made *at the beginning of each period* is called an *annuity due*. Because of the timing of interest payments, the calculations are different for the two types. Suppose, for example, you deposit $2,000 a year in an IRA. Over the course of 20 years, you will deposit a total of $40,000, regardless of when payments are made. At the end of the term, however, the balance in the account will be larger if you make the deposits on January 1 each year (annuity due) than if you make them on December 31 (ordinary annuity), because interest begins to accrue earlier on each payment.

Most loans and mortgages are ordinary annuities, with payments at the end of each period. Payments may be due the first of the month or at the beginning of a quarter, but those payments are actually for the *preceding* period. Your mortgage payment due June 1, for example, is actually for the month of May. Payments for leases, rentals, and periodic investments, on the other hand, are usually made at the *beginning* of each payment period, and thus are annuities due.

All annuities involve five variables:

Future value   The balance at the end of the term if all interest is reinvested.

Present value	The principal of a loan or the current (discounted) value of a future series of payments.
Payment	The amount paid each period.
Term	The number of periods.
Interest	The rate at which interest accrues each period, or the periodic interest rate.

Generally, if you know the periodic interest rate and two of the other four variables, you can determine the value of remaining variables. There is, however, no mathematical formula for calculating the interest rate when you know the values of the other variables; interest must be determined by trial and error. In Chapter 3, you will learn to set up data tables that allow you to look up interest rates. You can also use the @Function for internal rate of return (@IRR) to calculate the rate for an annuity, even though it is designed to calculate interest for an uneven series of payments, as explained in Chapter 4.

The mathematical formulas governing annuities are fairly complex, but 1-2-3's financial @Functions greatly simplify the calculations. All of the functions are designed for ordinary annuities; some are based on future value, others on present value. However, you can easily adapt them for any annuity. The mathematical equations for the calculations underlying the annuity @Functions are omitted here. You will find them in the guide to @Functions in Chapter 9. Ordinary annuities are covered first.

Before you begin making calculations, you should understand one feature all annuities have in common: the period must be the same for payment, interest rate, and term. The next section explains how to reconcile periods when the given values differ.

Matching Interest Periods with Payment Periods

The payment determines the period in annuity calculations. If payments are monthly, then interest must be compounded monthly, and the term must be expressed in months. If payments are quarterly, then the compounding period and term must be adjusted accordingly, and so on. The models in this chapter make these conversions automatically, but you will have to make them on your own if you do not break the calculations down into steps as the models do. A model using continuous compounding is provided at the end of the chapter.

Suppose, for example, that a bank advertises a 30-year mortgage at 12% APR. The term is expressed in years, the payments are monthly, and the nominal interest rate (APR) cannot be used directly in annuity calculations. Interest may be compounded monthly, daily, or even continuously.

Reconciling the term with the payment period is rarely a problem. In this case, there are 12 payment periods per year for 30 years, so the term is 360 months (12 × 30). If the term is given as eight quarters and payments are monthly, the term is 24 months (3 × 8), since there are three months in each quarter. If, for some reason, the term is expressed as 36 months and the payments are semiannual, then the term is six halves (36/6) since there are six months in a half. And so on. (Continuous compounding is explained at the end of the chapter.) After making your annuity computations, you can always make an additional calculation to return the term to its original form.

Converting annual interest to periodic interest is just as simple when the rate is given as APR and the compounding period is the same as the payment period, as is the case in the mortgage example. If the APR is 12%, with monthly compounding and payment periods, then the periodic rate is 1% (12%/12). If payments and compounding are quarterly, then the quarterly rate is 3% (12%/4) and so on.

Not all annual interest rates divide so evenly. For example, If the APR is 10%, with monthly compounding, the periodic rate is 0.833333...% (10%/12). To avoid rounding errors, make your interest calculations within your worksheet. 1-2-3 bases calculations on 15 decimal places, regardless of the display. Even if you format your worksheet to display zero or two decimal places, the underlying values remain intact. You can make unrounded periodic rate calculations either by including the calculation within a formula or by making the calculation in a separate cell and incorporating it in the formula as a cell reference.

To focus on the methodology of annuity calculations, most of this chapter uses examples in which the payment periods and compounding periods coincide, and the models are set up to make the appropriate interest calculations. Real life is not always so neat. For example, many loans compound interest daily but require monthly payments. You might run into a situation where interest is expressed as 1% per month, but payments are quarterly. Sometimes interest is even compounded continuously. In such cases, you will need to calculate the *effective* interest rate for the payment period. This is explained at the end of the chapter, with instructions for modifying the basic models, under *Continuous Compounding*.

Working with Loans and Other Ordinary Annuities

Mortgages and other loans are the most common examples of ordinary annuities. However, the same calculations apply to any series of even payments at the end of each period at a fixed interest rate. Calculations for annuities due, with payments at the beginning of each period, are explained later in this chapter.

1-2-3 provides four @Functions for analyzing ordinary annuities, as summarized in Table 2.1. These make most loan and mortgage calculations quite simple, and you can adapt them to many other purposes. Again, all of these functions assume *even payments at the end of each period*. In addition, the payment period, interest period, and term must always match.

Table 2.1. @Functions for Ordinary Annuities.

Function	Result
@PMT(*principal,interest,term*)	Calculates the payment, given the principal, periodic interest rate, and term.
@PV(*payment,interest,term*)	Calculates the present value, given the payment amount, periodic interest rate, and term.

Table 2.1. Continued.

Function	Result
@FV(*payment,interest,term*)	Finds the future value, given the payment amount, periodic interest rate, and term.
@Term(*payment,interest,FV*)	Calculates the term required to reach a future value, given the payment amount, interest rate, and future value.

Calculating Loan Payments

A mortgage payment, usually calculated with monthly compounding, is one of the simplest examples of using the @PMT function. You can also use @PMT to calculate the payment for any fixed-rate loan when the compounding period is the same as the payment period or to figure periodic payments derived from an annuity purchased for a lump sum.

Using @PMT to Determine Loan Payments

Using @PMT to calculate the payment for an ordinary annuity is quite straightforward. You must know the principal (or present value), periodic interest rate, and term. As always, the periods for payment, interest, and term must match. To make the calculation, enter:

```
@PMT (principal,interest,term)
```

Suppose you want to calculate the payment on a $100,000 mortgage at 11.3% annual interest (APR), compounded monthly, for 30 years. The periodic (monthly) interest rate is 0.113/12, and the term is 30*12. To determine the payment, enter:

```
@PMT(100000,0.113/12,30*12)
```

Answer: $975.06.

Building a model will allow you to make as many calculations as you want without reentering the formula.

Building a Model

Even using @PMT, you have to enter a lot of data in a single cell to calculate a payment. You can easily build a model that allows you to vary the principal, interest, and term without revising the main calculation, as shown in Figure 2.1.

All you have to do is to enter the variables in cells B1-B4, as shown in the examples below. The model calculates the periodic interest rate in B5 and the number of periods in B6.

	A	B
1	Principal (PV)	
2	Annual Interest (APR)	
3	Years	
4	Periods/Year	
5	Payment	@PMT(B1,B7,B8)
6		
7	Periodic Interest	+B2/B4
8	Number of Periods	+B3*B4

Figure 2.1. Calculating the payment on a loan.

Note: The formulas in B5 and B7 will return ERR messages until you enter data in the model because of division by zero.

Examples

Calculating a Mortgage Payment

Suppose you want to calculate the payment for a $150,000 mortgage for 30 years at 11.25% interest, compounded monthly. All you have to do is to plug the values into the model shown in Figure 2.1. The solution is shown in Figure 2.2.

	A	B
1	Principal (PV)	$150,000.00
2	Annual Interest (APR)	11.25%
3	Years	30
4	Periods/Year	12
5	Payment	$1,456.89
6		
7	Periodic Interest	0.94%
8	Number of Periods	360

Figure 2.2. Calculating the payment for a $150,000 mortgage at 11.25% interest.

A Shorter Term with Lower Interest

The same mortgage company also offers a 15-year fixed-rate loan at 11% interest, compounded monthly. How much higher will the payment be on a $150,000 mortgage?

To solve the problem, change the annual interest rate to 11% (enter 0.11) and the number of years to 15.

Answer: The payment is $1,704.90, or $248.01 more than the payment for the 30-year mortgage in the first example. Bear in mind, however, that the interest portion of the payment—and thus your tax deduction—will decline more rapidly with the 15-year mortgage, increasing the difference in the actual monthly cost of the two mortgages. Calculations for the net cost of loans are discussed in Chapter 6.

Finding Payments to Reach a Goal

The last section explains calculating payments for a present value ordinary annuity, such as a loan. You can also use @PMT to calculate how much you must pay each period to reach a *future value* or goal, given the number of periods and the interest rate. For example, you might want to know how much you must set aside each month to build a retirement nest egg or a college fund for your children. In business, companies sometimes set up sinking funds, with regular deposits, to pay off a bond issue or other future obligation with a fixed amount.

Remember that ordinary annuity calculations assume that payments are made *at the end of each period.* For example, if you deposit $2,000 each calendar year in an IRA, the following calculations will assume the deposit is made at the end of the year. If you will begin making payments immediately, you will need to use the formulas for annuities due, as explained in the next chapter.

Using @PMT to Reach a Goal

The @PMT function is designed to compute the payment for a present value ordinary annuity, such as a loan. But suppose you want to know how much you must set aside on a regular basis to reach a goal within a certain time? To adapt @PMT to a future value calculation, simply enter the term as a negative value:

```
@PMT(future value,interest,-term)
```

You can think of this as calculating the payments *backwards* from the future value at the end of the term. This formula returns the periodic payment as a *negative* value. To convert the result to a positive value, add a minus sign (-) or the @ABS function (absolute value) at the beginning of the formula:

```
-@PMT(future value,interest,-term)
```

or

```
@ABS(@PMT(future value,interest,-term))
```

As always, you must reconcile periods for payment, interest, and term. For example, to compute the monthly payment required to accumulate $100,000 in 10 years at 9% APR, compounded monthly, enter:

```
-@PMT(100000,0.09/12,-10*12)
```

Answer: $516.76.

Building a Model

If you already have a model for calculating payments on a present value ordinary annuity, you can easily adapt it for payments to reach a future value. All you have to do is to change the label in A1 to Future Value and enter two minus signs in the formula in B5, as shown in Figure 2.3.

	A	B
1	Future Value	
2	Annual Interest (APR)	
3	Years	
4	Periods/Year	
5	Payment	-@PMT(B1,B7,-B8)
6		
7	Periodic Interest	+B2/B4
8	Number of Periods	+B3*B4

Figure 2.3. Calculating the future value of an ordinary annuity.

As before, you enter the variables in B1-B4. The model calculates periodic interest in B7, number of periods in B8, and the payment in B5. Earlier, we calculated the monthly payment required to accumulate $100,000 in 10 years at 9% APR. Figure 2.4 shows this example calculated on the model.

Note: The model will return ERR messages until you enter values in B3 and B4 because of division by zero.

	A	B
1	Future Value	$100,000.00
2	Annual Interest (APR)	9.00%
3	Years	10
4	Periods/Year	12
5	Payment	$516.76
6		
7	Periodic Interest	0.75%
8	Number of Periods	120

Figure 2.4. To reach a goal of $100,000 in 10 years at 9% APR, you must deposit $516.76 at the end of each month.

If you prefer, you can set up a model that will calculate payments for both present value and future value ordinary annuities, as shown in Figure 2.5.

	A	B
1	Value (PV or FV)	
2	Annual Interest (APR)	
3	Years	
4	Periods/Year	
5	Payment	@ABS(@PMT(B1,B7,B8))
6		
7	Periodic Interest	+B2/B4
8	Number of Periods	+B3*B4

Figure 2.5. A model for calculating the payments required for a present value or future value ordinary annuity.

Note: Again, the model will return ERR messages until you enter values in B3 and B4 because of division by zero.

In this model, you must enter the term (Years) in B3 as a positive number to calculate payments based on present value. To compute payments based on future value, enter the term as a negative value, as shown in Figure 2.6.

	A	B
1	Value (PV or FV)	$100,000.00
2	Annual Interest (APR)	9.00%
3	Years	-10
4	Periods/Year	12
5	Payment	$516.76
6		
7	Periodic Interest	0.75%
8	Number of Periods	-120

Figure 2.6. To calculate the future value of an ordinary annuity, enter the term as a negative value in this model.

To calculate the payment required to pay off a present value of $100,000, simply change the entry in B3 (Years) from -10 to 10. The answer is $1,266.76. Obviously, a higher payment is required to retire a current obligation of $100,000 over 10 years than to accumulate $100,000 over the same period.

The examples below use the second model, so you have to enter term as a negative value for future value calculations.

Examples

Setting Money Aside to Meet an Obligation (Sinking Fund)

Smurf Builders must pay off a $2.5 million obligation in 4 1/2 years. It wants to set aside a certain amount each quarter so that the money will be available when the time comes. This type of arrangement is sometimes called a sinking fund. If Smurf can earn 10% annual interest, compounded quarterly, what are the payments? Simply fill in the values in the model shown in Figure 2.5. The solution is shown in Figure 2.7.

	A	B
1	Value (PV or FV)	$2,500,000.00
2	Annual Interest (APR)	10.00%
3	Years	-4.5
4	Periods/Year	4
5	Payment	$111,675.20
6		
7	Periodic Interest	2.50%
8	Number of Periods	-18

Figure 2.7. Establishing a sinking fund to pay off a $2.5 million obligation.

Comparing Investments

Smurf Builders finds an alternative investment with monthly payments
that will pay 11.7% APR, compounded monthly. What are the payments
now? Just enter the Annual Interest (APR) as .117 and the Periods/Year
as 12.

Answer: $35,393.56.

Determining the Present Value of Future Payments

The present value, or principal, of a loan is always given; it is simply the
amount you borrow. By definition, the principal is the present value of
the payments over the term of the loan at the stated interest rate. In some
situations, however, it is useful to calculate the present value of a series
of equal payments.

For example, the manual for 1-2-3 Version 2.2 poses the problem of a
lottery winner faced with a choice between $400,000 in cash or 20 annual
payments of $50,000. Or, you may be considering spending $2,500 to
install storm windows, figuring that they will reduce your annual fuel
bill by 15%. Perhaps you want to know how much you need to invest in
a 20-year retirement annuity to receive monthly payments of $5,000. Or,
again, your company may be considering purchasing a piece of equipment
that costs $20,000 and will reduce production costs by $5,000 a year.

In real life, such questions are complicated by many variables, such as inflation, changing interest rates, taxes, depreciation, salvage value, and so on. In concept, however, it is a simple matter to calculate the present value of an even series of payments, given the interest rate and term. Remember that payments for an ordinary annuity are at the end of the period, not the beginning.

Using @PV to Find Present Value

Calculating the present value of a series of even payments at a fixed interest rate is easy with 1-2-3. The @PV function does all the work for you. Enter the calculation this way:

```
@PV(payment,interest,term)
```

Suppose you want to purchase a lump sum retirement annuity that pays $5,000 for 20 years at 10% APR. How much will the annuity cost? Since the payment is monthly, the periodic (monthly) interest rate is 0.10/12 and the term is 20*12. To solve the problem, enter:

```
@PV(5000,0.10/12,20*12)
```

Answer: $5,000 a month for 20 years at 10% interest has a present value of $518,123.09, so that is what you should expect to pay for the annuity.

Building a Model

The model shown in Figure 2.8 calculates the present value of a series of even payments, given the payment, periodic interest rate, and term. In the previous example, these calculations were made within the @PV formula. Here, they are made in separate cells. In B7, the formula +B2/B4 calculates Periodic Interest by dividing Annual Interest (APR) by

Periods/Year. In B8, +B3*B4 calculates the Number of Periods by multiplying Years by Periods/Year.

	A	B
1	Payment	
2	Annual Interest (APR)	
3	Years	
4	Periods/Year	
5	Present Value	@PV(B1,B7,B8)
6		
7	Periodic Interest	+B2/B4
8	Number of Periods	+B3*B4

Figure 2.8. Calculating the present value of a series of even payments.

To use the model, enter the payment, APR, term, and periods per year in B1..B4. The model calculates periodic interest in B7, periods in B8, and the payment in B5. Remember that the payment comes at the end of each period.

> **Note:** The model will return ERR messages until you enter values for Annual Interest (APR) and Payments/Year, because of division by zero.

Examples

Pricing a Retirement Annuity

We've already seen that the present value of $5,000 at the end of each month for 20 years at 10% interest is $518,123.09. Suppose you need only $4,000 a month, but can earn only 8% APR. To find the answer, just enter the new values in the model shown in Figure 2.8. Figure 2.9 shows how the calculation looks.

	A	B
1	Payment	$4,000.00
2	Annual Interest (APR)	8.00%
3	Years	20
4	Payments/Year	12
5	Present Value	$478,217.17
6		
7	Periodic Interest	0.67%
8	Number of Payments	240

Figure 2.9. The present value of $4,000 per month for 20 years.

Finding How Much You Can Borrow

You can afford $1,500 a month in mortgage payments. The current rate for 30-year mortgages is 11.2%. How much can you afford to borrow? Again, you simply enter the values in the model shown in Figure 2.8. The solution is shown in Figure 2.10.

The answer, $155,044.16, does not include the likely additional costs,

	A	B
1	Payment	$1,500.00
2	Annual Interest (APR)	11.20%
3	Years	30
4	Payments/Year	12
5	Present Value	$155,044.16
6		
7	Periodic Interest	0.93%
8	Number of Payments	360

Figure 2.10. Solving for a loan amount, given a monthly payment, APR, and term.

such as escrow payments for taxes and insurance, title search, inspection, and points. Escrow payments for taxes and insurance can be a substantial portion of your actual monthly payment, so you may want to deduct them from the payment you can afford in this calculation. Suppose you plan on putting 10% down, in addition to the front-end charges. The amount you can borrow is 90% of the cost of the house you can afford. Thus, you can buy a house that costs $172,271 ($155,044/0.90): if $155,044 = 90% of x, then $x = $155,044/0.90$.

Evaluating an Investment in New Equipment

The Better Mousetrap Company offers a new device that can save your company $2,500 a quarter over the next five years. If your company's capital cost—the rate at which you can acquire funds—is 14.5%, what is the break-even price of the device, not counting the tax write-off for depreciation and assuming no salvage value at the end of five years?

In this case, enter 2500 for the Payment, 0.145 for APR, 5 for Years, and 4 for Payments/Year.

Answer: $35,132.47, a figure you can use as a starting point for deciding whether the new device is worth the price.

Calculating How Regular Payments Add Up: Future Value

The @FV function calculates the future value of a series of even payments *made at the end of each period*, given a payment, periodic interest rate, and term. You might, for example, deposit $2,000 in your IRA at the end of each year. @FV will tell you much you will have accumulated at any interval. As another example, businesses sometimes make periodic end-of-period deposits into a sinking fund in expectation of retiring a bond issue or other debt obligation.

In many common situations, however, payments are made *at the beginning of each period.* Leases and periodic investments are examples. In these cases, @FV will not provide the right answer; you will need the calculation for an annuity due, rather than an ordinary annuity. Annuities due are discussed in the second half of this chapter.

Using @FV to Calculate Future Value

To use @FV to calculate the future value of an even series of payments, given the interest rate and term, enter the formula in this format:

```
@FV(payment,interest,term)
```

The interest rate must match the periods of the term. Suppose you plan to deposit $7,500 at the end of each quarter, for five years, at an APR of 14%, the periodic (quarterly) interest rate is 0.14/4, and the term is 5*4. To calculate the amount in the fund after five years, enter:

```
@FV(7500,.14/4,5*4)
```

Answer: $212,097.61.

Building a Model

The model for calculating the future value of an ordinary annuity is similar to the one for calculating present value (Figure 2.8). If you already have a present value model, you can simply change the @Function entry and the label for the calculation, then save the worksheet under a new name.

The model in Figure 2.11 calculates the future value of a series of even payments at the end of each period, given the term and APR. Enter the payment, APR, years, and periods per year in B1-B4. The main formula, in B5, is the basic @FV function for calculating future value. The format, remember, is: @FV(payment,interest,term). In B7, the formula +B2/B4 calculates Periodic Interest by dividing APR by Periods/Year. In B8, +B3*B4 calculates the Term in B7. To use the model, simply fill in Payment, Annual Interest (APR), and Years in B1..B3. The model makes the rest of the calculations automatically.

	A	B
1	Payment	
2	Annual Interest (APR)	
3	Years	
4	Periods/Year	
5	Future Value	@FV(B1,B7,B8)
6		
7	Periodic Interest	+B2/B4
8	Number of Periods	+B3*B4

Figure 2.11. A model for calculating the future value of end-of-period payments.

> **Note:** The model will return ERR messages until you enter data because of division by zero.

Examples

Investing to Reach a Goal

The Robber Baron Investment Club is experimenting in the stock market. Members plan to invest a total of $2,500 a month. We've already seen that $7,500 deposited at the end of each quarter for five years at 14% APR is $212,097.61. How will the investment club fare by comparison if it earns 14% APR compounded monthly? The calculation is shown in Figure 2.12. Even though the total payments are the same in both examples, the difference between monthly and quarterly payments and compounding adds $3,390.21 to the total at the end of five years.

	A	B
1	Payment	$2,500.00
2	Annual Interest (APR)	14.00%
3	Years	5
4	Payments/Year	12
5	Future Value	$215,487.81
6		
7	Periodic Interest	1.17%
8	Number of Payments	60

Figure 2.12. The future value of an even series of payments.

Saving for Retirement with an IRA

You are 35 years old. If you deposit $2,000 in an IRA at the end of each year for 30 years, how much will the account be worth when you retire at 65 if the effective interest rate (not APR) is 10% per year? An effective interest rate, remember, is the rate for the period, after compounding. See Chapter 1 for an explanation of effective interest rate. The solution is shown in Figure 2.13.

	A	B
1	Payment	$2,000.00
2	Annual Interest (APR)	10.00%
3	Years	30
4	Payments/Year	1
5	Future Value	$328,988.05
6		
7	Periodic Interest	10.00%
8	Number of Payments	30

Figure 2.13. Calculating the future value of an IRA.

> **Note:** At this writing, you can claim a tax deferral on contributions to an IRA only if neither you nor your spouse is covered by an employer-sponsored retirement plan or if your income is below certain limits, depending on your filing status. However, tax on the interest earned in an IRA will be deferred for anyone, even if the contributions are taxable. Thus, an IRA can be a profitable investment for funds you will not need until you retire.

Finding the Time Required to Reach a Goal

In most cases, the term—or number of payments—is given in loans and other ordinary annuities. However, if you know the payment, periodic interest rate, and future value (or present value), you can easily calculate the number of payments with the @TERM function. (@CTERM, recall, calculates the term of a lump-sum investment.)

@TERM is set up to calculate the number of payments required to reach a future value. However, you can easily adapt @TERM to figure the number of payments required to pay off a present value. Thus, you can use @TERM to determine either how long it will take to reach a goal (future value) or how long it will take to pay off a debt (present value). Again, payments are assumed to come at the end of each period.

Since @TERM is designed to calculate the term to reach a future value, that calculation is covered first. Next comes the basic method for calculating term based on a present value, such as the principal of a loan. Finally, we will build a model that can handle either calculation.

Using @TERM to Reach a Goal

@TERM calculates how long it will take to reach a goal or any other future value, given regular payments at the end of each period, a constant interest rate, and the future value or goal. Again, the payment period must match the period for the interest rate; if the payments are monthly, then interest must be calculated on a monthly basis, and so on. To calculate how long it will take to reach a goal, enter the data this way:

```
@TERM(payment,interest,future value)
```

Suppose you plan to set aside $1,000 at the end of each month at 9.5% interest (APR), compounded monthly. How long will it take to accumulate $100,000? (Of course, you might want to take inflation into account. Ways of addressing that problem are covered in Chapter 6.) Since payments are monthly, the periodic (monthly) interest rate is 0.095/12. You can make the calculation this way:

```
@TERM(1000,0.095/12,100000)
```

Answer: 73.95 months.

Using @TERM to Find the Term of a Loan

The @TERM function calculates the term required to reach a future goal, given the payment and interest rate. To calculate the term required to pay off a present value, such as a debt, you need to make some adjustments.

You can use @TERM to calculate the term for a present value ordinary annuity by entering the present value as a negative number. However, that calculation returns a negative number for term. To compensate, begin the formula with either @ABS (absolute value) or a minus sign (-):

```
@ABS(@TERM(payment,interest,-present value))
```

or

```
-@TERM(payment,interest,-present value)
```

The latter, obviously, requires fewer keystrokes.

Suppose you borrow $10,000 and agree to pay $300 a month at 10% APR, compounded monthly. How long will it take to pay off the loan? The interest period must match the payment period, so you must divide the APR by 12 (.10/12) to get the periodic interest rate. Enter:

```
-@TERM(300,.10/12,-10000)
```

Answer: 39.2 months.

Building a Model

You could build separate models for calculating the term of a future value ordinary annuity and the term for a present value ordinary annuity. However, one model will serve both purposes if you use the @ABS function, rather than a minus sign, to correct the sign for the present value annuity. The @ABS function will have no effect on future value terms, since absolute values are positive by definition, but the function will correct the sign in the present value calculation. The model is shown in Figure 2.14.

	A	B
1	Payment	
2	Value (FV or -PV)	
3	Annual Interest (APR)	
4	Periods/Year	
5	Term	@ABS(@TERM(B1,B8,B2))
6	Years	+B5/B4
7		
8	Periodic Interest	+B3/B4

Figure 2.14. A model for calculating term for either a future value ordinary annuity or a present value ordinary annuity.

To use the model, enter the future value as a positive number or the present value as a negative number. The other variables in B1..B5 are filled in as usual. The model calculates periodic interest in B8 and the number of periods (term) in B5. It also converts the number of periods to years in B6. The latter is optional.

Note: Until you enter values in B1..B4, the formulas will return ERR messages, because of division by zero.

Examples

Setting Aside Funds to Reach a Goal

Smurf Builders plans to buy a $150,000 crane in a few years. Toward that end, the company plans to deposit $3,500 at the end of each month at 12% APR, compounded monthly. How many deposits will it take to accumulate $150,000? And how many years is that? (The calculation is a little more complicated if you want to take inflation into account. Solutions are provided in Chapter 6.)

In this case, you enter the value ($150,000) in the model as a positive number, because it is a *future value*, as shown in Figure 2.15. The answer is 35.85 months, or 3 years.

	A	B
1	Payment	$3,500.00
2	Value (FV or -PV)	$150,000.00
3	Annual Interest (APR)	12.00%
4	Periods/Year	12
5	Term	35.85
6	Years	3.0
7		
8	Periodic Interest	1.00%

Figure 2.15. Calculating term for a future amount.

Pacing Retirement Income

You purchase a lump-sum annuity for $130,000 to help finance your retirement and want monthly payments of $1,500. If the interest rate is 9.2%, compounded monthly, how many monthly payments will you receive?

This time, enter the value as a negative number (-130000), as shown in Figure 2.16, because this is the *present value* of the annuity. The answer is 143 monthly payments, or 11.9 years.

	A	B
1	Payment	$1,500.00
2	Value (FV or -PV)	($130,000.00)
3	Annual Interest (APR)	9.20%
4	Periods/Year	12
5	Term	142.98
6	Years	11.9
7		
8	Periodic Interest	0.77%

Figure 2.16. Calculating the number of payments for a present value annuity.

Retiring a Debt

A client has run up a bill of $4,535 and is unable to pay. He agrees to pay $200 a month at 15% APR. How long will it take to retire the debt? Again, this is a *present value* calculation, so enter -4535 as the value.

Answer: 27 (26.83) months or 2.2 years.

Calculating a Loan Balance

A loan is the most typical ordinary annuity. As payments are made, the balance, or present value of the remaining payments, declines. The present value might also be referred to as the outstanding principal. There are many situations in which you need to know how much you still owe on a loan. To calculate your equity in your home, for example, you will need to know the balance on the mortgage.

Using @PV to Calculate a Loan Balance

1-2-3 does not offer an @Function for calculating the balance of a loan or other ordinary annuity, but you can easily adapt the @PV function to the task. The outstanding balance of a loan is simply the present value of the remaining payments. Thus, you can calculate balance by using @PV to make the calculation. The only adjustment required is to determine the remaining number of payments:

```
@PV(payment,interest,term-payments made)
```

Suppose you borrow $15,000 to buy a car at 12.95% APR, compounded monthly, for 48 months. You decide to trade the car in after making 28 monthly payments of $402.04. What is the balance of the loan? Remember that you must divide the APR by 12 to obtain the monthly interest rate. Enter:

```
@PV(402.04,0.1295/12,48-28)
```

Answer: $7,197.53. Thus, if you can sell the car for $9,200, you will have enough left over to make a down payment of about $2,000 on a new one.

Building a Model

The model for calculating the outstanding balance of an ordinary annuity (Figure 2.17) is similar to the one for calculating present value shown in Figure 2.14. If you already have a present value model, you may want to start with that, using the /Worksheet Insert Row command to insert a row after Payments/Year, so you can enter Payments Made in A6. You can also add a line for principal and a payment calculation, as shown, although you don't need to know the original amount of a loan to calculate the balance. Again, Periodic Interest and Number of Payments are calculated in B9 and B10, based on the entries for Annual Interest (APR), Years, and Payments/Year.

	A	B
1	Principal	
2	Payment	@PMT(B1,B9,B10)
3	Annual Interest (APR)	
4	Years	
5	Payments/Year	
6	Payments Made	
7	Balance	@PV(B2,B9,B10-B6)
8		
9	Periodic Interest	+B3/B5
10	Number of Payments	+B4*B5

Figure 2.17. A model for calculating the balance of a loan.

Note: The model will return ERR messages until you enter data because of division by zero.

Examples

Finding the Outstanding Balance of a Loan

We have already calculated the balance after 28 payments on a 48-month loan of $15,000 at 12.95% APR, compounded monthly. (Answer: $7,197.53.) With the model shown in Figure 2.17, you can easily determine the balance of any loan after any number of periods by filling in new values. Figure 2.18 shows the calculation for a $20,000 loan for five years at 14.95% APR, compounded monthly. At the end of the first year (after 12 payments), the balance is $17,092.86.

	A	B
1	Principal	$20,000.00
2	Payment	$475.27
3	Annual Interest (APR)	14.95%
4	Years	5
5	Payments/Year	12
6	Payments Made	12
7	Balance	$17,092.86
8		
9	Periodic Interest	1.25%
10	Number of Payments	60

Figure 2.18. The balance of a 48-month loan after 28 payments.

Figuring Your Equity in Your Home

The house you bought 6 1/2 years ago for $219,000, with a $175,000 mortgage, was recently appraised at $339,000. To apply for a second mortgage, you need to calculate your equity in the house—its value less the balance of the mortgage. The mortgage is 30 years at 11.9% interest. What is the balance after 80 payments? The solution is shown in Figure 2.19.

	A	B
1	Principal	$175,000.00
2	Payment	$1,786.61
3	Annual Interest (APR)	11.90%
4	Years	30
5	Payments/Year	12
6	Payments Made	80
7	Balance	$168,793.85
8		
9	Periodic Interest	0.99%
10	Number of Payments	360

Figure 2.19. The balance of a mortgage after 80 payments.

The sad truth is that, after 80 payments of $1,786.61, the balance of the mortgage has been reduced by only $6,206.15. During the early years of such a long loan, most of the payments are for interest. Still, you can easily calculate your equity in the house: $339,000 - $168,793.85 = $170,206.15.

Working with Leases and Other Beginning-of-period Payments (Annuties Due)

Ordinary annuities, including most loans, are based on payments at the end of each period, as explained in the first part of this chapter. Many payments, such as those for leases and periodic investments, occur at the beginning of each period.

Suppose, for example, that you plan to make annual deposits of $2,000 in an IRA, beginning next calendar year. Ordinary annuity calculations will assume that the deposit is made December 31, and no interest will accumulate for the first year. On the other hand, annuity due calculations assume that the deposit is made January 1, and interest on the initial deposit will be included for the first year.

There is a similar difference between loan and lease calculations. Even though a loan payment may be due the first of the month, the payment usually is for the previous period. A lease payment, however, is typically in advance, and the payment you make at the beginning of the month is for the month just beginning. Formulas for ordinary annuities and annuities due calculate interest accordingly.

Otherwise, annuities due are quite similar to ordinary annuities. Payments must be equal for each period. In addition, the periods must correspond for payment, periodic interest, and term. If payments are monthly, for example, interest must be compounded monthly, and the term must be expressed in months. If the compounding period and payments differ—if interest is compounded daily and payments are monthly, for example—you must calculate the *effective* interest rate for the payment period. This is explained under *What to Do When Payment Periods and Interest Periods Differ* at the end of this chapter.

Adapting @Functions for Beginning-of-period Payments

1-2-3 provides four @Functions for making annuity calculations: future value (@FV), payment (@PMT), present value (@PV), and term (@TERM).

Since all are designed for ordinary annuities, they assume that payments are made at the end of each period. The difference between an ordinary annuity and an annuity due is simply a shift in the timing of interest. With a little simple arithmetic, you can easily adapt the functions to make annuity due calculations.

The formats for adapting the @Functions for annuities due are shown in Table 2.2. These calculations are described in more detail in the sections and examples below. You can adjust @FV, @PMT, and @PV to work for annuities due simply by multiplying or dividing the result by $(1+i)$, where i is the periodic interest rate. @TERM is slightly different—you must divide the *future value*, not the entire formula, by $(1+i)$. Thus, the change occurs within the function argument: @TERM($pmt,i,FV/(1+i)$).

In addition, by switching a few signs, you can use @PMT to calculate payments to reach a future value or @TERM to calculate the number of periods based on a present value. For example, the formula for calculating beginning-of-period payments to reach a future value is: -@PMT($FV,i,-term$)/($1+i$). Note that the formula will return a negative value for payment if you omit either of the minus signs.

Table 2.2. Using @Functions for Annuities Due.

Function	How to Use It
Future Value	@FV($pmt,i,term$)*($1+i$)
Present Value	@PV($pmt,i,term$)*($1+i$)
Payment (*PV*)	@PMT($PV,i,term$)/($1+i$)
Payment (*FV*)	-@PMT($FV,i,-term$)/($1+i$)
Term (*FV*)	@TERM($pmt,i,FV/(1+i)$)
Term (*PV*)	-@TERM($pmt,i,-PV/(1+i)$)

where *pmt* is the payment per period; *i* is the interest per period; *PV* is the present value or principal; *term* is the number of periods; and *FV* is the future value.

Because these calculations are so similar to those for ordinary annuities, you can easily adapt the models we have already created for ordinary annuities. You can call up your ordinary annuity model and save it under a new name. Then use Edit (F2) to add the appropriate operator (* or /) and $(1+i)$ to your @FV, @PV, @PMT, and @TERM functions, using the appropriate cell reference for the interest rate.

Calculating Payments to Reach a Goal

Regular savings or investments are one of the most common applications of future value of annuities due. If you deposit $100 a month for 15 years at 6.3% interest (APR), how much will you have? If you add $2,000 at the beginning of each year to your IRA, how much will the account be worth when you retire in 20 years?

Given the unpredictability of interest rates, inflation, and so on, the difference between payments at the beginning of the period and the end of the period (ordinary annuity) may not be enough to worry about. Nevertheless, an annuity due more closely reflects the actual series of transactions. Where interest, payment, and term are set by contract, of course, only the annuity due calculation yields the correct result.

Using @FV to Determine Future Value

The @FV function calculates the future value of an ordinary annuity, with end-of-period payments. However, the future value of an annuity due is simply @FV multiplied by $(1+i)$, where i is the periodic interest rate. Thus, you can solve for future value of an annuity due by entering a formula in this format:

```
@FV(payment,interest,term)*(1+interest)
```

Again, it is important to remember that the periods must match for interest, payment, and term. Suppose you deposit $100 a month for 15 years at 6.3% interest (APR), compounded monthly. The term is 180 months (15*12), and the monthly interest rate is 0.525% (6.3% /12). You can make the calculation by entering:

```
@FV(100,.063/12,5*12)*(1+0.063*12)
```

Answer: $29,994.00.

Building a Model

The model for calculating the future value of an annuity due is almost the same as the one for ordinary annuities shown in Figure 2.11. Just multiply the future value by (1 + *interest*), as shown in Figure 2.20.

	A	B
1	Payment	
2	Annual Interest (APR)	
3	Years	
4	Payments/Year	
5	Future Value	@FV(B1,B7,B8)*(1+B7)
6		
7	Periodic Interest	+B2/B4
8	Number of Payments	+B3*B4

Figure 2.20. A model for calculating the future value of an annuity due.

> **Note:** Periodic Interest (B7) returns an ERR message until you fill in a value for payments a year because of division by zero. If payments are annual, enter 1.

To use the model, fill in values in B1..B4. The model calculates periodic interest and number of payments in B7 and B8, plugging those values into the future value formula as cell references.

Examples

Saving to Reach a Goal

We've already seen that you will accumulate $29.994.00 if you deposit $100 at the beginning of each month for 15 years at 6.3% APR, compounded monthly. With the model shown in Figure 2.20, you can fill in any values for Payment Annual Interest (APR), Years, and Payments/Year. Figure 2.21, for example, shows the calculation for monthly payments of $5,000 for 10 years at 11.6% APR.

	A	B
1	Payment	$5,000.00
2	Annual Interest (APR)	11.60%
3	Years	10
4	Payments/Year	12
5	Future Value	$1,134,419.11
6		
7	Periodic Interest	0.97%
8	Number of Payments	120

Figure 2.21. The future value of $5,000 at the beginning of each month.

Building an IRA

At the beginning of each year, you deposit $2,000 in an IRA and expect to earn an effective annual interest rate of 8%. How much will be in the account when you retire in 20 years?

The model allows you to vary payments, interest, term, and periods as long as the periods are consistent. Since compounding is annual here, enter 1 for Payments/Year, as shown in Figure 2.22.

	A	B
1	Payment	$2,000.00
2	Annual Interest (APR)	8.00%
3	Years	20
4	Payments/Year	1
5	Future Value	$98,845.84
6		
7	Periodic Interest	8.00%
8	Number of Payments	20

Figure 2.22. The future value of an IRA.

How Much Is It Worth Now?: Finding the Present Value of Future Payments

The present value of an annuity due is the current value of a series of even payments, or the amount you would have to deposit today to generate a series of even payments, at a fixed interest rate for a given term. The period must be the same for interest, payments, and term.

For example, the winner of a $1 million lottery might receive the prize as 20 annual payments of $50,000. The payments total $1 million, but the current value of the prize is considerably less. The present value calculation yields the equivalent lump sum.

More practically, you can use the present value calculation to evaluate a lease. Theoretically, the present value of a lease equals the purchase price if you can borrow money at the same rate the lessor charges. In real life, comparing a purchase to a lease is apt to be complicated by many factors, including taxes, depreciation, and the residual value of the property at the end of the lease. But a simple present value calculation is a starting point for comparing cash flows in a lease-purchase decision.

Using @PV to Determine Present Value

The only difference between an annuity due and an ordinary annuity is that the payments for an annuity due come at the beginning of each period instead of at the end. You can adapt the @PV function to determine the present value of an annuity due by multiplying the standard calculation by $(1+i)$, where i is the periodic interest rate. Thus, you can enter the formula in a single cell in this format:

@PV(*payment,interest,term*)*(1+*interest*)

For example, to calculate the present value of $50,000 a year for 20 years at 8% effective annual interest, enter:

@PV(50000,0.08,20)*(1+0.08)

Answer: $530,179.96.

Remember that periods must coincide for payments, interest rate, and term.

Building a Model

To determine the present value of an annuity due, you need to know the payment, the periodic interest rate, and the term. The periods must be the same for payments, interest, and term. The model shown in Figure 2.23 makes all of the necessary calculations.

	A	B
1	Payment	
2	Annual Interest (APR)	
3	Years	
4	Payments/Year	
5	Present Value	@PV(B1,B7,B8)*(1+B7)
6		
7	Periodic Interest	+B2/B4
8	Number of Payments	+B3*B4

Figure 2.23. A model for the present value of an annuity due.

The formulas in B7 and B8 calculate the Periodic Interest and Number of Payments. These results are incorporated in the formula in B5, where the basic @PV calculation—@PV(*payment,interest,term*)—is multiplied by (1+*interest*). To complete the model, fill in the values for payment, APR, years, and payments per year.

> **Note:** The model returns ERR messages for present value and periodic interest until you enter values for annual interest (APR) and payments/year because of division by zero.

Examples

Comparing Lump-sum with Periodic Payments

We have been using an example in which $1 million lottery pays $50,000 a year for 20 years and the winner can earn interest at an effective annual rate of 8%. Suppose, instead, that the lottery pays $3,333.33 a month for 25 years, and the winner earns 6.5% APR, compounded monthly. What is the present value of the prize? The solution is shown in Figure 2.24.

	A	B
1	Payment	$3,333.33
2	Annual Interest (APR)	6.5%
3	Years	25
4	Payments/Year	12
5	Present Value	$496,349.23
6		
7	Periodic Interest	0.54%
8	Number of Payments	300

Figure 2.24. The present value of $3,333.33 a month for 25 years at 6.5% APR, compounded monthly.

Deciding Whether to Lease or Buy: A Simplified Example

Your company needs a personal computer network. You can purchase the system for $24,366.25, or you can lease it for five years with monthly payments of $560, paid at the beginning of each month. If capital costs the company 12% APR, compounded monthly, which is the better deal, assuming the system has no salvage value after five years and ignoring the tax effects? The solution is shown in Figure 2.25.

	A	B
1	Payment	$560.00
2	Annual Interest (APR)	12.00%
3	Years	5
4	Payments/Year	12
5	Present Value	$25,426.57
6		
7	Periodic Interest	1.00%
8	Number of Payments	60

Figure 2.25. Calculating the present value of a lease.

The present value of the lease is $25,426.57, so it would be less expensive to buy the system for $24,366.65, other things being equal. In real life you would have to consider, at the least, depreciation, taxes, and salvage value.

Calculating Lease Payments and Other Payments Based on Present Value

The payment for a present value annuity due is similar to a loan payment, except that the payment is made at the beginning of each period instead of at the end. Perhaps the most common example is the periodic payment on a lease. You can use the same method to compare periodic deposits to a lump sum investment.

Using @PMT to Calculate Payments

The @PMT function calculates payments based on the present value of an ordinary annuity, with end-of-period payments. You can easily adapt it to compute payments required at the beginning of each period. You will need to know the present value, the periodic interest rate, and the term. The periods must be the same for payment, interest, and term.

The payment for a present value annuity due is the ordinary annuity payment divided by $(1+i)$, where i is the periodic interest rate. Thus, you can adapt @PMT for payments at the beginning of each period this way:

```
@PMT(present value,interest,term)/(1+interest)
```

Suppose you want to lease a $20,000 computer system for five years at 15% APR, compounded monthly. (Assume that the computer will have no salvage value at the end of the lease.) Remember, you must convert the percentage rate and term to monthly periods. Enter the formula this way:

```
@PMT(20000,0.15/12,5*12)/(1+.15/12)
```

Answer: $469.92.

Building a Model

The model for determining the payment for a present value annuity due is almost identical to the one for the payment of an ordinary annuity. The critical difference is the formula for calculating the payment. The model for annuities due is shown in Figure 2.26.

	A	B
1	Present Value	
2	Annual Interest (APR)	
3	Years	
4	Periods/Year	
5	Payment	@PMT(B1,B7,B8)/(1+B7)
6		
7	Periodic Interest	+B2/B4
8	Number of Periods	+B3*B4

Figure 2.26. A model for calculating the payment for a present value annuity due.

Periodic Interest and Number of Periods are calculated in B7 and B8. To use the model, just fill in values for present value, APR, years, and periods/year. The model makes all of the calculations.

> **Note:** The model returns ERR messages until you enter values for Years and Periods/Year because of division by zero.

Examples

Determining Lease Payments

We have already calculated the monthly payment for a $20,000 computer system for five years at 15% APR, compounded monthly. Like all of the examples in this chapter, the example assumes that the computer system has no value at the end of the lease. Figure 2.27 shows the calculation on the model.

	A	B
1	Present Value	$20,000.00
2	Annual Interest (APR)	15.00%
3	Years	5
4	Periods/Year	12
5	Payment	$469.92
6		
7	Periodic Interest	1.25%
8	Number of Periods	60

Figure 2.27. Calculating the payment for a simple lease.

Varying the Terms of a Lease

You can freely vary any of the values in the first four rows of the model. Suppose, for example, the lease is for six years, instead of five, with the other terms remaining the same. What is the monthly payment? Just change the value in B3 to 6.

Answer: $417.68.

To calculate the quarterly payment, with interest compounded quarterly, for a five year lease, leave Years at 5 and change Periods/Year to 4.

Answer: $1,387.22.

Comparing Regular Payments with Lump-sum Investment

A lump sum investment of $1,000 will return $7,210 in 20 years at 10% interest, compounded quarterly. What is the equivalent quarterly investment at 10% APR, compounded quarterly? The solution is shown in Figure 2.28.

	A	B
1	Present Value	$1,000.00
2	Annual Interest (APR)	10.00%
3	Years	20
4	Periods/Year	4
5	Payment	$28.32
6		
7	Periodic Interest	2.50%
8	Number of Periods	80

Figure 2.28. Calculating payments equivalent to a lump-sum investment.

In other words, depositing $28.32 at the beginning of each quarter at 10% APR, compounded quarterly, for 20 years is equivalent to depositing a single sum of $1,000 at the same interest and term.

Figuring Payments Required to Reach a Goal

The @PMT function calculates the payment required at the end of each period, based on present value. You can easily adapt it to calculate the payments required at the beginning of each period to reach a goal or future value. Payments made at the beginning of each period will be slightly lower because the payments are earlier.

The same calculations apply to payments required to reach any goal, whether it is a retirement reserve, a college fund, or a sinking fund to meet a future obligation, such as a balloon payment on a loan. You will need to know the future value, the periodic interest rate, and the term. As with any annuity, payments must be the same for each period, and periods must be consistent for payment, interest rate, and term.

Using @PMT to Determine Payments Reach a Goal

The payment required to reach a goal with an annuity due is equivalent to the payment for an ordinary annuity divided by $(1+i)$, where i is the periodic interest rate. This reflects the fact that payments come in at the beginning of the first period, rather than at the end.

The @PMT function is designed to calculate the payments for a loan, a present value ordinary annuity. As explained earlier in this chapter, you can adapt @PMT to calculate end-of-period payments to reach a goal by entering the term as a negative value and reversing the sign of the entire formula:

```
-@PMT(future value,interest,-term)
```

or

```
@ABS(@PMT(future value,interest,-term))
```

These formulas assume payments at the end of each period. To adapt them for annuities due, you must divide by $(1+i)$, where i is the periodic interest rate:

```
-@PMT(future value,interest,-term)/(1+i)
```

or

```
@ABS(@PMT(future value,interest,-term))/(1+i)
```

Suppose you want to set aside a certain amount at the beginning of each month, with a goal of generating a $100,000 college fund for your daughter in 10 years, and you can earn 9% APR, compounded monthly. Since the period is monthly, the periodic interest rate is 0.09/12, and the term is -10*12. To make the calculation, enter:

```
-@PMT(100000,0.09/12,-10*12)/(1+0.09/12)
```

Answer: $512.91, only slightly less than the $516.76 required if payments are made at the end of the month.

Building a Model for Present and Future Value

Setting up a model is particularly useful for calculating payments for a future value annuity due, because the adaptation of the @PMT function is somewhat elaborate. You can adapt any of the other payment models; the model for calculating payments for an future value ordinary annuity (Figure 2.3) is the closest. The model for calculating payments required at the beginning of each period to reach a goal is shown in Figure 2.29.

	A	B
1	Future Value	
2	Annual Interest (APR)	
3	Years	
4	Periods/Year	
5	Payment	-@PMT(B1,B7,-B8)/(1+B7)
6		
7	Periodic Interest	+B2/B4
8	Number of Periods	+B3*B4

Figure 2.29. A model for calculating payments at the beginning of each period to reach a future value.

To use the model, enter values in B1..B4. The model calculates Periodic Interest and Number of Periods in B7 and B8, and the Payment in B5. Enter the term (Years) as a positive value. The formula in B5 automatically reverses the sign. The payment calculation to reach a goal of $100,000 in 10 years at 9% APR, compounded monthly, is shown in Figure 2.30.

Note: The model returns ERR messages until you enter data in B1..B4 because of division by zero.

	A	B
1	Future Value	$100,000.00
2	Annual Interest (APR)	9.00%
3	Years	10
4	Periods/Year	12
5	Payment	$512.91
6		
7	Periodic Interest	0.75%
8	Number of Periods	120

Figure 2.30. Calculating payments (annuity due) to reach a goal of $100,000 in 10 years.

If you prefer, you can use the absolute value version of the payment formula (Figure 2.5) to build a model that can be used to calculate payments for either present value or future value annuities due, as shown in Figure 2.31. In this model, you must enter the term (Years) as a negative number to calculate payments to reach a future value. To calculate payments based on present value, such as lease payments, enter the term as a positive number. This model is used in the following examples.

	A	B
1	Value (PV or FV)	
2	Annual Interest (APR)	
3	Years (PV +, FV -)	
4	Periods/Year	
5	Payment	@ABS(@PMT(B1,B7,B8))/(1+B7)
6		
7	Periodic Interest	+B2/B4
8	Number of Periods	+B3*B4

Figure 2.31. A model for calculating payments for a future value or a present value annuity due.

> **Note:** Again, the model returns ERR messages until you enter values in B1..B4 because of division by zero.

Examples

Saving for a Down Payment (Future Value)

You plan to make a $25,000 down payment on a house in 3 1/2 years. How much must you set aside each month if you can earn 7.8% APR, compounded monthly? Since this is a future value, enter the term as a negative number, as shown in Figure 2.32.

	A	B
1	Value (PV or FV)	$25,000.00
2	Annual Interest (APR)	7.80%
3	Years (PV +, FV -)	-3.5
4	Periods/Year	12
5	Payment	$516.25
6		
7	Periodic Interest	0.65%
8	Number of Periods	-42

Figure 2.32. Calculating payments to reach a future value.

Figuring Lease Payments (Present Value)

Abercrombie Brokers plans to lease a building to Fitch & Co. The present value of the first year's payments must be $68,500. What are the monthly payments, using an APR of 12.3%, compounded monthly? This is a present value calculation, so you must enter the term (in this case one year) as a positive number, as shown in Figure 2.33.

	A	B
1	Value (PV or FV)	$68,500.00
2	Annual Interest (APR)	12.30%
3	Years (PV +, FV -)	1
4	Periods/Year	4
5	Payment	$6,033.91
6		
7	Periodic Interest	1.03%
8	Number of Periods	12

Figure 2.33. To calculate payments based on present value with this model, enter term as a positive value.

Finding the Term for Leases and Other Annuities Due

The term for an annuity due is similar to the term for a loan or other ordinary annuity. You might, for example, want to know how many deposits of $1,000 you must make at the beginning of each month to accumulate $1 million. That is a future value calculation. You can also use the formulas in this section to determine the term of a lease, based on the property's present value. In either case, you need to know the amount of the payment, the present value or future value, and the periodic interest rate.

Because the formulas are similar for calculating term for a future value and for a present value, the model in this section is designed for either purpose. For a future value, you will enter the amount as a positive number. For a present value, the amount is negative. The @TERM function calculates the term for an ordinary annuity. To adapt it to annuities due, you must divide that amount by $(1+i)$, where i is the periodic interest rate.

Before setting up the model, let's look at using @TERM for future value and present value annuities due.

Using @TERM for Future Value

The @TERM function calculates the number of periods required to reach a future value for an ordinary annuity, given the payment and periodic interest rate. To determine the term required to reach a future value, with payments at the beginning of each period, divide the future value by $(1+i)$, where i is the periodic interest rate. You can enter the formula in this format:

```
@TERM(payment,interest,future value/(1+i))
```

Suppose, for example, that you plan to deposit $2,000 a month at 6.8% interest (APR), compounded monthly. How long will it take to accumulate $1 million? Since compounding is monthly, the periodic interest rate is 0.068/12. You can make the calculation this way:

```
@TERM(2000,0.068/12,1000000/(1+0.068/12))
```

Answer: 237.06 months, or just under 20 years.

Using @TERM for Present Value

You can also adapt @TERM to calculate the term for a present value annuity due, such as a lease, provided you know the payment, the periodic interest rate, and the present value. To make the calculation, enter the present value as a negative number. Again, to adapt @TERM from an ordinary annuity to an annuity due, you must divide the present value by $(1+i)$, where i is the periodic interest rate. Enter the formula in this format:

```
@TERM(payment,interest,-present value/(1+i))
```

However, this formula returns the term as a negative value. To convert the term to a positive value, you need to reverse the sign for the entire formula. You can do this either by placing a minus sign (-) at the beginning of the formula, or by using the @ABS function to calculate the absolute value of the formula:

```
-@TERM(payment,interest,-present value/(1+i))
```

or

```
@ABS(@TERM(payment,interest,-present value/(1+i)))
```

Suppose, for example, that Frejus Equipment purchases a gasoline-powered electric generator for $17,500. The company requires a 20% return on its investment, compounded quarterly, and the customer proposes to pay $1,500 a quarter. Assuming that the generator will have no value at the end of the lease, how long must the customer lease the equipment? Since payments are quarterly, the periodic rate is 0.20/4. You can use either version of the formula to make the calculation:

```
-@TERM(1500,0.20/4,-17500/(1+0.20/4))
```

or

```
@ABS(@TERM(1500,0.20/4,-17500/(1+0.20/4)))
```

Answer: 16.62 quarters or, effectively, 4 1/4 years.

Building a Model for Present and Future Value

You can set up a model for calculating the term of either a future value annuity due or of a present value annuity due, using the absolute value version of the present value formula. Since absolute value is, by definition, positive, the @ABS function has no effect on the future value calculation. In the model shown in Figure 2.34, enter the value as a positive value for a future value annuity due, or as a negative number for a present value annuity due.

To use the model, fill in the values in B1..B4. Again, enter the value as a positive number for a future value, as a negative number for a present value. The model calculates the term (number of periods) in B5, the number of years in B6, and the periodic interest rate in B8.

	A	B
1	Payment	
2	Value (FV or -PV)	
3	Annual Interest (APR)	
4	Periods/Year	
5	Term	@ABS(@TERM(B1,B8,B2/(1+B8))
6	Years	+B5/B4
7		
8	Periodic Interest	+B3/B4

Figure 2.34. A model for calculating term of an annuity due.

Note: The model returns ERR messages until you enter data in B1..B4 because of division by zero.

Examples

Finding the Time Required to Reach a Goal

We've already seen that it takes just under 20 years to accumulate $1 million if you deposit $2,000 at the beginning of each month at 6.8% interest (APR), compounded monthly. Suppose you can earn 8.9% (APR), compounded monthly. How long is the term then? Since this is a future value calculation, enter 1000000 as a positive value. The solution is shown in Figure 2.35.

	A	B
1	Payment	$2,000.00
2	Value (FV or -PV)	$1,000,000.00
3	Annual Interest (APR)	8.90%
4	Periods/Year	12
5	Term	208.89
6	Years	17.4
7		
8	Periodic Interest	0.74%

Figure 2.35. Calculating the term required to reach a goal of $1 million.

At 8.9% APR, it takes about 2 1/2 less years to accumulate $1 million than at 6.8% APR. You can freely vary any of the values in B1..B4.

Calculating Payments from a Retirement Fund

When you retire, you have $500,000 invested, earning 12% APR. If you withdraw $5,000 at the beginning of each month, how long will the money hold out? What if you withdraw $7,500 a month? Since this is a present value annuity due, enter -500000 for the value, as shown in Figure 2.36.

	A	B
1	Payment	$5,000.00
2	Value (FV or -PV)	($500,000.00)
3	Annual Interest (APR)	12.00%
4	Periods/Year	12
5	Term	463.82
6	Years	38.7
7		
8	Periodic Interest	1.00%

Figure 2.36. Determining time a retirement fund will last.

You will be able to withdraw $5,000 a month for almost 464 months, or nearly 39 years. If you invest just $5,000 more before you retire, you can withdraw $5,000 a month forever, because that's the amount of interest that will be generated each month after the first withdrawl.

To determine how long the money will last if you withdraw $7,500 at the beginning of each month, enter 7,500 in B1.

Answer: 108.44 months, or slightly more than nine years.

Note: This model returns ERR messages for Term and Years (in B5 and B6) if the payment is less than the interest on the principal, because the interest will cover the payments forever. That is, the term is inifinity. In the example, you will get ERR messages if the payment is $4,950 or less. If this were an ordinary annuity, you would get ERR messages with payments of $5,000 or less.

How Much Is It Worth Now?: Present Value of Leases and Other Annuities Due

The balance of an annuity due is the present value of the remaining payments at a given interest rate. You might use this calculation, for example, to compute the current value of a lease when you are deciding whether to replace a piece of equipment or whether to buy out a lease. The interest rate may not be the rate for the original lease. If your company is acquiring a lease, for example, you might require a higher rate than was originally negotiated. If so, the current value of the lease will be lower.

Using @PV to Calculate Present Value

The @PV function calculates the present value of a series of even payments at the end of each period. To adapt the function to calculate the balance of an annuity due, with payments at the beginning of each period, you need to make two adjustments:

1. Subtract the payments already made from the original term; and

2. Multiply the result of the formula by $(1+i)$, where i is the periodic interest rate.

Thus, to calculate the balance of an annuity due, enter:

```
@PV(payment,interest,term-payments)*(1+interest)
```

Suppose Capital Services buys State Office Equipment. State Office has leased a copier to a customer for $50 a month for five years. The customer has already made 27 payments. State originally calculated the payments at 13% APR, compounded monthly, but Capital requires a return of 15%.

What is the value of the lease to Capital if the copier has no salvage value at the end of the lease?

Thirty-three monthly payments remain on the lease (60-27), and the periodic interest rate is 0.15/12, since interest is compounded monthly. To determine the present value of the lease to Capital, enter:

```
@PV(50,0.15/12,60-27)*(1+0.15/12)
```

Answer: $1,362.06.

Building a Model

The model for calculating the balance of an annuity due is just like the one for determining present value (Figure 2.23), except that it adds the calculation for remaining payments. You can also adapt the model for determining the balance of an annuity due (Figure 2.17). The model for calculating the balance of an annuity due is shown in Figure 2.37.

	A	B
1	Payment	
2	Annual Interest (APR)	
3	Years	
4	Payments/Year	
5	Payments Made	
6	Balance	@PV(B1,B8,B9-B5)*(1+B8)
7		
8	Periodic Interest	+B2/B4
9	Number of Payments	+B3*B4

Figure 2.37. A model for calculating the balance, or present value, of an annuity due.

To use the model, fill in values in B1..B4. The model calculates the Balance in B6, taking into account the number of payments remaining. It also figures Periodic Interest in B8 and the original Number of Payments in B9.

Examples

Finding the Present Value of a Lease

We have already calculated the present value of a lease on a copier. The customer has made 27 monthly payments of $50 out of 60. If Capital Services, the new owner of the leasing company, requires a return of 15% APR, the present value of the lease is $1,362.06. But what if Capital requires a return of 20%? To solve the problem, enter 0.20 as Annual Interest, as shown in Figure 2.38. To earn a 20% return, Capital should pay only $1,282.31 to take over the lease. The higher rate of return reduces the present value.

	A	B
1	Payment	$50.00
2	Annual Interest (APR)	20.00%
3	Years	5
4	Payments/Year	12
5	Payments Made	27
6	Balance	$1,282.31
7		
8	Periodic Interest	1.25%
9	Number of Payments	60

Figure 2.38. The present value of a lease at midterm.

Buying Out a Contract

The coach of a major university is a winner, but he has run afoul of NCAA regulations. He will soon begin the third year of his five-year contract at $100,000 a year. The school decides that he must go, but that the university must honor the contract. As a compromise, the coach agrees to accept a lump sum equal to the present value of the remaining three years of his contract, at 10% interest, compounded annually. How much must the university pay?

The coach has a five-year contract for $100,000 a year. In annual terms, he has already received two payments. The analysis of the remainder of the contract, assuming 10% annual interest, is shown in Figure 2.39. The present value of the contract is $273,553.72.

	A	B
1	Payment	$100,000.00
2	Annual Interest (APR)	10.00%
3	Years	5
4	Payments/Year	1
5	Payments Made	2
6	Balance	$273,553.72
7		
8	Periodic Interest	10.00%
9	Number of Payments	5

Figure 2.39. Buying out a five-year contract after two years.

What to Do When Payment Periods and Interest Periods Differ

In real life, the interest compounding period may not match the payment periods for loans or other annuities. A common example is daily interest with monthly payments. This calculation is often used for car loans, among others. Less commonly, interest may be compounded daily or monthly with quarterly or annual payments. Banks often calculate interest daily, regardless of when you make deposits. Thus, to make calculations for regular deposits, you may need to use annuity due formulas, with daily interest and monthly, quarterly, or annual payments.

In all of these cases, you must convert the periodic interest rate to the effective rate for the payment period. For daily interest and monthly payments, for example, you need the effective monthly interest rate.

The last chapter included the equation for calculating an effective interest rate—the rate for a given period after compounding:

```
effective rate = (1+i)^n - 1
```

where i is the periodic interest rate, and n is the number of periods.

This equation is easily adapted to annuities where the compounding period does not match the payment period. If compounding is daily and payments are monthly, for example, you need to calculate the *effective* monthly rate. Then you can use the effective monthly rate as the monthly periodic rate for any annuity calculation. The principle is the same for any combination of compounding periods and payment periods.

Here's the equation:

```
i = (1+APR/c)^(C/P) - 1
```

where i is the effective periodic interest rate; *APR* is the annual percentage rate; c is the compounding periods per year; and p is the payments per year.

This formula simply uses the basic formula for converting an APR to an effective rate to compute the effective interest rate for the payment period. Suppose you want to figure the effective monthly rate for a loan at 12% APR, compounded daily, with monthly payments. You can enter the formula in a 1-2-3 cell this way:

```
(1+.12/365)^(365/12)-1
```

The effective monthly rate is 1.004851%. (The difference between daily and monthly compounding is not much; the monthly rate for 12% APR, compounded monthly, is exactly 1%.)

The formula first calculates the daily interest rate (12%/365 = about 0.033%), then the number of days per payment period (365/12 = about 30.42, the average number of days in a month). Thus, the effective monthly rate is approximately $(1+0.033\%)^{30.42}$.

For example, suppose you take out a car loan for $15,000 for five years at 12% APR, compounded daily. What is the monthly payment? You can make an accurate calculation by plugging the effective interest rate formula into the @PMT function:

```
@PMT(15000,(1+.12/365)^(365/12)-1,60)
```

Answer: $334.11.

You should include the entire calculation in a single cell or make the calculations on your worksheet and include them in the formula as cell references. Otherwise, rounding will yield a slightly inaccurate result. In this case, for example, rounding the daily interest rate 0.33...% to 0.3% reduces the monthly payment to $326.13. In fact, it would be more accurate simply to use a monthly rate of 1% (12% APR compounded monthly). A 1% monthly rate is not much different from 1.004851% (12% APR compounded daily), but it yields a monthly payment of $333.67.

Of course, if you're going to do this often, you might want to build a model.

Building a Model

You can quite easily incorporate a calculation for reconciling compounding periods with payment periods in any of the models in this chapter. You will need to add a new row for the number of compounding periods and a different formula for calculating periodic interest.

Figure 2.40 shows the model for calculating payments for an ordinary annuity, such as a loan. Note that the model is very similar to Figure 2.1. (You can use the /Worksheet/Insert/Row command to insert the Compounding/Year row. 1-2-3 will adjust the cell references automatically.)

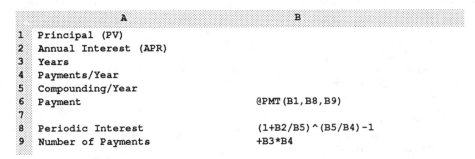

	A	B
1	Principal (PV)	
2	Annual Interest (APR)	
3	Years	
4	Payments/Year	
5	Compounding/Year	
6	Payment	@PMT(B1,B8,B9)
7		
8	Periodic Interest	(1+B2/B5)^(B5/B4)-1
9	Number of Payments	+B3*B4

Figure 2.40. Calculating payments when the payment period and the compounding period differ.

> **Note:** The model returns ERR messages until you enter values in B3..B5 because of division by zero.

For clarity, Payments has also been substituted for Periods in A4 and A9. You can use the same method to adapt any of the other models in this chapter for calculations when periods for payments and compounding differ.

This model works for any compounding and payment periods—daily compounding with monthly payments, monthly compounding with quarterly payments, quarterly compounding with annual payments, and so on.

Examples

A Car Loan with Daily Interest (Ordinary Annuity)

You borrow $15,000 to finance a car. The term is five years at 13.95% interest, compounded daily. What is the monthly payment? In the model, enter the amount, APR, years, payments per year, and compounding periods as shown in Figure 2.41.

	A	B
1	Principal (PV)	$15,000.00
2	Annual Interest (APR)	13.95%
3	Years	5
4	Payments/Year	12
5	Compounding/Year	365
6	Payment	349.25
7		
8	Periodic Interest	1.17%
9	Number of Payments	60

Figure 2.41. Calculating monthly payments with daily interest compounding.

The payment is $349.25. To get the payment with monthly compounding, change Compounding/Year to 12. The answer is $348.64—not that much different.

A Loan with Quarterly Payments and Monthly Interest (Ordinary Annuity)

Abercrombie Catering borrows $23,125 for new equipment. Interest is 14.3%, compounded monthly, with quarterly payments for six years. To compute the quarterly payment, enter the values shown in Figure 2.42.

	A	B
1	Principal (PV)	$23,125.00
2	Annual Interest (APR)	14.30%
3	Years	6
4	Payments/Year	4
5	Compounding/Year	12
6	Payment	$1,457.93
7		
8	Periodic Interest	3.62%
9	Number of Payments	24

Figure 2.42. Quarterly payments with monthly compounding.

Total payments, incidentally, come to $34,990.32. To calculate monthly payments, change Payments/Year from 4 to 12. The monthly payment is $480.23, or a total of $34,576.56 over the life of the loan.

Annual Deposits with Daily Compounding (Annuity Due)

You deposit $2,000 at the beginning of each year in an IRA. Your bank pays 7.23% APR, compounded daily. How much will be in the account when you retire in 17 years? Since payments are made at the beginning of each period, this is an annuity due. You can adapt the model in Figure 2.20 to accommodate the difference in periods, as shown in Figure 2.43.

	A	B
1	Payment	
2	Annual Interest (APR)	
3	Years	
4	Payments/Year	
5	Compounding/Year	
6	Future Value	@FV(B1,B8,B9)*(1+B8)
7		
8	Periodic Interest	(1+B2/B5)^(B5/B4)-1
9	Number of Payments	+B3*B4

Figure 2.43. A model for calculating future value of an annuity due when payment periods and compounding periods differ.

To solve the problem, fill in the values in B1..B5, as shown in Figure 2.44. As usual, you will see ERR messages until you fill in these values, because of division by zero.

	A	B
1	Payment	$2,000.00
2	Annual Interest (APR)	7.23%
3	Years	17
4	Payments/Year	1
5	Compounding/Year	365
6	Future Value	$69,334.15
7		
8	Periodic Interest	7.50%
9	Number of Payments	17

Figure 2.44. Calculating the future value of an annuity due with annual payments and daily compounding.

Adapting Models for Continuous Compounding

Some financial institutions compound interest continuously, rather than periodically. Continuous compounding, of course, generates more interest than periodic compounding.

1-2-3 does not provide an @Function for calculating continuous interest, but you can use @EXP to calculate the effective periodic interest rate with continuous compounding. You can use the effective rate in any calculation, just as you would any periodic rate. This is the equation:

$$i = e^r - 1$$

where i is the effective periodic interest rate; e is a constant, the base for natural logarithms; and r is the nominal periodic interest rate.

For example, if the APR is 10%, the nominal monthly interest rate is 10%/12, and the effective monthly rate is $e^{(0.10/12)} - 1$.

Using @EXP to Calculate an Effective Interest Rate

Fortunately, the value of e is built into the @EXP function. The constant e (about 2.718282) is used as the base for natural logarithms. @EXP(x) returns the value of e raised to the power x, or e^x. (See Chapter 9 for an explanation of @EXP and logarithms.) Thus, to calculate the effective monthly rate with continuous compounding when the APR is 10%, enter:

```
@EXP(0.10/12)-1
```

Answer: The effective monthly rate is about 0.8368%. By comparison, the effective monthly rate with monthly compounding is about 0.8333% (0.10/12), and with daily compounding, it is about 0.8367%. The latter is calculated with this formula: (1+0.10/365)^(365/12)-1.

Once you have calculated the effective periodic rate, you can use it in any of the formulas or models in this chapter. As with all interest rate calculations, to avoid rounding errors, you should include the entire calculation in the formula. One way is to include the calculation within a formula. As an alternative, you can make the calculation in a separate cell and include it in a formula as a cell reference.

Suppose, for example, that you borrow $21,333.32 to finance a car at 13.55% APR for six years. What are the monthly payments if interest compounded continuously? How does that compare with monthly and daily compounding?

You can use @EXP to determine the effective monthly interest rate:

```
@EXP(0.1355/12)-1
```

The effective monthly rate is about 1.14%. Again, to avoid rounding errors, you should make the effective interest calculation within your formula or make the computation in a different cell and include it in the formula as a cell reference. (The effective monthly rate is actually 1.1355658...%.) To determine the monthly payment, enter:

```
@PMT(21333.32,@EXP(0.1355/12-1,6*12))
```

Answer: $435.34. For monthly compounding, the formula @PMT(21333.32,0.1355/12,6*12) yields a payment of $434.46. For daily compounding, the formula @PMT(21333.32,0.1355/365,6*365) returns a payment of $435.31.

Building a Model

You can adapt any of the models in this chapter for continuous interest calculations by modifying the periodic interest calculation. While the effective monthly rate for 12% APR, compounded monthly, is 1% (12%/12), for example, the effective monthly rate for 12% APR, compounded continuously is @EXP(0.12/12)-1.

For example, to adapt the payment model for ordinary annuities (Figure 2.1), simply change the entry in B7, the periodic interest calculation to @EXP(B2/B4)-1. The result is shown in Figure 2.45.

As usual, you fill in the values in B1..B4, and the model makes the rest of the calculations.

	A	B
1	Principal (PV)	
2	Annual Interest (APR)	
3	Years	
4	Periods/Year	
5	Payment	@PMT(B1,B7,B8)
6		
7	Periodic Interest	@EXP(B2/B4)-1
8	Number of Periods	+B3*B4

Figure 2.45. A model for calculating payments for annuities due with continuous compounding

If you are adapting a model for different payment periods and compounding periods, like the payment model for an ordinary annuity shown in Figure 2.40, you can use the /Worksheet/Insert/Row command to insert rows for continuous interest calculations, as shown in Figure 2.46.

	A	B
1	Principal (PV)	
2	Annual Interest (APR)	
3	Years	
4	Payments/Year	
5	Compounding/Year	
6	Payment	@PMT(B1,B9,B11)
7	Payment (Continuous)	@PMT(B1,B10,B11)
8		
9	Periodic Interest	(1+B2/B5)^(B5/B4)-1
10	Continuous Interest	@EXP(B2/B4)-1
11	Number of Payments	+B3*B4

Figure 2.46. A model for calculating payments for an ordinary annuity when compounding periods and payment periods differ or when compounding is continuous.

Again, fill in the values in B1..B5, and the model makes the rest of the calculations. In this case, the number of compounding periods per year (B5) has no effect on the continuous compounding calculations. However, for the sake of consistent presentation, the number of payments per year should be the same as the number of compounding periods for continuous interest problems.

Note: Both of these models return ERR messages until you fill in the blanks in column B because of division by zero.

Examples

Comparing Compounding Methods on a Retirement Fund (Ordinary Annuity)

You purchase a retirement annuity for $100,000 and want payments to continue for 15 years. If payments are made at the end of each month and APR is 11.2%, how much are the payments if compounding is monthly, daily, and continuous? Since payments are at the end of each period, these are ordinary annuity calculations.

Figure 2.47 shows the calculations for monthly and continuous compounding, using the model in Figure 2.46. For daily compounding, enter 365 for Compounding/Year in B5.

	A	B
1	Principal (PV)	$100,000.00
2	Annual Interest (APR)	11.20%
3	Years	15
4	Payments/Year	12
5	Compounding/Year	12
6	Payment	$1,149.19
7	Payment (Continuous)	$1,152.50
8		
9	Periodic Interest	0.93%
10	Continuous Interest	0.94%
11	Number of Payments	180.00

Figure 2.47. Payments on an ordinary annuity with monthly and continuous compounding.

Answers: $1,149.19 with monthly compounding, $1,152.39 with daily compounding, and $1,152.50 with continuous compounding.

Comparing Compounding Methods for Savings (Annuity Due)

You deposit $1,000 at the beginning of each month at 8.6% APR. How much will accumulate in 20 years if interest is compounded monthly, daily, and continuously?

In this example, you can adapt the model for determining future value for an annuity due when payment and compounding periods differ (Figure 2.43) by inserting the calculations for continuous compounding in row 7 and row 10. The model shown in Figure 2.48 calculates the effective periodic interest rate in B10, then incorporates it in the future value formula for annuities due in B7. As with the previous model, varying compounding per year has no effect on the continuous compounding calculations, but matching the compounding period to the payment period will yield a more consistent presentation.

	A	B
1	Payment	
2	Annual Interest (APR)	
3	Years	
4	Payments/Year	
5	Compounding/Year	
6	Future Value	@FV(B1,B9,B11)*(1+B9)
7	Future Value (Continuous)	@FV(B1,B10,B11)*(1+B10)
8		
9	Periodic Interest	(1+B2/B5)^(B5/B4)-1
10	Continuous Interest	@EXP(B2/B4)-1
11	Number of Payments	+B3*B4

Figure 2.48. A model for determining future value of an annuity due when periods for payments and compounding differ, and when compounding is continuous.

Note: Again, the model returns ERR messages until you enter values in B1..B5 because of division by zero.

Figure 2.49 shows the future value of $1,000 deposited at the beginning of each month, with monthly and continuous compounding. For daily compounding, enter 365 in B5 for compounding/year.

	A	B
1	Payment	$1,000.00
2	Annual Interest (APR)	8.60%
3	Years	20
4	Payments/Year	12
5	Compounding/Year	12
6	Future Value	$639,486.78
7	Future Value (Continuous)	$641,996.65
8		
9	Periodic Interest	0.72%
10	Continuous Interest	0.72%
11	Number of Payments	240

Figure 2.49. The future value of $1,000 deposited at the beginning of each month, with monthly and continuous compouding.

Answers: $639,486.78 with monthly compounding, $641,913.57 with daily compounding, and $641,996.65 with continuous compounding.

Conclusion

This chapter has explained a variety of calculations involving loans, leases, savings, and other transactions involving a regular series of payments. The models and examples allow you to make calculations whether payments occur at the end of each period (ordinary annuities) or at the beginning (annuities due).

The basic annuity calculations require that interest, payments, and term be calculated at the same interval. However, you have also seen how to reconcile these periods when they don't match, and even to make calculations with continuous compounding.

These calculations, along with the lump-sum problems discussed in Chapter 1, cover a wide range of financial situations. They are the building blocks of the models we will set up in the following chapters. Chapters 6 and 8 provide more elaborate examples involving the time value of money. Meanwhile, the next chapter explains how to set up tables to analyze transactions and to compare options, and Chapter 4 tells you how to analyze cash flow when payments are uneven or come at erratic intervals.

3

Setting Up Tables for Decision Making

The last two chapters described how to make calculations involving compound interest and annuities. With the models in those chapters, you can make most of the calculations you will want to make, but you have to change the variables one at a time and make each calculation separately. In order to evaluate financial options, it is often useful to look at how more than one variable affects a decision and to see the outcomes on a single worksheet. This is called sensitivity analysis.

For example, suppose your company is considering several alternatives for a $100,000 investment. The interest rate may be anywhere from 7.5% to 9.5% APR, and you may be able to choose a term anywhere from one to 20 years. Or you may want to review the payments on a loan, given various interest rates and terms.

This chapter describes two ways to do just that. The first is to set up a model and table with the /Data Table 2 command. Data tables are a quick and elegant solution, but they have a minor disadvantage: you have to repeat the /Data Table 2 command to recalculate when you change any of the values in the model. The second option is to set up a table by copying formulas into a range of cells. This may take slightly longer to set up, but the worksheet recalculates automatically when you change values.

Using Data Tables to Compare Options

Data tables are easier to create than they are to explain. As with most 1-2-3 applications, the best way to learn is to do. Once you have set up a data table, you should be able to create others without difficulty.

1-2-3 provides two types of data tables. /Data Table 1 allows you to experiment with one variable in any number of formulas. /Data Table 2 allows you to experiment with two variables in a single formula. In the following example, we want to look at two variables, interest rate (APR) and term, to see how various possibilities affect the future value of a lump-sum investment, so /Data Table 2 is the appropriate choice.

Setting up a data table involves two basic steps. The first is to build a model for the main calculation, such as the future value of a lump sum. The second is to create the table itself, based on that model.

Comparing Investments

Figure 3.1 shows the future value of $100,000, with monthly compounding, terms ranging from 1 to 20 years, and APR ranging from 7.5% to 9.5%. The top eight rows of the worksheet contain the model we saw in Figure 1.1 for calculating the future value of a lump sum at varying interest rates, terms, and compounding periods. The lower part of the worksheet, occupying the range A12..F20, is the data table itself, allowing you to compare future values of a lump sum at different terms and interest rates.

	A	B	C	D	E	F
1	Present Value	$100,000.00				
2	Annual Interest (APR)	7.50%				
3	Years	10				
4	Periods/Year	12				
5	Future Value	$211,206.46				
6						
7	Periodic Interest	0.63%				
8	Number of Periods	120				
9						
10						
11		Years	APR			
12	+B5		7.50%	8.00%	8.50%	9.00%	9.50%
13		1	107,763	108,300	108,839	109,381	109,925
14		2	116,129	117,289	118,459	119,641	120,835
15		3	125,145	127,024	128,930	130,865	132,827
16		4	134,860	137,567	140,326	143,141	146,010
17		5	145,329	148,985	152,730	156,568	160,501
18		10	211,206	221,964	233,265	245,136	257,606
19		15	306,945	330,692	356,265	383,804	413,459
20		20	446,082	492,680	544,124	600,915	663,606

Figure 3.1. A data table comparing future values of a lump sum at varying interest rates and terms.

Building a Model

The worksheet in Figure 3.1 includes no formulas other than the ones in the basic future value model at the top of the worksheet and the simple cell reference +B5 in A12. The interest rates in B12..G12 and the Years in A13..A20 are simple value entries. The amounts in B13..F20 are calculated directly by the /Data Table 2 command.

The first step in creating the worksheet is to set up a model that calculates the future value of a lump sum, given present value, APR, term in years, and periods per year, using the model shown in Figure 1.1. As before, you fill in the values in B1..B4, and the model calculates the rest. As we saw in Chapter 1, the formula for calculating the future value of a lump sum is:

$$FV=PV(1+i)^n$$

where *PV* is the present value; *i* is the periodic interest rate (APR/periods per year); and *n* is the number of periods (years × periods per year).

This formula is in B5, with cell references for the appropriate variables:

```
+B1*(1+B7)^B8
```

B1 is the present value; B7 calculates the periodic interest rate (+B2/B4); and B8 calculates the number of periods (+B3*B4).

Annual percentage rate (B2) and Years (B3) are the variables you will be experimenting with in the data table, and the values you enter there will not affect the table. However, you should fill in *some* value for Present Value and Periods/Year before you set up the data table. If you leave Periods/Year blank, the table will return ERR messages; if you omit Present Value, it will return all 0's. The table will not recalculate automatically if you make a change later, unless you repeat the /Data Table command.

Setting Up the Data Table

Once you have built a model, you will have to add three more important components before setting up the data table itself. In a data table 2, the first variable, or input, is always defined by the left column of the table (here, A12..A20), the second is always defined in the top row (here, A12..F12), and the formula is always in the top left cell of the table (here, A12).

Enter the years range in A13..A20 and the APR range in B12..F12. (You can use the /Data Fill command if the intervals are regular, as they are in the APR range.) Here, the years range is 1-5, 10, 15, and 20, and the APR range is set at intervals of 0.5 percentage points from 7.5% to 9.5%. You can use any values you want or extend the ranges.

Next, enter +B5 in B12 to define the formula entered in B5 as the formula for the data table. The formula in B5 is the basic future value formula, expressed as +B1*(1+B7)^B8.

Now, this is an important point. Remember that left column of the table defines the variations for input variable 1, and the top row defines variations for input variable 2—in this case Years and APR, respectively. In the model at the top of the table, Years is entered in B3 and APR in B2. Neither B3 nor B2 appears in the formula you have just entered, nor do they appear in the formula in the reference cell, B5. That doesn't matter here, because the values for years and APR are included in the formulas B7 and B8, which do appear in the formula in B5.

This will become clearer as you complete the following steps. With the model, table formula, and input ranges completed, you can set up the table as follows:

1. Use the /Data Table 2 command to select a two-variable data table.

2. When the command line asks you to Enter table range, enter A12..F20 (move the cursor to A12, press period, then move the cursor to F20, and press Enter).

3. When asked to Enter input cell 1, type B3 and press Enter. This is Years, and the table will substitute the values in the left column of the table for years in the formula.

4. When asked to Enter input cell 2, type B2 and press Enter. The table will substitute the values in row 12 for APR in the formula.

When you complete the /Data Table sequence, 1-2-3 automatically calculates the values within the table. Again, you should be aware that the table will not recalculate automatically if you change information on your worksheet. If you make any change that requires recalculation, you must repeat the Data Table sequence. Simply enter the /Data Table 2 command again, and then continue to press Enter until the program finishes redefining the table. 1-2-3 will automatically enter the table range and input cells you defined earlier.

Comparing Loan Payments

You can easily adapt /Data Table 2 to any of the models described in the first two chapters of this book. First set up or retrieve the model, and then set up the data table using the steps described above. This section explains how to set up a data table for loan payments with varying terms and interest rates.

Suppose you want to figure the payments for a $100,000 loan at varying interest rates and terms, with monthly compounding. Start with the loan payment model in Figure 2.1, and then set up a data table 2, as shown in Figure 3.2. The payment is shown with APR ranging from 10% to 12%,

	A	B	C	D	E	F
1	Principal (PV)	$100,000.00				
2	Annual Interest (APR)	10.00%				
3	Years	30				
4	Periods/Year	12				
5	Payment	$877.57				
6						
7	Periodic Interest	0.83%				
8	Number of Periods	360				
9						
10		Years	APR			
11	+B5		10.00%	10.50%	11.00%	11.50%	12.00%
12		3	3,227	3,250	3,274	3,298	3,321
13		4	2,536	2,560	2,585	2,609	2,633
14		5	2,125	2,149	2,174	2,199	2,224
15		6	1,853	1,878	1,903	1,929	1,955
16		10	1,322	1,349	1,378	1,406	1,435
17		15	1,075	1,105	1,137	1,168	1,200
18		20	965	998	1,032	1,066	1,101
19		25	909	944	980	1,016	1,053
20		30	878	915	952	990	1,029

Figure 3.2. A data table 2 showing payments for a loan (annuity due) at varying rates and terms.

with periods ranging from 3-6 years, then at 5-year intervals from 10 years to 30 years.

In this example, the data table occupies the range A11..F20. the formula that governs the table is entered in A11. As always, it goes at the top left corner of the table. The formula is entered as +B5, referring to the formula in that address, which is @PMT(B1,B7,B8). When you vary the years and APR in that formula, given the values in A12..A20, and the APR, given in B11..B12, you get the payments shown in the table.

To set up the table, follow these steps:

1. Set up the model for calculating payments of an ordinary annuity, as described in Chapter 2 (see Figure 2.1).

2. Enter the labels Years in A10 and APR in B10.

3. Enter the values for term in A12..A20.

4. Enter values for APR in B11..F11.

5. Enter the /Data Table 2 command.

6. Select A11..F20 as the table range.

7. Select B3 (Years) as input cell 1.

8. Select B2 (APR) as input cell 2.

The result should look like the example in Figure 3.2. This table shows the payments on a $100,000 loan at varying terms and interest rates. As before, if you change any of the values in the model, you must repeat the /Data Table 2 command to recalculate the table.

You can quite easily adapt this model to calculate the payments for varying principal and interest rates, while keeping the term of the loan constant. Suppose, for example, that you are planning to buy a house and want to calculate payments on a 30-year mortgage with APR ranging from 10% to 12% and principal at $5,000 intervals ranging from $100,000 up.

You can set up the table as just described, with variations of principal listed in A12..A20. This time, when you enter the /Data Table 2 command, input cell 1 is B1, which will translate into the principal variables listed in column A; input cell 2 is B2, representing the APR values listed in row 11. The result is shown in Figure 3.3.

	A	B	C	D	E	F
1	Principal (PV)	$100,000.00				
2	Annual Interest (APR)	10.00%				
3	Years	30				
4	Periods/Year	12				
5	Payment	$877.57				
6						
7	Periodic Interest	0.83%				
8	Number of Periods	360				
9						
10	Principal	APR				
11	+B5	10.00%	10.50%	11.00%	11.50%	12.00%
12	100,000	878	915	952	990	1,029
13	105,000	921	960	1,000	1,040	1,080
14	110,000	965	1,006	1,048	1,089	1,131
15	115,000	1,009	1,052	1,095	1,139	1,183
16	120,000	1,053	1,098	1,143	1,188	1,234
17	125,000	1,097	1,143	1,190	1,238	1,286
18	130,000	1,141	1,189	1,238	1,287	1,337
19	135,000	1,185	1,235	1,286	1,337	1,389
20	140,000	1,229	1,281	1,333	1,386	1,440

Figure 3.3. Varying principal and interest for a 30-year mortgage with data table 2.

Using Formulas to Set Up Tables

You can achieve the same effect as the data tables just described by copying formulas that use cell references. This method may be easier to learn, particularly if you already understand copying and absolute and relative cell references and have no other need to set up data tables. (See the note on absolute references below for an explanation of absolute and relative references.) Formula-based tables also have the advantage of automatically recalculating when you change values anywhere on the worksheet.

Analyzing a Lump–sum Investment

Suppose you want to calculate how much $100,000 will be worth at a future date, varying the term and the annual percentage rate. The model shown in Figure 3.4 uses formulas to make the calculation for terms ranging from one to 30 years at interest rates ranging from 7.5% t0 9.5%. (For a different compounding period, simply change the entry in B2 for Periods/Year.)

	A	B	C	D	E	F
1	Present Value	$100,000.00				
2	Periods/Year	12				
3						
4						
5	Years	APR				
6		7.50%	8.00%	8.50%	9.00%	9.50%
7	1	107,763	108,300	108,839	109,381	109,925
8	2	116,129	117,289	118,459	119,641	120,835
9	3	125,145	127,024	128,930	130,865	132,827
10	4	134,860	137,567	140,326	143,141	146,010
11	5	145,329	148,985	152,730	156,568	160,501
12	10	211,206	221,964	233,265	245,136	257,606
13	15	306,945	330,692	356,265	383,804	413,459
14	20	446,082	492,680	544,124	600,915	663,606
15	30	942,153	1,093,573	1,269,250	1,473,058	1,709,486
16						
17						
18						
19						
20						

Figure 3.4. A table for future value of a lump sum with varying APR and term.

The underlying formulas for column B are shown in Figure 3.5. (Only the relative references differ in the remaining columns.) The formulas are not anywhere near as complicated as they might look at first.

You know that the formula for future value of a lump sum is:

$$PV*(1+i)^n$$

where *PV* is the present value; *i* is the periodic interest rate; and *n* is the number of periods.

	A	B
1	Present Value	$100,000.00
2	Periods/Year	12
3		
4		
5	Years	APR
6		7.50%
7	1	+$B$1*(1+B$6/$B$2)^($B$2*$A7)
8	2	+$B$1*(1+B$6/$B$2)^($B$2*$A8)
9	3	+$B$1*(1+B$6/$B$2)^($B$2*$A9)
10	4	+$B$1*(1+B$6/$B$2)^($B$2*$A10)
11	5	+$B$1*(1+B$6/$B$2)^($B$2*$A11)
12	10	+$B$1*(1+B$6/$B$2)^($B$2*$A12)
13	15	+$B$1*(1+B$6/$B$2)^($B$2*$A13)
14	20	+$B$1*(1+B$6/$B$2)^($B$2*$A14)
15	30	+$B$1*(1+B$6/$B$2)^($B$2*$A15)

Figure 3.5. Copyable formulas for calculating the future value of a lump sum.

That's all the formula in B7 is. Only the absolute references, indicated by the dollar signs, make it look difficult. You don't even have to enter the dollar signs at first, as you are about to see. Once you have entered one formula, you will copy the rest.

Let's take a closer look at the formula in B7:

```
$B$1*(1+B$6/$B$2)^($B$2*$A7)
```

Stripped of absolute references, this looks much simpler:

```
B1*(1+B6/B2)^(B2*A7)
```

where B1 is the present value (currently $100,000); B6/B2 is the periodic interest rate (here, 7.5%/12 periods/year); and B2*A7 is the number of periods (12 periods*1 year).

This formula calculates the future value after one year for $100,000 at 7.5% APR, compounded monthly ($107,763).

Similar formulas will work in all of the cells of the table, but you need to adjust the absolute and relative references. With the absolute references, you can copy the formula across the table in a single step. The references to $B$1 and $B$2 are absolute, meaning they remain constant. In the reference to B$6, the column is relative, but the row is absolute. When you copy, the formula will select the APR from row 6 of the current column. Similarly, in the reference to $A7, the column is absolute, but the row is relative. When you copy, the formula will select Years from the current row in column A. As a result, this single formula allows you to pluck Present Value from B1, Periods/Year from B2, Years from A7..A15, and APR from B6..F6. The results are automatically plugged into the future value formula, and *voila!* you have made 45 calculations with one formula.

Here's how to set up the model:

1. Type the labels as shown in A1 and A2 and the corresponding values for your base case in B1 and B2. In this case, you want to know the future value of 100000, and Periods/Year is 12, to yield monthly compounding.

2. Enter the labels Years in A5 and APR in B5. You may want to use the /**R**ange Label **R**ight command to justify the labels, so they will line up with the figures below.

3. Enter values for APR in B6..F6 and for term in years in A7..A15. If intervals are even, the /**D**ata **F**ill command will speed up the procedure.

4. Enter the basic formula in B7, the upper left corner of the range that will contain calculated values:

    ```
    B1*(1+B6/B2)^(B2*A7)
    ```

5. Now adjust the absolute and relative references. With the cursor still at B7, press F2 to edit the formula. Move the cursor to the first cell reference, B1, and press F4 once to make the reference absolute ($B$1). Continue editing the cell references until the formula looks like this:

    ```
    $B$1*(1+B$6/$B$2)^($B$2*$A7)
    ```

6. Finally, you will copy the formula across the entire table. With the cursor in B7, enter the /Copy command and Press Enter to accept B7..B7 as the range to copy FROM. Then, press period (.) to define B7 as the upper left cell of the copy range and move the cursor to F15 and press Enter to establish B7..F15 as the range to copy TO.

When the formulas are copied, the result should look like Figure 3.4. You now have a model you can use to calculate future value of a lump sum with any present value, any number of periods per year, and any ranges for term in years and APR. You are free to enter any values for Present Value and Periods/Year in B1 and B2, APR in B6..F6, or Years in A7..A15. If you expand the table, however, you will need to repeat step 6 to copy the formula into the new cells in the table. If you opt for a smaller table, you may want to use /Range Erase to eliminate extraneous calculations.

A Note on Absolute and Relative Cell References

When you enter a cell reference, 1-2-3 assumes you are referring to the relative position of the cell. For example, if you enter +B2 in A1, the value in A1 will equal the value in B2. However, when you copy the formula +B2 from A1 to another cell, 1-2-3 assumes you meant "over one, down one." If you enter +C2 in A1, the program will interpret that as "over two, down one," and so on. Thus, if you copy the formula +B1 from A1 to, say, D5, the value in D5 will equal the one in E6—over one, down one.

Fortunately, you are not locked in to relative cell references when you copy formulas. You can make the reference absolute, so that your formula returns the value in B2, for example, no matter where you copy it. You can also use mixed references, holding either the column or the row constant, but leaving the other relative.

You can use dollar signs ($) to fix the column, the row, or both when you copy formulas. For example, +$B$2 will return the value in B2, no matter where you copy the formula. When you copy +B$2 to a new cell, the column will be relative, but the reference will always be to row 2. If you copy +B$2 from A1 to C3, for example, the entry in C3 will be +D$2—over one column, row 2. To keep the column constant with a relative row reference, enter +$B2. Copied from A1 to C3, that formula yields +$B4—column B, down one.

You can type the dollar signs if you want, but it's easier to use F4 to set absolute references, either when you're typing them or while you are in the edit mode. Suppose you enter +B2 in A1. To make the reference absolute place the cursor on the entry and press F4 once to get +$B$2. Press F4 again to get +B$2, again for +$B2, and again to return to +B2.

Absolute and relative references allow you to create tables quickly. The next section explains how to set up a table of loan payments by copying the formula, rather than using the /Data Table command.

Loan Payments with Varying Terms and Interest

You can use the method described above to create tables using any formula using two (or more) variables. Figure 3.6 is a table of loan payments with interest rates ranging from 10% to 12% and for terms of one to 30 years.

	A	B	C	D	E	F
1	Principal (PV)	$100,000.00				
2	Periods/Year	12				
3						
4						
5	Years	APR				
6		10.00%	10.50%	11.00%	11.50%	12.00%
7	3	3,227	3,250	3,274	3,298	3,321
8	4	2,536	2,560	2,585	2,609	2,633
9	5	2,125	2,149	2,174	2,199	2,224
10	6	1,853	1,878	1,903	1,929	1,955
11	10	1,322	1,349	1,378	1,406	1,435
12	15	1,075	1,105	1,137	1,168	1,200
13	20	965	998	1,032	1,066	1,101
14	25	909	944	980	1,016	1,053
15	30	878	915	952	990	1,029
16						
17						
18						
19						
20						

Figure 3.6. Payments on a loan with varying term and interest rate.

Remember, the function for calculating payments for an ordinary annuity is:

@PMT(*principal,interest,term*)

To set up the table:

1. Enter the labels for Principal and Periods/Year in A1 and A2 and the corresponding values in column B.

2. Enter the labels for Years and APR in A5 and B5.

3. Use the /**D**ata **F**ill to enter the APR variables in B6..F6, then enter the years range in A7..A15.

4. In B7, enter this formula:

    @PMT($B$1,B$6/$B$2,$A7*$B$2)

   The values in B1 and B2, principal and periods per year, remain constant throughout the worksheet. The periodic interest rate is the value listed in row 6 divided by periods per year, and the term is the number of years listed in column A times periods per year.

5. To copy the formula across the table, use the /**C**opy command, with B7..B7 as the range to copy FROM and B7..F15 as the range to copy TO.

The result should look like Figure 3.6.

Conclusion

You can use either data tables or broad-scale copying to create tables for many types of financial situations where you want to test the effect of one or more variables. Which you choose depends on personal preference and the situation.

Data tables are perhaps the more elegant solution, and they may allow you to avoid absolute and relative cell references. However, they do not recalculate automatically. In addition, you are limited to a single variable with data table 1 and two variables and a single formula with data table 2.

Tables made by copying formulas across ranges are more flexible and recalculate automatically. On the other hand, you have to contend with absolute and relative cell references, and some tables will take longer to set up. The choice is yours.

4

Analyzing Return on Investment

Chapter 2 explains how to make many calculations involving annuities. Annuity payments are by definition the same for each period. Unless regular payments are set by contract, however, business decisions usually involve variable cash flows, so annuity calculations do not apply. For example, new business ventures and expansions are generally predicated on growth. Investments in stocks and bonds ebb and flow. Returns on real estate investments vary with expenses, depreciation, repairs, vacancies, and eventual sale, even if the cash flow is fixed by leases.

1-2-3 provides two @Functions for analyzing variable cash flows. @NPV (net present value) calculates the current value of a series of cash flows, given a constant interest rate and regular intervals. @NPV is similar to @PV (present value), except that it allows for varying periodic payments, while @PV is designed for annuities, with regular payments. The second function is @IRR (internal rate of return), which calculates the *periodic* rate of return, given an initial outlay and a series of cash flows at regular intervals.

You can also use @IRR to calculate the interest rate for an annuity. You may have noticed that Chapter 2 did not include a method for that calculation. That's because there is no mathematical formula for calculating the interest rate of an annuity, and 1-2-3 provides no @Function for that purpose. Although the @IRR calculation is usually applied to uneven cash flows, it really doesn't matter whether payments are regular or irregular as long as they occur at regular intervals.

Since you can use the same model for calculating IRR and NPV, we will do both at once, after a brief introduction to @NPV and @IRR. The two functions also share many of the same rules, discussed after the model below.

Analyzing an Investment with @NPV

Net present value (NPV) is the present value of series of cash flows at a given interest rate. That rate is sometimes called the "hurdle rate"—the return you require to consider an investment worth making. If the NPV is greater than the initial investment, you expect to earn more than the hurdle rate; if it is lower, the return will not be as high.

Unlike most @Functions, you cannot make an NPV calculation in a single cell; you must list the cash flows in consecutive cells of your worksheet. Once you have entered the cash flows, you can solve for NPV by entering a formula in this format:

```
@NPV(interest,range)
```

where *interest* is the hurdle rate, and *range* is the range of cells containing the cash flows after the initial investment.

Measuring Return with @IRR

By definition, the IRR is the interest rate at which NPV equals the positive value of the initial investment. There is no mathematical formula for making this calculation, so 1-2-3 solves the problem by testing interest rates until the problem is resolved, starting with your best guess as to what the IRR might be.

As with NPV, you cannot calculate IRR in a single cell. You must first list the cash flows, beginning with the original outlay, entered as a negative number. Once these values are entered, you can calculate IRR by entering a formula in this format:

```
@IRR(guess,range)
```

where *guess* is your best estimate of IRR, and *range* is the range of cells containing the cash flows.

In most real-life situations a guess of 10% will yield the correct answer, but 1-2-3 will return an ERR message if it cannot find the correct IRR within 0.0000001 in 30 calculations.

Building a Model for @NPV and @IRR

The first step to making an NPV or IRR calculation is to enter the expected cash flows in contiguous cells of your worksheet. Once that is done, you can simply enter the appropriate function and argument anywhere in the worksheet.

Suppose, for example, that H.J. Jones Stationers plans to buy a $10,000 computer system to automate its bookkeeping, which is now done by hand. The company projects after-tax savings of $2,000 the first year, $2,500 the second, $4,000 the third, and $4,500 in each of the fourth and fifth years. The required return, or hurdle rate, is 15%. What is the NPV and IRR?

A model for making the calculation is shown in Figure 4.1. Remember that @NPV and @IRR are entered in these formats:

`@NPV(interest,range)`

and

`@IRR(guess,range)`

Since the cash flows are listed on an annual basis, the 15% Hurdle Rate is an annual figure. In B2, the formula is @NPV(B1,B6..B10). This formula retrieves the hurdle rate from B1 for interest and sets the range as B6..B10. Note that Initial Outlay (B5) is *not* included in the range. (See the second example below for an explanation of how to include an initial outlay in an NPV calculation, as businesses sometimes prefer to do.)

The @IRR formula is in B3: @IRR(0.1,B5..B10). Here, the guess at the percentage rate is 0.1 or 10%. As mentioned earlier, a guess of 10% will work in most practical situations. The range is B5..B10, which *does* include the Initial Outlay (B5). (@IRR will return an ERR message unless the sign of the cash flows changes at least once.)

The final calculation in the model, in B12, determines the NPV using the calculated IRR in B3. This simply illustrates that the IRR is in fact the rate at which NPV equals the initial investment.

	A	B
1	Hurdle Rate	15.00%
2	Net Present Value	@NPV(B1,B6..B10)
3	Internal Rate of Return	@IRR(0.1,B5..B10)
4		
5	Initial Outlay	(10,000)
6	Year 1	2,000
7	Year 2	2,500
8	Year 3	4,000
9	Year 4	4,500
10	Year 5	4,500
11		
12	NPV using IRR	@NPV(B3,B6..B10)

Figure 4.1. Calculating the NPV and IRR for series of uneven cash flows.

Figure 4.2 shows the results of the calculations in Figure 4.2. NPV is $11,070 using a hurdle rate of 15%; IRR is 18.81%; and NPV using the IRR calculated in B3 is $10,000. Since NPV at 15% is greater than the initial outlay, the company will earn more than the hurdle rate. The IRR shows just what that return is—18.81%.

	A	B
1	Hurdle Rate	15.00%
2	Net Present Value	$11,070
3	Internal Rate of Return	18.81%
4		
5	Initial Outlay	(10,000)
6	Year 1	2,000
7	Year 2	2,500
8	Year 3	4,000
9	Year 4	4,500
10	Year 5	4,500
11		
12	NPV using IRR	$10,000

Figure 4.2. The results of the NPV and IRR calculations in Figure 4.1.

There are several important items to note in this model. The first is that there are six cash flows in the model, even though it spans only five years.

The time line below makes this clearer. The initial outlay, a negative cash flow, occurs at period 0; that is to say, immediately. The cash flows come at the end of each period:

($10,000)	$2,000	$2,500	$4,000	$4,500	$4,500
⊥	⊥	⊥	⊥	⊥	⊥
0	1	2	3	4	5

The initial outlay, at period 0, is included in the range for IRR, but not in the range for NPV. Like most financial calculators, @IRR assumes that the first cash flow occurs immediately. Unlike most financial calculators, however, @NPV assumes that the first cash flow occurs at the end of the first period, thus excluding the initial outlay. This is why 1-2-3 defines IRR as the rate at which NPV equals the original outlay, while many finance texts define IRR as the rate at which NPV equals 0.

A second important point is that both functions assume that the cash flows span the life of the project being assessed. The H.J. Jones Stationers case essentially assumes that the new computer will be tossed in the scrap heap at the end of five years. By contrast, if the company expected to sell the computer for $5,000, net of taxes, at the end of the fifth year, the last cash flow would be $9,500 instead of $4,500, and NPV and IRR would be correspondingly higher. The same principle applies even to a savings account. If you omit the value of the original asset at the end of the period, both NPV and IRR will be meaningless—and probably depressing.

There are additional critical factors to consider, including:

1. Periods must be equal in NPV and IRR calculations. If cash flows are timed erratically, use the shortest interval as the basic period and enter 0 for each intervening period. For example, if you expect to receive $100 in January, $200 in June, $1,000 in July, and $5,000 in December, the period must be monthly. Enter 0 in each month with no cash flow.

2. As with annuities, periods must match for interest rates and payments. If payments are monthly or quarterly, for example, the NPV hurdle rate and the IRR guess must be the *effective* interest

rate for the appropriate period. (A guess of 10% will still usually work for @IRR, however.) For the same reason, IRR returns a *periodic* interest rate; i.e., if payments are monthly, then the IRR will be monthly. You may want to convert it to an annual rate. Reconciling periods and calculating effective interest rates is explained in detail in Chapter 2.

3. Remember that all cash flows (except the initial outlay for IRR) are assumed to come *at the end of each period*. If payments come at the beginning of each period, as in the case of a lease, you will need to adjust the NPV and IRR formulas, as discussed in the next section. This also means that you should use appropriate payment periods when comparing options. In the H.J. Jones case, for example, the model assumes the savings occur on the last day of each year. Actually, of course, the savings would be spread throughout the year. With more frequent compounding, the IRR would be slightly higher. In other words, a project analyzed on an annual model is at a slight disadvantage against one analyzed on a monthly model. (Of course, your projections are likely to be off by more than the difference produced by the two methods anyway.)

4. It is a mathematical fact of life that there are as many correct answers for IRR as there are changes in the sign of the cash flows. The most important implication of this is that the sign must change *at least once*; the IRR range must include at least one negative cash flow and one positive one. Otherwise, @IRR returns an ERR message. The rule of signs also means that results may be unpredictable—and invalid—if cash flows switch back and forth between positive and negative in the IRR model.

Adjusting the Timing of Cash Flows

As already noted, @NPV and @IRR assume that cash flows come at the end of each period—the last day of the month, quarter, or year. Sometimes, as with leases, payments come at the beginning of each period. You can easily adapt @NPV and @IRR for such cases.

NPV is simply the sum of the present values of the payments, with each payment discounted for the appropriate number of periods. When cash flows occur at the beginning of each period, the present value of the first payment equals the first payment, because interest does not come into play—$100 received today is worth exactly $100. Thus, you can simply add the first payment to the NPV of the remaining payments:

```
first payment + @NPV(interest,range)
```

This has the effect of moving the entire stream of payments forward one period. Of course, you must make sure that the first payment is not included in the range, so it won't be counted twice.

In the case of @IRR, the first cash flow—the initial outlay—already occurs at period 0, or immediately. If the first payment also comes at period 0, simultaneously, you can calculate IRR by deducting the initial payment from the original outlay and moving the remaining payments forward one period.

Suppose, as a simplified example, that Acme Leasing Company buys a truck for $12,000 and immediately leases for $3,000 a year, payable at the beginning of each year for five years. For the purpose of this calculation, the initial outlay is –$9,000 (–$12,000 + $3,000), followed by *four* annual payments of $3,000. If the truck has a residual value at the end of the lease, that cash flow comes at the beginning of the sixth year, when the leasing company gets the truck back. Once you have entered these values in a column or row, you can calculate IRR as usual.

These methods are illustrated in the examples that follow. In the examples, annual cash flows are used to keep the number of periods manageable for the sake of illustration. Monthly or quarterly periods could easily be substituted, using the appropriate periodic interest rate conversions described in Chapter 2.

Examples

Buying an Asset and Selling It at the End of a Project

H.J. Jones Stationer has already seen that a $10,000 computer is a sound investment, using the calculation shown in Figures 4.1 and 4.2. The results: a NPV of $11,070, assuming a hurdle rate of 15%, and an IRR of 18.81%. That computer will have no market value at the end of five years.

Now the company finds a more sophisticated computer for $12,500. It will produce the same after-tax savings in bookkeeping—$2,000 the first year, $2,500 the second, $4,000 the third, and $4,500 each of the last two years. However, the company should be able to sell the system for $3,000, net of taxes, at the end of five years. Which computer is the better investment?

H.J. Jones's analysis of the more expensive computer is shown in Figure 4.3. The calculation is identical, except that the initial outlay is increased to –$12,500 and $3,000 is added to the cash flow for Year 5, because the computer will be sold at the end of the year. Thus, the final cash flow is $7,500, instead of $4,500.

	A	B
1	Hurdle Rate	15.00%
2	Net Present Value	$12,561
3	Internal Rate of Return	15.17%
4		
5	Initial Outlay	(12,500)
6	Year 1	2,000
7	Year 2	2,500
8	Year 3	4,000
9	Year 4	4,500
10	Year 5	7,500
11		
12	NPV using IRR	$12,500

Figure 4.3. Calculating NPV and IRR with a salvage value.

The second computer also meets H.J. Jones's criteria. The NPV is greater than the original cost, and the IRR is larger than the company's required rate of return. However, the IRR, 15.17%, is only slightly higher than the hurdle rate, and the NPV, $12,561, is only slightly more than the original cost. The less expensive computer appears to be the better buy.

Including Initial Cost in Net Present Value

In the last example, the NPV of the first computer is $11,070, compared with $12,561 for the second. But that doesn't mean the second is the better choice. Common sense says that a $10,000 investment worth $11,070 is better than a $12,500 investment worth $12,561, but the numbers are not directly comparable.

Often, it is useful to compare the NPV of two investments *including* the original outlay. @NPV cannot do this internally. But the present value of the initial outlay equals the amount of the outlay, since it occurs immediately. All you have to do is add the original outlay to the NPV of the remaining cash flows.

In our model, the initial outlay is entered in B5, so you can simply add the value in that cell to the NPV formula in B2. Now the formula in B2 looks like this:

```
+B5+@NPV(B1,B6..B10)
```

where B1 is the hurdle rate, and B6..B10 is the range of cash flows.

Now the model returns a NPV of $1,070 for the first computer and $61 for the second, and the numbers are more directly comparable. For NPV using IRR at the bottom of the worksheet, you must add B5 (the original outlay) to the formula in B12:

```
+B5+@NPV(B3,B6..B10)
```

The model now returns $0 for both investments, as suggested by many finance texts.

@NPV and @IRR for Payments at Irregular Intervals

You are considering a $100,000 investment that promises no return—positive or negative—for the first three years. You should receive $75,000 in the fourth year and $150,000 in the fifth, at which point the deal will be closed out. You require a return of 13%. What are the NPV and IRR?

Again, periods must remain constant in @NPV and @IRR calculations, even though cash flows can vary. The solution here is simply to enter 0 as the cash flow for the first three years, as shown in Figure 4.4. If the periods were months or quarters, you could use the same tactic or convert the cash flows to an annual basis.

	A	B
1	Hurdle Rate	13.00%
2	Net Present Value	$127,413
3	Internal Rate of Return	19.07%
4		
5	Initial Outlay	(100,000)
6	Year 1	0
7	Year 2	0
8	Year 3	0
9	Year 4	75,000
10	Year 5	150,000
11		
12	NPV using IRR	$100,000

Figure 4.4. Calculating NPV and IRR when the timing of cash flows is uneven.

Selling an Asset at the End of a Lease

Let's go back to the Acme Leasing Company example. The company buys a truck for $12,000 and leases for $3,000 for five years, with payments at the beginning of each year. At the beginning of the sixth year, when the lease has expired, Acme sells the truck for $5,000. What are the NPV and IRR? (Assume that the lease payments and sale price are net of taxes.)

Unless you want to include the initial outlay in your NPV calculation, as described in the second example, you will have to make the calculations separately here, because the outlay and the first payment occur at the same time. The outlay is not included for calculating NPV, but it is for IRR.

The NPV is the first payment, plus the net present value of the remaining payments, including the sale of the truck. The initial outlay is irrelevant to the calculation, except as a comparison for the NPV. Figure 4.5 shows the NPV of the series of payments, assuming a hurdle rate of 15%. The only formula in the model is the NPV calculation in B2:

```
+B5+@NPV(B1,B6..B10)
```

where B5 is the first payment, and B6..B10 is the range of subsequent payments, from the payment for Year 2 to the sale of the truck at the beginning of Year 6.

	A	B
1	Hurdle Rate	15.00%
2	Net Present Value	$14,051
3	Initial Outlay	(12,000)
4		
5	Year 1	3,000
6	Year 2	3,000
7	Year 3	3,000
8	Year 4	3,000
9	Year 5	3,000
10	Year 6	5,000

Figure 4.5. Calculating NPV of a lease.

If you *do* want to include the initial outlay in NPV, you can make that calculation along with IRR. The time line for the payments is shown below:

```
($12,000)
    3,000   $3,000   $3,000   $3,000   $3,000   $5,000
     ⊥        ⊥        ⊥        ⊥        ⊥        ⊥
     0        1        2        3        4        5
```

Thus, the cash flow for year 1 is -$9,000 (-$12,000 + $3,000), followed by four annual payments of $3,000, and a final payment of $5,000. Figure 4.6 calculates both the IRR and the NPV *including the initial outlay.*

	A	B
1	Hurdle Rate	15.00%
2	Net Present Value	$2,051
3	Internal Rate of Return	23.59%
4		
5	Year 1	(9,000)
6	Year 2	3,000
7	Year 3	3,000
8	Year 4	3,000
9	Year 5	3,000
10	Year 6	5,000
11		
12	NPV using IRR	($0)

Figure 4.6. NPV (including initial outlay) and IRR with payments at the beginning of

There are three formulas in this model:

```
Net Present Value (B2) = +B5+@NPV(B1,B6..B10)

Internal Rate of Return (B3) = @IRR(0.1,B5..B10)

NPV using IRR (B12) = +B5+@NPV(B3,B6..B10)
```

In the NPV formula, we have simply added the first cash flow, taking into account the initial outlay, to the NPV of the remaining cash flows (Year 2 – Year 6), assuming the hurdle rate entered in B1. For IRR, we have simply moved the payments forward by combining the first cash flow with the initial outlay (–$12,000 + $3,000). In the final formula, the calculated IRR in B3 is substituted for the hurdle rate in the NPV formula. The result, by definition, will be 0.

Note: ($0) appears in parentheses, indicating a negative number, because an extremely small rounding error has yielded a slightly negative result—($0.000000000038465), to be more exact. Despite 1-2-3's precision, you do occasionally get this sort of infinitesimal deviation.

Using @IRR to Calculate the Interest Rate of a Loan

The ad in the paper says a dealer will sell you a car for $23,119.45 or for 72 monthly payments of $476.39 with no money down. What is the monthly interest rate?

This is an ordinary annuity with a present value, or principal, of $23,119.45. As already noted, there is no mathematical formula or @Function for calculating the interest rate of an annuity, but you can press @IRR into service for the purpose. Although @IRR is designed for uneven cash flows, it doesn't matter if the payments are all the same. (Admittedly, it might be easier to use a financial calculator for this one.)

A worksheet that calculates the solution is shown in Figure 4.7. Since all of the payments are $476.39, you can enter that value in B2 and copy it to D2..D73.

	A	B	C	D
1	Cost	$23,119.45		(23,119.45)
2	Payment	$476.39		476.39
3	Internal Rate of Return	1.17%		476.39
4	APR	14.00%		476.39
5	Effective Annual Rate	14.93%		476.39
6				476.39
7				476.39
8				476.39
	***			
71				476.39
72				476.39
73				476.39

Figure 4.7. Using @IRR to calculate the rate for a loan (ordinary annuity).

The formulas at the top of the worksheet are shown in Figure 4.8. (There are no formulas after row 5.) To set up the worksheet:

1. Enter the labels in column A, the cost in B1, and the payment in B2.

2. In D1, enter -B1. This is the cost of the car, expressed as a negative value, since this is an outflow.

3. Now use the /Copy command to copy the payment from B2 to D2..D73. This represents the 72 monthly payments of $476.39.

4. To calculate IRR in B3, enter @IRR(0.01,D1..D73). This is the guess (1%) and the range for the original outlay and the 72 monthly payments. (One hopes the monthly rate will be closer to 1% per month than to 10%. However, as noted earlier, 10% works in most real life situations. And, in fact, you get the same result if you enter 0.1, or 10%.)

5. The payments are monthly, so the IRR is the monthly rate of return. To calculate APR in B4, enter 12*B3. This yields an APR of 14.00%.

6. The effective annual rate of return for monthly compounding, remember, is $(1+i)^{12}-1$. To make this calculation in B5, enter (1+B3)^12-1, yielding 14.93%.

	A	B	C	D
1	Cost	23119.45	-B1	
2	Payment	476.39		476.39
3	Internal Rate of Return	@IRR(0.01,D1..D73)		476.39
4	APR	12*B3		476.39
5	Effective Annual Rate	(1+B3)^12-1		476.39

Figure 4.8. Formulas for calculating the interest rate of a loan.

As you can see, the *monthly* IRR is 1.17%, and the APR is 14.00%. The latter, of course, is the APR used to calculate the monthly payment in the first place. It's also the APR you should find in the small print at the bottom of the car ad if the dealer compounds monthly. The effective annual rate for 14% APR, compounded monthly, is 14.93%.

Conclusion

In this chapter, you have learned to analyze investments using @NPV and @IRR, even if the payments do not occur at regular intervals. The chapter also explains how to use these functions to determine the interest rate for a series of regular payments, a calculation you can't readily make with basic math or @Functions.

None of these calculations take depreciation into account, and that is often a major consideration in analyzing business options. Depreciation is the topic of the next chapter.

5

Calculating Depreciation

This chapter focuses on depreciation calculations for tax purposes. It makes no pretense of being comprehensive. Rather, the purpose is to suggest ways to adapt 1-2-3 to make the necessary calculations. The tax law prescribes depreciation methods depending on the type of property and when it was placed in service. You may want to seek the advice of an accountant. Once you have decided on a method, however, the calculations are generally straightforward.

The Internal Revenue Service's rules for calculating depreciation of business property changed several times during the 1980s. To judge from the past, it is likely that Congress will change the law again. The examples and models in this chapter are based on the rules in effect for the 1989 tax year. Absent changes in the law, the same methods will work for subsequent years. If the law does change, you should be able to adapt the examples and models to reflect the changes.

The next section gives a brief overview of how depreciation methods have evolved. The rest of the chapter explains how to use 1-2-3 for the most common methods of calculating depreciation.

Choosing a Depreciation Method

In accounting and tax reporting, depreciation has little to do with the market value of an asset. The purpose of depreciation calculations is to allocate the cost of an asset over its useful life. A property used in business, such as rental real estate, will be depreciated on the books, even if its market value is actually increasing. Even when the market value of an asset declines, accounting rules or the tax law govern depreciation calculations, regardless of market value.

Suppose, for example, that your company invests $20,000 in equipment that will save $7,500 a year in labor costs for each of the next five years. You don't really lose $12,500 the first year and make $7,500 in future years. The IRS won't think so, in any case. You need a reasonable method of spreading the cost of the asset over the benefits it produces, and that's what depreciation calculations do. The depreciation method you use depends on the tax rules and circumstances.

Straight-line depreciation is the most straightforward method. You simply divide the cost of the asset by its useful life. If you expect to throw your $20,000 computer system in the trash heap after five years, for example, you would figure depreciation at $4,000 a year ($20,000/5=$4,000). If you expect to sell the system for $5,000 after five years, you might depreciate it at $3,000 per year, since ($20,000-$5,000)/5=$3,000. In this case, $5,000 would be the system's salvage value.

For financial statements and other internal purposes, accounting rules generally require businesses to use straight-line depreciation to allocate the cost of an asset over the period that it generates revenues or savings. Although you also have the option of using straight-line depreciation for tax purposes, it is usually advantageous to claim depreciation as rapidly as possible, because a $100 write-off in hand now is worth more than a $100 write-off that can be claimed next year.

Over the years, several methods of accelerating depreciation have been used. The concept of accelerated depreciation entered tax accounting during World War II. Large investments were required in plants that, without major modifications, would have little civilian use after the war, so the government allowed businesses to calculate depreciation over not less than six years. In 1954, Congress approved two methods of accelerated depreciation, known as double-declining balance and sum-of-the-years' digits. Both methods provide higher depreciation deductions early in the life of the asset, but lower write-offs later. 1-2-3 provides @Functions for these methods, even though they have been superceded by newer ways of calculating accelerated depreciation for tax purposes. These functions, @DDB and @SYD, and their underlying formulas are discussed at the end of this chapter.

Beginning in 1981, new business property had to be depreciated for tax purposes under the Accelerated Cost Recovery System, or ACRS. ACRS allowed businesses to accelerate depreciation in the early years of an asset's life. It also fixed the lives of various classes of property and eliminated salvage value from depreciation calculations for tax purposes. Businesses still had the option of electing straight-line depreciation under ACRS. Except for real estate, nearly all ACRS property will have been fully depreciated by the 1990 tax year. The exceptions are few, the rules are complex (which ones apply depends on exactly when a property was placed in service), and 1-2-3's @Functions are not readily adaptable to ACRS calculations. Therefore, ACRS is not discussed in detail here. If you are still depreciating property under ACRS, consult an adviser or a tax guide, such as *J.K. Lasser's Your Income Tax.*

For property placed in service after 1986, depreciation for tax purposes is governed by what is known as the Modified Accelerated Cost Recovery System (MACRS, pronounced "makers"). MACRS is explained in the following sections. Toward the end of the chapter, there is a more detailed discussion of straight-line depreciation and 1-2-3's @Functions for depreciation.

Adapting 1-2-3 to the Modified Accelerated Cost Recovery System

Under the Modified Accelerated Cost Recovery System (MACRS), most business equipment is depreciated over five years, using tables provided by the IRS. Five-year property includes cars, light trucks, computers, typewriters, and other office equipment. A seven-year period is used for furnishings, such as desks, files, and refrigerators. For most businesses, all equipment will be depreciated over five or seven years; exceptions apply only to highly specialized properties. (A few classes of specialized manufacturing equipment are depreciated over three years, and some other specialized assets have recovery periods longer than seven years. Three-year property includes certain special equipment for the manufacture of food and beverages, rubber products, plastics, fabricated metal, and motor vehicles. Other three-year property includes breeding hogs, racehorses more than two years old when acquired, and other horses more than 12 years old. Properties with depreciation lives of more than seven years include, among other things, water transportation vessels and equipment, petroleum refining equipment, equipment used in tobacco manufacturing, municipal sewage plants, and telephone distribution plants. These are quite specifically defined by the Internal Revenue Code.)

Rental real estate placed in service after 1986 is depreciated by the straight-line method, over 27.5 years for residential properties and 31.5 years for commercial and other nonresidential real estate.

Under MACRS, all property is treated as if it were acquired midyear, *unless* more than 40% of the depreciable property acquired during a given year was placed in service during the final quarter. In the latter case, *all* property for the year is treated as if it were placed in service in the middle of the quarter in which it was acquired. This will be explained shortly.

If you need to figure depreciation only occasionally for a few items, the easiest solution is to use simple multiplication of the original cost by the depreciation factors listed in the IRS tables. With the exception of @VDB (variable declining balance, which is available only with Release 3), 1-2-3's depreciation @Functions are not readily adaptable to MACRS calculations. The formulas underlying MACRS are understandable but not simple. A full explanation of using @VDB for MACRS calculations is provided in Chapter 9. @VDB can handle the MACRS calculations, but even users of Release 3 may it easier to use the methods described below.

First, we will look at MACRS depreciation under the midyear and midquarter rules, using the IRS tables. Later, we will explain the calculations underlying the MACRS tables, and then set up a model that uses 1-2-3 lookup tables to calculate depreciation automatically.

Using the IRS Tables for MACRS Depreciation

Unless there are heavy purchases in the final quarter of the tax year, MACRS treats all new depreciable property as if it were placed in service at midyear. If your business buys a new computer, for example, you may claim six months of depreciation—and only that amount—whether the machine was bought on January 1 or December 31. Unless more than 40% of purchases for a given year were in the last quarter, MACRS depreciation for each property is calculated according to the percentages shown in Figure 5.1.

Year	3-Year Property	5-Year Property	7-Year Property
1	33.33%	20.00%	14.92%
2	44.45%	32.00%	24.49%
3	14.81%	19.20%	17.49%
4	7.41%	11.52%	12.49%
5		11.52%	8.93%
6		5.76%	8.92%
7			8.93%
8			4.46%

Figure 5.1. The IRS table for MACRS depreciation of property placed in service after 1986.

The midyear rule does not apply if more than 40% of the depreciable property acquired during the tax year is placed in service in the last quarter. Instead, all property acquired that year is depreciated as if it were placed in service in the middle of the quarter in which it was acquired. If your business meets the 40% test some years but not others, then you must use the midquarter rule for years in which it applies and the midyear rule when it does not.

Under the midquarter rule, property bought during the first quarter is depreciated for 7/8 of the first year, property in the second quarter 5/8, property in the third quarter 3/8, and property in the fourth quarter 1/8. This is because 1/8 of the year has passed at the middle of the first quarter, 3/8 at the middle of the second, and so on. The IRS tables for depreciating property under the midquarter rule are shown in Figure 5.2.

Note: Factors for the midyear convention are added in the right column of Figure 5.2. The midyear rates are not used in years when the midquarter rule applies, but setting up the table this way can be useful if you want to set up a lookup table, as explained later.

5-Year Property

Year	First Quarter	Second Quarter	Third Quarter	Fourth Quarter	Midyear
1	35.00%	25.00%	15.00%	5.00%	20.00%
2	26.00%	30.00%	34.00%	38.00%	32.00%
3	15.60%	18.00%	20.40%	22.80%	19.20%
4	11.01%	11.37%	12.24%	13.68%	11.52%
5	11.01%	11.37%	11.30%	10.94%	11.52%
6	1.38%	4.26%	7.06%	9.58%	5.76%

7-Year Property

Year	First Quarter	Second Quarter	Third Quarter	Fourth Quarter	Midyear
1	25.00%	17.85%	10.71%	3.57%	14.29%
2	21.43%	23.47%	25.51%	27.55%	24.49%
3	15.31%	16.76%	18.22%	19.68%	17.49%
4	10.93%	11.97%	13.02%	14.06%	12.49%
5	8.75%	8.87%	9.30%	10.04%	8.93%
6	8.74%	8.87%	8.85%	8.73%	8.92%
7	8.75%	8.87%	8.86%	8.73%	8.93%
8	1.09%	3.33%	5.53%	7.64%	4.46%

Figure 5.2. Midquarter and midyear depreciation factors for five-year and seven-year property.

In the examples below, the depreciation factors shown in Figures 5.1 and 5.2 are used to calculate the annual depreciation for specific properties. Before we get to the examples, however, there are two other considerations to take into account when you calculate depreciation: first-year expensing and the alternative minimum tax.

Expensing Property for the Current Tax Year

If purchases of depreciable property are relatively small, you can count them as simple expenses, rather than depreciating the assets. This has the advantage of giving you an immediate tax write-off and saves the trouble of accounting for depreciation in subsequent years.

In general, you can elect to deduct up to $10,000 of the cost of business equipment placed in service during the current tax year rather than depreciating it under the MACRS formula. For example, if you purchase a computer for $6,300 and a desk for $1,265, you can deduct the entire amount, $7,565, as a straight business expense, rather than depreciating the property over five and seven years, respectively, provided they are used entirely for business.

If the total cost of depreciable property placed in service during the year exceeds $10,000 you can still deduct $10,000 as an expense and depreciate the balance under regular MACRS rules. For example, if you purchase $23,000 worth of office furniture, you can claim $10,000 as an expense and depreciate the $13,000 balance over seven years, since furnishings fall in the seven-year category.

First-year expensing is subject to these limitations, among others:

1. If qualifying depreciable property placed in service during the year exceeds $200,000, the allowable expense deduction is reduced by the excess. For example, if the total is $205,000, the maximum expense deduction is $5,000. If the total exceeds $210,000, no first-year expensing is allowed, so you must depreciate all new property under the MACRS rules.

2. Real estate does not qualify.

3. Special rules apply to computers, automobiles, partnerships, S corporations, and married couples filing separately.

4. Total first-year expensing may not exceed business income, calculated without regard to the expense deduction. Excess may be carried forward to the next year.

When these qualifications are met, first-year expensing will increase deductions for the current tax year but reduce depreciation deductions later. If you have doubts, consult a tax expert.

A Note about Alternative Minimum Tax

The alternative minimum tax (AMT) is designed to prevent wealthy people from taking excessive advantage of various tax write-offs. It may apply if you claim substantial deductions for accelerated depreciation and other tax benefits associated with certain types of investments. If the AMT applies to you, you will have to use a different method for calculating depreciation. The AMT rules are too complicated to go into here. If you think you may be subject to AMT, check the instructions on Form 6251 or consult a tax adviser.

Examples

The following examples calculate depreciation for individual items with simple multiplication and the depreciation factors shown in Figures 5.1 and 5.2. The basic 1-2-3 depreciation @Functions are discussed at the end of the chapter. There is a special section on Release 3's @VDB function (variable declining balance) in Chapter 9.

Calculating Simple Midyear Depreciation

Hot Type Desktop Publishing purchases a high-resolution laser printer for $18,000 in March 1989. It is the only depreciable property placed in service during the year. What is the depreciation schedule under MACRS?

The printer is a five-year property, and the midyear rule applies, because less than 40% of total assets were placed in service in the last quarter. To calculate depreciation schedule, multiply the cost by the midyear depreciation factors for five-year property from Figure 5.1, as shown in Figure 5.3.

	A	B	C	D
1	Property	Laser Printer		
2	Year in service	1989		
3	Cost	$18,000.00		
4	Class	5-year		
5	==
6		Year	Factor	Depreciation
7		1989	20.00%	$3,600.00
8		1990	32.00%	5,760.00
9		1991	19.20%	3,456.00
10		1992	11.52%	2,073.60
11		1993	11.52%	2,073.60
12		1994	5.76%	1,036.80
13			=======================
14		Total	100.00%	$18,000.00

Figure 5.3. A depreciation schedule for simple midyear depreciation under MACRS.

The Depreciation calculation in column D is simply the Factor in C multiplied by the Cost in B3. You can simplify setting up the worksheet by incorporating the original cost as an absolute reference. The formula in D7, for example, is $B$3*C7, an absolute reference to Cost in B3 and a relative reference to the Factor in column C. Now you can simply copy the formula down column D.

Sorting Properties by Class

As of the 1989 tax year, IRS Form 4562 requires you to break down depreciation for property placed in service during the current year by class (for example, five-year, seven-year, residential rental property, and nonresidential real property). Depreciation for all MACRS property placed in service before the current year (but after 1986) is reported on a separate line, and depreciation for property placed in service before 1987 is reported on still another line. Thus, five-year and seven-year property must be listed separately.

Suppose, for example, that in the current tax year your company spends $8,000 for a new computer, $5,000 for a new copier, $15,000 for new office furniture, and $800 for a new refrigerator for the office kitchen. (Assume that less than 40% of total purchases of depreciable property occurred in the last quarter.) The computer and copier are five-year property, and the furniture is seven-year property.

The calculation is shown in Figure 5.4. The formulas in column F simply multiply the depreciation factor (taken from Figure 5.1) times the cost for each item, listed in column B. Once you have entered a formula for a class of property, you can use the /Copy command to copy the formula vertically. Relative cell references will automatically select the correct cost for each line. The formulas in B14 and B15 simply use @SUM to add up the totals for each class, as required by Form 4562. The results are shown in Figure 5.5.

	A	B	C	D	E	F
1				MACRS		
2	Tax Year	1989				
3						
4						
5				Year in	Dep.	
6	Property	Cost	Class	Service	Year	Depreciation
7	============	================	========	==================	=============	==============
8	Computer	8,000.00	5-year	1989	1	0.2*B8
9	Copier	5,000.00	5-year	1989	1	0.2*B9
10	Furniture	15,000.00	7-year	1989	1	0.1429*B10
11	Refrigerator	800	7-year	1989	1	0.1429*B11
12						
13	Totals					
14	5-year	@SUM(F8..F9)				
15	7-year	@SUM(F10..F11)				

Figure 5.4. Depreciating property under MACRS.

If you prefer not to sort properties by class and year as you enter them, you can enter the data at random, and then use /Data Sort to arrange the entries by year and/or class. If you plan to copy formulas in column F, you

	A	B	C	D	E	F
1				MACRS		
2	Tax Year	1989				
3						
4						
5				Year in	Dep.	
6	Property	Cost	Class	Service	Year	Depreciation
7	==
8	Computer	8,000.00	5-year	1989	1	1,600.00
9	Copier	5,000.00	5-year	1989	1	1,000.00
10	Furniture	15,000.00	7-year	1989	1	2,143.50
11	Refrigerator	800	7-year	1989	1	114.32
12						
13	Totals					
14	5-year	2,600.00				
15	7-year	2,357.36				

Figure 5.5. The results of calculations for five-year and seven-year property placed in service in the current year.

should sort the entries before making your depreciation calculations. The data range for the sort should include all of your data about depreciable properties, but not the labels above, or the sums below. If you are depreciating property placed in service over several years, the primary sort key is column D, Year in Service, and the sort order is descending. The secondary key is column C, Class, with an ascending sort order. If all property was placed in service during the current year, column C becomes the primary key.

Working with Midquarter Depreciation and Depreciation in Earlier Years

Suppose that more than 40% of the equipment your company bought in 1989 was placed in service in the last quarter. Using the items listed in the last example, the computer ($8,000) was bought in the third quarter, the copier ($5,000) in the second, the refrigerator ($800) in the first, and the furniture ($15,000) in the fourth. In addition, you are still using the midyear rule to depreciate a $787 typewriter bought in 1988 and a CAD system purchased for $42,365 in 1987. What is the depreciation for 1989?

The midquarter rule applies for the items bought in 1989, because more than 40% of the total was placed in service in the fourth quarter. Thus, each item is treated as if it were placed in service in the middle of the quarter it was acquired. The furniture and refrigerator are seven-year property; the copier and computer are five-year property. The typewriter and CAD system are five-year property, in their second and third years of depreciation, respectively.

From Figure 5.2, you can see that the depreciation factors are:

Computer (third quarter)	15.00%
Copier (second quarter)	25.00%
Furniture (fourth quarter)	3.57%
Refrigerator (first quarter)	25.00%
Typewriter (year 2)	32.00%
CAD system (year 3)	19.20%

Figure 5.6 shows the calculations. In column G, depreciation is calculated by multiplying the depreciation factors from Figure 5.2 by the cost of each item in column B. For example, the formula in G11 for the computer depreciation is simply 0.15*B11, where 0.15 is the first-year midquarter depreciation factor for five-year property placed in service during the third quarter and B11 is the original cost of the computer.

The totals at the bottom of the worksheet simply use @SUM to add up the totals for each category.

First-year Expensing with Leftover Depreciation

On April 15, Bob's Garage buys a computerized engine analyzer for $16,575. The company elects to claim a first-year expense of $10,000 and to depreciate the remainder over five years. (Assume the midyear rule applies.)

The worksheet in Figure 5.7 shows the calculation. Elected Cost is the IRS's term for the amount you elect to claim as a first-year expense. The entries are very simple:

	A	B	C	D	E	F	G
1					MACRS		
2	Tax Year		1989				
3							
4							
5					Year in		Dep	
6	Property	Cost	Class	Service	Qtr	Year	Depreciation
7	==
8		1989					
9							
10	Five-Year						
11	Computer	8,000.00	5-year	1989	3	1	1,200.00
12	Copier	5,000.00	5-year	1989	2	1	1,250.00
13							
14	Seven-Year						
15	Furniture	15,000.00	7-year	1989	4	1	535.50
16	Refrigerator	800.00	7-year	1989	1	1	200.00
17							
18	Previous years						
19	Typewriter	787.00	5-year	1988	MY	2	251.84
20	CAD System	42,365.00	5-year	1987	MY	3	8,134.08
21							
22	Totals						
23							
24	1989						
25	Five-year	2,450.00					
26	Seven-year	735.50					
27							
28	Previous years	8,385.82					
29							
30							

Figure 5.6. Calculating midquarter depreciation by multiplication.

	A	B	C	D
1			Depreciation	Elected Cost/
2	Property	Cost	Factor	Depreciation
3	==
4	Engine Analyzer	16,575.00		10,000.00
5	Balance (5-year)	6,575.00	20.00%	1,315.00
6				============
7	Total			$11,315.00

Figure 5.7. Claiming a first-year expense and depreciating the balance.

B4: 16,575.00	original cost of the analyzer.
D4: 10,000.00	the elected cost.
B5: +B4–D4	original cost less elected cost.
C5: .20	the first-year depreciation factor for five-year property.
D7:+D4+D5	adds up the total.

Thus, Bob's Garage can claim both an expense deduction of $10,000 and a depreciation deduction of $1,315 the first year it uses the analyzer.

How the MACRS Calculation Works

For most purposes, the easiest way to determine MACRS depreciation factors is to consult the IRS tables, but it is worth understanding how the tables are constructed. The tables use the double-declining balance method of calculating accelerated depreciation, switching to a modified version of straight-line depreciation when the latter yields a higher result. This will become clearer as we walk through the calculations.

Figure 5.8 shows the calculation for a five-year property that cost $10,000, using the midyear rule. The DDB column calculates each year's depreciation using the double-declining-balance method. The SLN column uses straight-line depreciation to depreciate the remaining balance over the remaining life of the property. (As we will see shortly, the formulas for these calculations are not exactly the ones used by @DDB

	A	B	C	D	E
1	Year	DDB	SLN	Dep	Balance
2	0				10,000.00
3	1	2,000.00	1,000.00	2,000.00	8,000.00
4	2	3,200.00	1,777.78	3,200.00	4,800.00
5	3	1,920.00	1,371.43	1,920.00	2,880.00
6	4	1,152.00	1,152.00	1,152.00	1,728.00
7	5	691.20	1,152.00	1,152.00	576.00
8	6	230.40	576.00	576.00	0.00

Figure 5.8. MACRS depreciation for $10,000 worth of five-year properties, such as office equipment and computers.

and @SLN, which are discussed at the end of this chapter.) The Dep column selects the larger of the two, and the Balance column calculates the amount remaining to be depreciated, which is the basis for the next year's calculations. DDB is used for the first three years, since it yields more depreciation then. In the fourth year, SLN equals DDB. In the fifth and sixth years, the SLN method is used.

Figure 5.9 shows how the model works. The beginning balance, $10,000 is entered in E2. In the first year, the formulas for DDB and SLN are divided by 2, to reflect a half-year's depreciation. In the next column, the formulas use @IF to select the larger of the amounts calculated by the two methods. Column E simply subtracts the depreciation from the old balance to figure a new one.

	A	B	C	D	E
1	Year	DDB	SLN	Dep	Balance
2	0				10,000.00
3	1	+E2*2/5/2	+E2/5/2	@IF(B3>C3,B3,C3)	+E2-D3
4	2	+E3*2/5	+E3/4.5	@IF(B4>C4,B4,C4)	+E3-D4
5	3	+E4*2/5	+E4/3.5	@IF(B5>C5,B5,C5)	+E4-D5
6	4	+E5*2/5	+E5/2.5	@IF(B6>C6,B6,C6)	+E5-D6
7	5	+E6*2/5	+E6/1.5	@IF(B7>C7,B7,C7)	+E6-D7
8	6	+E7*2/5	+E7	@IF(B8>C8,B8,C8)	+E7-D8

Figure 5.9. Formulas for calculating MACRS for five-year property.

The DDB calculation is similar to the one used by @DDB, except that the depreciation for the first and last years is prorated, and there is no easy way to do that with @DDB. Here is the formula:

$$DDB = \frac{2*Balance}{Life}$$

For each year, the remaining balance is multiplied by 2 and divided by the life of the property, hence the derivation of the term "double-declining balance." The remaining balance must be calculated for each year. In the first year, the basic formula is divided by 2 to calculate a half year's depreciation. In subsequent years, a full year's depreciation is claimed, and division by 2 is omitted.

The calculations in the SLN column are a modified version of basic straight-line depreciation (the method used by @SLN). The basic SLN formula is simply the cost of the asset divided by the asset's useful life. In this case, that would yield a figure of $2,000 per year ($10,000/5). Here, the remaining balance is divided by the remaining life:

$$SLN = \frac{Balance}{Remaining\ Life}$$

In the first year, only a half year's depreciation is allowed, so the basic formula is divided by 2 ($10,000/5/2 = $1,000). The result is less than the $2,000 calculated with in the DDB column, so the Balance at the beginning of the second year is $8,000. Now, the Remaining Life is 4.5 years, so the SLN calculation for the second year is $8,000/4.5 = $1,777.78. The SLN column continues to use the latest balance from column E and divide by the remaining life, so the divisor is 3.5 for the third year, 2.5 for the fourth, and 1.5 for the fifth. In the last year, SLN is simply the remaining balance (+E7), because dividing by the remaining life (0.5 years) would yield more depreciation than the balance.

A model for any other depreciation period could be constructed the same way. The only difference would be the number of years in which a full year's depreciation is calculated. For midquarter depreciation, you would change the calculations for prorating the first year and the remaining life in the SLN column.

That's the way the IRS model works. If you want to build an automatic MACRS model, rather than simply multiplying by the IRS's annual factors as discussed earlier, it's easier to use an @VLOOKUP table, as explained in the next section.

Building a Model for MACRS Depreciation

If you need to figure depreciation only occasionally for a few items, the simple multiplication using the depreciation factors in Figures 5.1 and 5.2 is the easiest solution. For more frequent work, you can build a model to calculate depreciation automatically. This model is also an opportunity to use two of 1-2-3's more interesting @Functions, @VLOOKUP and @@ (the latter is new in Release 2.0). The following sections explain how to use these functions, and then how to set up a model based on the tables in Figure 5.2.

Note: A different model, using @HLOOKUP but not @@, is provided in Chapter 9.

Using @VLOOKUP to Retrieve Information from a Table

@VLOOKUP is perfectly suited to extracting information from a table like the MACRS table in Figure 5.2. Once you have set up a table, you can enter the function in this format:

`@VLOOKUP (criterion, range, column-offset)`

where *criterion* is the lookup criterion (e.g., depreciation year); *range* is the range of the table; and *column-offset* identifies the column from which the value will be selected.

The function searches down the first column of the table until it finds the largest value not greater than the criterion, and then selects the value *x* columns to the right, as specified by the column-offset. For example, if you have used /Range Name to label the table in Figure 5.1 MACRS, you could enter @VLOOKUP(3,MACRS,2) to find the third-year depreciation factor for five-year property—down 3 rows, over 2 columns. The function returns 19.20%.

Using @@ to Identify a Range

The @@ function is an indirect cell pointer. In a formula, @@ allows you to refer to a cell that contains a label identifying a cell or range. (Without @@, a reference to a cell containing a label evaluates to 0; with a simple cell reference, you get the label in the cell referred to.) @@ is entered in this format: @@(cell), where the argument is the address of a cell that contains a label identifying another cell address. The @@ function returns the contents of the range identified by the label. This is one of the 1-2-3 functions you pretty much have to try in order to understand it. Here's a quick tutorial:

1. In cell A1 of a blank worksheet enter the label B1 (not the formula +B1).

2. In B1, enter the value 10.

3. In C1, enter the formula +A1.

4. In D1, enter the formula @@(A1).

Your worksheet now looks like this (the labels in A1 and C1 are right-justified for appearance):

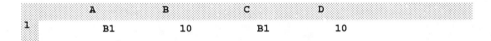

Figure 5.10. Using @@ to retrieve data.

In column C, the formula +A1 simply returns the label in A1, which has a numerical value of 0 if incorporated in a longer formula. (+A1+B1 = 10, since the value of A1 is 0 and the value of B1 is 10.) However, in column D, the formula @@(A1) returns the value 10 because the label in column A names the cell B1. (Thus, @@(A1)+B1 = 20.) On the other hand, @@(B1) or @@(A2) returns an ERR message, because neither cell contains a label that names a cell or range.

The next section explains how to build a model for calculating MACRS depreciation using @@, @VLOOKUP, and a single, copiable formula.

Building a MACRS Model with @VLOOKUP and @@

Most often, MACRS property other than real estate is depreciated under the midyear convention. However, if you fall under the midquarter rule for one or more years and the midyear rule in others, you will have to use both methods to calculate depreciation for the current year. You can build a model that will calculate MACRS depreciation either way.

The first step in building the model is to enter the lookup tables shown in Figure 5.11. Their exact location on the worksheet is not important, but the rest of the model will be easier to set up if you place the tables below and to the right of your calculations. After copying the tables onto your worksheet, use the /Range Name Create command to name the numerical portions of the tables 5-year and 7-year, respectively. The top right corner of each range is 1 in the Year column. The bottom left is the last entry under Midyear.

	I	J	K	L	M	N
21	5-Year Property					
22		First	Second	Third	Fourth	
23	Year	Quarter	Quarter	Quarter	Quarter	Midyear
24	=========	==========	==========	==========	==========	==========
25	1	35.00%	25.00%	15.00%	5.00%	20.00%
26	2	26.00%	30.00%	34.00%	38.00%	32.00%
27	3	15.60%	18.00%	20.40%	22.80%	19.20%
28	4	11.01%	11.37%	12.24%	13.68%	11.52%
29	5	11.01%	11.37%	11.30%	10.94%	11.52%
30	6	1.38%	4.26%	7.06%	9.58%	5.76%
31						
32						
33	7-Year Property					
34		First	Second	Third	Fourth	
35	Year	Quarter	Quarter	Quarter	Quarter	Midyear
36	==========	==========	==========	==========	==========	==========
37	1	25.00%	17.85%	10.71%	3.57%	14.29%
38	2	21.43%	23.47%	25.51%	27.55%	24.49%
39	3	15.31%	16.76%	18.22%	19.68%	17.49%
40	4	10.93%	11.97%	13.02%	14.06%	12.49%
41	5	8.75%	8.87%	9.30%	10.04%	8.93%
42	6	8.74%	8.87%	8.85%	8.73%	8.92%
43	7	8.75%	8.87%	8.86%	8.73%	8.93%
44	8	1.09%	3.33%	5.53%	7.64%	4.46%

Figure 5.11. Setting up lookup tables for MACRS.

Now go to A1 and set up the top of the model as shown in Figure 5.12, entering information about depreciable property in columns A–E. (You can adjust column widths and range formats to your preferences; that will not affect the calculations.) To meet the requirements of IRS Form 4562, you should separate properties placed in service during the current year by class, as shown. Properties placed in service in earlier years can be lumped together.

	A	B	C	D	E	F	G
1						MACRS	
2	Tax Year	1989					
3							
4							
5				Year in		Dep	
6	Property	Cost	Class	Service	Qtr	Year	Depreciation
7	==
8	1989						
9							
10	Five-Year						
11	Computer	8,000.00	5-year	1989	3	1	1.200.00
12	Copier	5,000.00	5-year	1989	2	1	1,250.00
13							
14	Seven-Year						
15	Furniture	15,000.00	7-year	1989	4	1	535.50
16	Refrigerator	800.00	7-year	1989	1	1	200.00
17							
18	Previous years						
19	Typewriter	787.00	5-year	1988	5	2	251.84
20	CAD System	42,365.00	5-year	1987	5	3	8,134.08
21							
22	Totals						
23							
24	1989						
25	Five-year	2,450.00					
26	Seven-year	735.50					
27							
28	Previous years	8,385.92					
29							
30	Total		11,571.42				

Figure 5.12. Separating properties by year and class for depreciation.

To avoid unnecessary complexity, the model is limited to five-year and seven-year property, which includes most business property other than real estate. Also for the sake of simplicity, it uses 1, 2, 3, and 4 to designate the quarter a property was placed in service when the midquarter rule applies, and 5 designates property that falls under the midyear convention.

Figure 5.13 shows the formulas in columns F and G of Figure 5.11. (For the formulas at the bottom of the worksheet, simply use @SUM to calculate totals for the indicated categories.)

	F	G
5	Dep	
6	Year	Depreciation
7	=======	===
8		
9		
10		
11	+$B$3−D11+1	+B11*@VLOOKUP (F11, @@ (C11) , E11)
12	+$B$3−D12+1	+B12*@VLOOKUP (F12, @@ (C12) , E12)
13		
14		
15	+$B$3−D15+1	+B15*@VLOOKUP (F15, @@ (C15) , E15)
16	+$B$3−D16+1	+B16*@VLOOKUP (F16, @@ (C16) , E16)
17		
18		
19	+$B$3−D19+1	+B19*@VLOOKUP (F19, @@ (C19) , E19)
20	+$B$3−D20+1	+B20*@VLOOKUP (F20, @@ (C20) , E20)

Figure 5.13. Formulas in columns F and G of the MACRS depreciation model.

The formulas in column F calculate the depreciation year by subtracting the year in service (column D) from the tax year (B3) and adding 1. Thus, if the year in service is 1989, the property is in the first year of depreciation. For example, the computer listed in row 11 went in service during the current tax year, so the depreciation year is 1 (+$B$3-D11+1 = 1). Cell references to the tax year are absolute ($B$3), because the reference is constant for all entries. Once you have entered this formula once, you can copy it into any cell in column D.

The most important calculations in the model are in column G, where @VLOOKUP formulas figure the depreciation for each item. Again, once you have entered one formula, you can copy it anywhere in the column. All cell references are relative. The formula in G11 is +B11*@VLOOKUP(F11,@@(C11),E11), so when you copy it to G12, it automatically becomes

```
+B12*@VLOOKUP (F12,@@ (C12) ,E12)
```

and so on.

The formulas in column G start with the original cost of the property, and then multiply that by the appropriate depreciation factor in the lookup tables shown in Figure 5.11. Remember that the format for the lookup function is:

```
@VLOOKUP (criterion, range, column-offset)
```

For example, the depreciation formula for the computer listed in row 11 is +B11*@VLOOKUP(F11,@@(C11),E11). Here's how the formula breaks down:

+B11*	Selects the cost of the item from column B (in this case $8,000) and multiplies.
@VLOOKUP(	Specifies the @VLOOKUP function.
F11	Specifies the depreciation year in column F (here, it's 1) as the lookup criterion.
@@(C11),	Selects the lookup table named by the column in C (here, '5-year).
E11)	Uses the value for Qtr in column E to specify the column-offset (in this case, 3) and closes the formula with a parenthesis.

This model may seem fairly complicated, but it actually takes only a few minutes to set up once you understand the @VLOOKUP and @@ functions. Note that the formulas in column G will return ERR messages if there is no named range that matches the label in column C.

Calculating Straight-line Depreciation

The simplest and most straightforward depreciation method, of course, is straight-line depreciation. Companies generally use straight-line depreciation for calculating earnings and profits, even if they use accelerated depreciation for tax purposes, because straight-line depreciation spreads cost evenly over the resulting revenues. In most cases, you can also elect straight-line depreciation for tax purposes, provided you use the method consistently. This option is sometimes desirable, for example, in startups, where losses or low earnings may be expected initially, followed by higher earnings later.

The basic straight-line formula is just this:

$$\frac{Cost - Salvage\ Value}{Life}$$

This formula is incorporated in the @SLN function in this format:

```
@SLN(cost,salvage,life)
```

Suppose, for example, that Abracadabra Printers buys a new folding machine for $10,000. At the end of its life in five years, it is expected to have a salvage value of $2,000. The annual depreciation is

```
(10000-2000)/5
```

or

```
@SLN(10000,2000,5)
```

Either way, the annual depreciation is $1,600.

The only calculation that requires much further notice is prorating depreciation in the first and last years of the property's life. In concept, prorating depreciation is quite simple. If a property with a life of five years is placed in service on July 1, for example, you can simply claim a half year's depreciation the first year and a half year the sixth; depreciation on the folder would be $800 the first and last years. If the property is placed in service at the beginning of the second quarter, you figure a quarter's depreciation the first year and three quarter's the last—$400 and $1,200 in this case. And so on.

In practice, however, the tax laws require very specific conventions for prorating depreciation, depending on the type of property and when it was placed in service, so it is important to make sure you are using the right method for the property in question.

Using Straight-line Depreciation under MACRS

MACRS allows you to elect straight-line depreciation for business property, rather than using the IRS's modified double-declining balance method explained earlier. Most equipment, such as computers, typewriters, cars, and light trucks, is depreciated over five years. For furniture and fixtures, you can choose a life of either 7 or 10 years. Once you have elected straight-line depreciation for a property, you cannot change methods later. In addition, the same method must be used for all property in the same class (generally meaning with the same life) placed in service during the same year.

Salvage value is ignored under MACRS, and the midyear and midquarter rules apply for prorating, except for real estate. New business property other than real estate is treated as if it were placed in service at midyear unless more than 40% of the year's new depreciable property is placed in service in the last quarter. In the latter case, each property is treated as if it were placed in service at the midpoint of the quarter you began using it. (See *Midyear Rule* and *Midquarter Rule* above. Real estate depreciation under MACRS is explained below.)

Figure 5.14 shows the formulas for calculating the MACRS depreciation for a $10,000 computer over five years under the MACRS rules for straight-line depreciation. (Since depreciation is prorated in the first year, the calculation spills over into the sixth year.) The result is shown in Figure 5.15.

	A	B	C	D	E	F	G
1	Property	Computer					
2	Cost	$10,000.00					
3	Life	5					
4	Dep./Year	$2,000.00					
5							
6	===
7			Midyear		MidQtr Rule		
8		Year	Rule	1st Qtr	2nd Qtr	3rd Qtr	4th Qtr
9	===
10		1	1/2*$B$4	7/8*$B$4	5/8*$B$4	3/8*$B$4	1/8*$B$4
11		2	$B$4	$B$4	$B$4	$B$4	$B$4
12		3	$B$4	$B$4	$B$4	$B$4	$B$4
13		4	$B$4	$B$4	$B$4	$B$4	$B$4
14		5	$B$4	$B$4	$B$4	$B$4	$B$4
15		6	+$B$4-C10	+$B$4-D10	+$B$4-E10	+$B$4-F10	+$B$4-G10

Figure 5.14. Formulas for five-year MACRS straight-line depreciation, using the midyear rule and the midquarter rule.

	A	B	C	D	E	F	G
1	Property	Computer					
2	Cost	$10,000.00					
3	Life	5					
4	Dep./Year	$2,000.00					
5							
6	===
7			Midyear		MidQtr Rule		
8		Year	Rule	1st Qtr	2nd Qtr	3rd Qtr	4th Qtr
9	===
10		1	1,000	1,750	1,250	750	250
11		2	2,000	2,000	2,000	2,000	2,000
12		3	2,000	2,000	2,000	2,000	2,000
13		4	2,000	2,000	2,000	2,000	2,000
14		5	2,000	2,000	2,000	2,000	2,000
15		6	1,000	250	750	1,250	1,750

Figure 5.15. Depreciating a computer over five years under the MACRS straight-line method.

The main calculation in Figure 5.14 is Dep/Year in B4. It simply applies @SLN function to the cost and life of the property entered in B2 and B3. Under MACRS, the salvage value is always 0, so you enter 0 as the second value in the argument. (You could, of course, simply divide the cost by the life by entering +B2/B3.) Once you have made that calculation, you can copy it as an absolute reference (+$B$4) into cells C10..G15, depreciation years 2-5, when depreciation is not prorated.

In the first year of depreciation under the midyear rule, you take a half-year's depreciation, and the calculation in B10 is half the annual depreciation (1/2*$B$4). Under the midquarter rule, the proration factor is 7/8 (7/8*$B$4) for property placed in service in the first quarter, 5/8 for property placed in service in the second quarter, 3/8 for the third quarter, and 1/8 for property placed in service in the fourth quarter.

For the final year, shown in row 15, the first year's prorated depreciation is subtracted from the annual figure in B4. Using absolute and relative references as shown, you can copy the calculation from C15 across the rest of row 15.

Depreciating Real Estate under MACRS

Real estate placed in service after 1986 is depreciated under the straight-line method; salvage value is not considered in the calculation. Residential rental property is depreciated over 27.5 years, commercial property over 31.5 years. All real estate begins depreciating at the middle of the month it is placed in service. Thus, for the first year, you can claim 11.5 months of depreciation for property placed in service in January, 10.5 months for property in service in February, and so on.

Generally, structures are depreciable, but land is not. Thus, you must allocate the cost of the property between land and structures. Improvements after 1986 that increase the value of a structure are depreciated under MACRS, even if the rest of the structure is depreciated under rules for older properties.

In all but the first and last years, you can simply divide the original cost of the structure, excluding land, by the life. For example, for a $100,000 duplex (excluding land) placed in service after 1986, you could enter:

```
100000/27.5
```

Answer: $3,636.36.

For a commercial property, the depreciation period is 31.5 years. For a $2.5 million building (again, excluding land), the calculation is:

```
2500000/31.5
```

Answer: $79,365.07.

If you prefer, you can use the @SLN function, although that requires more keystrokes. The formulas for the two examples above are @SLN(100000,0,27.5) and @SLN(2500000,0,31.5). In both cases, you must enter 0 for the middle value of the argument, even though salvage value is not taken into account. The answers, of course, are the same.

Prorating the First and Last Years

Under MACRS, real estate is treated as if it were placed in service in midmonth. Thus, when a property is in service in January the proration factor is 11.5/12 for the first year and 0.5/12 for the last. For property placed in service in December the figures are reversed.

You can calculate the numerator by numbering the months and subtracting the month in service from 12.5, and then dividing by 12. The factor for January is (12.5-1)/12; for March it's (12.5-3)/12; for October it's (12.5-10)/12; and so on. This allows you to copy the formula across a row or down a column, using relative references to the months.

Figure 5.16 shows the proration factors for the first year, intervening years, and the last year for both residential rentals and commercial real estate. Figure 5.17 shows the formulas for the first three months. The cell references simply match the columns; you can copy these formulas across the entire 12 months using relative cell references.

With these models, you can calculate the depreciation for any real estate placed in service after 1986. Remember that only structures may be depreciated while land may not. Thus, you must divide the cost of the property between land and buildings. For real estate placed in service before 1987, the tax rules depend on exactly when the property was acquired.

	A	B	C	D	E	F	G	H	I	J	K	L	M
1	In Service	1	2	3	4	5	6	7	8	9	10	11	12
2														
3	Residential													
4														
5	First Year	3.485%	3.182%	2.879%	2.576%	2.273%	1.970%	1.667%	1.364%	1.061%	0.758%	0.455%	0.152%
6	Middle Years	3.636%	3.636%	3.636%	3.636%	3.636%	3.636%	3.636%	3.636%	3.636%	3.636%	3.636%	3.636%
7	Last Year	0.152%	0.455%	0.758%	1.061%	1.364%	1.667%	1.970%	2.273%	2.576%	2.879%	3.182%	3.485%
8														
9	Commercial													
10														
11	First Year	3.042%	2.778%	2.513%	2.249%	1.984%	1.720%	1.455%	1.190%	0.926%	0.661%	0.397%	0.132%
12	Middle Years	3.175%	3.175%	3.175%	3.175%	3.175%	3.175%	3.175%	3.175%	3.175%	3.175%	3.175%	3.175%
13	Last Year	0.132%	0.397%	0.661%	0.926%	1.190%	1.455%	1.720%	1.984%	2.249%	2.513%	2.778%	3.042%

Figure 5.16. Annual depreciation factors for real property placed in service after 1986.

	A	B	C	D
1	In Service	1	2	3
2	===
3	Residential			
4				
5	First Year	(12.5-B1)/12*B6	(12.5-C1)/12*C6	(12.5-D1)/12*D6
6	Middle Years	@SLN(1,0,27.5)	@SLN(1,0,27.5)	@SLN(1,0,27.5)
7	Last Year	+B6-B5	+C6-C5	+D6-D5
8				
9	Commercial			
10				
11	First Year	(12.5-B1)/12*B12	(12.5-C1)/12*C12	(12.5-D1)/12*D12
12	Middle Years	@SLN(1,0,31.5)	@SLN(1,0,31.5)	@SLN(1,0,31.5)
13	Last Year	+B12-B11	+C12-C11	+D12-D11

Figure 5.17. Formulas for calculating annual depreciation factors for real estate placed in service after 1986.

Depreciating Property Placed in Service before 1987

MACRS was preceded by the Accelerated Cost Recovery System (ACRS), which governs depreciation of assets placed in service before 1987 but after 1980. Because most ACRS equipment has now been fully depreciated and the rules changed several times for real estate, only a general explanation is provided here. IRS Publication 534 provides details.

Using 1-2-3's @DDB and @SYD Functions for Double-declining Balance and Sum-of-the-years' Digits

As mentioned earlier, for property placed in service from the 1950s through 1980, accelerated depreciation was often calculated by methods known as double-declining balance and sum-of-the-years' digits. Most of this property has now been fully depreciated and these methods are of limited use. Nevertheless, 1-2-3 retains @Functions for these depreciation methods, @DDB for double-declining balance and @SYD for sum-of-the-years' digits.

@DDB and @SYD calculate the depreciable basis of a property by subtracting a property's salvage value, if any, from its cost. They then use formulas to allocate that value over the life of the property. Their operation is quite simple as long as you depreciate an asset for a full year (or other whole period) during the first period the asset is in use. The calculation is somewhat more complicated when depreciation begins in

	A	B	C	D	E	F	G
1	Cost		$10,000.00				
2	Salvage Value		$1,200.00				
3	Life		5				
4							
5							
6	Year	@SLN	Balance	@DDB	Balance	@SYD	Balance
7	1	1,760.00	8,240.00	4,000.00	6,000.00	2,933.33	7,066.67
8	2	1,760.00	6,480.00	2,400.00	3,600.00	2,346.67	4,720.00
9	3	1,760.00	4,720.00	1,440.00	2,160.00	1,760.00	2,960.00
10	4	1,760.00	2,960.00	864.00	1,296.00	1,173.33	1,786.67
11	5	1,760.00	1,200.00	96.00	1,200.00	586.67	1,200.00

Figure 5.18. Comparing depreciation using @SLN, @DDB, and @SYD.

the middle of a period.

Figure 5.18 compares depreciation for an asset using @SLN (straight-line depreciation), @DDB, and @SYD. The asset cost $10,000 and has a life of five years, at the end of which it will have a salvage value of $1,200. The balance for each method is the book or undepreciated value of the asset at the end of each year. Notice that @DDB provides more rapid depreciation than the straight-line method in the early years but less toward the end of the asset's life. @SYD also accelerates depreciation, but less rapidly than @DDB.

With all three methods, the balance equals the salvage value when depreciation is finished. In each case, the balance is calculated by subtracting the current year's depreciation from the previous balance. The beginning balance is the cost, $10,000 in C1. Thus, the balance at the end of the first year under @SLN is +C1-B7. At the end of the second year, the balance is +C7-B8, and so on.

We have already seen that straight-line depreciation simply allocates depreciation evenly over the life of the asset. For example, if an asset costs $10,000, has a life of five years, and has a salvage value of $1,200 at the end of that time, the depreciable basis is $8,800, and the depreciation is $1,760 per year ($10,000 - $1,200 = $8,800; $8,800 / 5 = $1,760).

By way of review, @SLN is entered in this format:

```
@SLN(cost,salvage,life)
```

Cost and salvage can be any values; life can be any value but 0 (to avoid division by 0). Unlike the other methods, you do not have to include the period for which you are calculating depreciation because it is the same for all.

Calculating Double-declining Balance Depreciation with @DDB

The double-declining balance function is entered in this format:

```
@DDB(cost,salvage,life,period)
```

Unlike @SLN, @DDB requires you to enter the period in the argument because depreciation varies for each. Cost and salvage can be any value;

life can be any value greater than 2; and period can be any value greater than or equal to 1, but will generally be a whole number. @DDB accelerates depreciation using this formula:

$$\frac{(bv * 2)}{n}$$

where bv is the book or undepreciated value of the property, and n is the number of periods in the project's life.

This simply doubles the undepreciated balance at the beginning of each period and divides by the life of the property. Thus, the depreciation for the first period in the example is:

$$\frac{\$10,000 * 2}{5} \quad = \quad \$4,000$$

Notice that salvage value, entered in the argument, does not appear in the equation; 1-2-3 simply uses that figure to stop depreciation when the book value reaches the salvage value. One of the characteristics of this formula, however, is that the outcome will never reach 0, because you are dividing an ever-decreasing amount by the fixed life of the property. Thus, the method is usually switched to straight-line if the property is not fully depreciated at the end of its life.

Again, @DDB does not lend itself to prorating the first year's depreciation. If prorating is required, the simplest solution is to solve the problem mathematically, rather than using @DDB, as explained earlier under *How the MACRS Calculation Works* in this chapter.

Calculating Sum-of-the-Years' Digits with @SYD

1-2-3 uses a complicated-looking formula to calculate sum-of-the-years digits depreciation:

$$\frac{(c-s)*(n-p+1)}{n*(n+1) \, / \, 2}$$

where *c* is the cost; *s* is the salvage value; *n* is the life of the property; and *p* is the period for which depreciation is being calculated.

That formula is the mathematical expression of a simpler idea. To determine the denominator, add the whole numbers from 1 to the life of the property. For a five-year property, for example, the calculation is:

```
1+2+3+4+5 = 15
```

The numerator for the first year is the basis of the property multiplied by its life. For each subsequent year, the life is reduced by 1. Thus, for a five-year property the basis is multiplied by 5/15 the first year, 4/15 the second, 3/15 the third, 2/15 the fourth, and 1/15 the fifth.

It's much easier to enter @SYD in this format:

```
@SYD(cost,salvage,life,period)
```

Salvage can be 0, but life and period must be greater than or equal to 1. For example, to calculate the first year's depreciation for a $10,000 machine with a salvage value of $1,200 and a life of five years, enter:

```
@SYD(10000,1200,5,1)
```

Answer: $2,933.33.

With @SYD, you can prorate depreciation fairly easily for property that is placed in service during the year. For the first year, figure SYD as usual, then multiply by the fraction of the year the asset was used—0.25 for three months, 0.5 for six, 0.75 for nine, and so on. Suppose, for example, that a machine costs $7,500 has a salvage value of $750 after a life of five years, and is in service for nine months the first year. To calculate the first year's depreciation, enter:

```
@SYD(7500,750,5,1)*0.75
```

Answer: $1,687.50, or simply 75% of the first year's calculation under SYD.

At the end of the second depreciation year, the machine will have been in service for 1.75 years, a figure you can simply enter as the period in the @SYD calculation:

```
@SYD(7500,750,5,1.75)
```

The period is 2.75 for the third year, 3.75 for the fourth, and 4.75 for the fifth. For the sixth year, calculate the final year of SYD and multiply by the fraction of the year that the equipment *was not* in service the first year (in this case 0.25):

```
@SYD(7500,750,5,5)*0.25
```

Here are the results:

Year	SYD
1	$1,687.50
2	1,912.50
3	1,462.50
4	1,012.50
5	562.50
6	112.50
	========
Total	$6,750.00

Again, @DDB and @SYD are useful mainly for calculating accelerated depreciation for property placed in service before 1981. Since most property from that era has been fully depreciated, there are relatively few current applications for these functions. Nevertheless, they are there when you need them.

Conclusion

This concludes the first part of this book. At this point, you should have a basic understanding of 1-2-3's financial functions. The remainder of the book is devoted to using the methods to solve real-life problems.

6

More Examples for Loans, Leases, and Savings

Chapter 2 explained the basic formulas and @Functions for annuities. For ordinary annuities, payments are at the end of each period. Loans are the typical example. 1-2-3's @Functions are set up for ordinary annuities. For annuities due, payments are at the beginning of each period, and you have to adapt the @Functions. Leases are the typical example of annuities due. You can calculate savings either way, depending on when deposits are actually made.

This chapter provides additional practical applications. Some combine annuity calculations with compound interest calculations. Examples include a mortgage amortization schedule, an annual loan analysis, loans with balloon payments, savings with a beginning balance, and leases in which the property has a residual value at the end of the lease.

The general approach changes somewhat at this point. It is generally assumed that you understand the basics of financial calculations, and now the focus is on applications. It is not possible to cover every possible variation, but you should be able to adapt the models here to your own purposes.

Setting Up a Loan Amortization Schedule

Most loans are ordinary annuities, fixed payments at the end of each period. While the payment is constant, the portions allotted to interest and principal vary with each period; as you pay off the loan, the interest component of each payment gradually declines, and the amount applied to principal increases.

Introductions to spreadsheets often include a loan schedule, showing how much of each payment goes to principal and interest and the balance at the end of each period. Such a schedule shows how a loan is amortized, or paid off, and setting up an amortization schedule is kind of fun—and easy. It is also an excellent exercise in designing a worksheet in stages. You don't have to work out every detail of the finished product in advance; you can work your way to a solution a step at a time, making adjustments as you go.

Even though you have to make calculations for 360 payments in the case of a 30-year mortgage, once you have set up the formulas for the first period, you can easily copy them to cover the rest of the schedule. The schedule also provides quite useful information, since you need to know the amount of interest for tax purposes. You also need to know the balance of the loan when you apply for credit, sell your house, or want to determine your net worth.

Figure 6.1 shows the first few months and last few months of an amortization schedule for a 30-year mortgage. Just for the fun of it, we've played around with @DATEVALUE and the /Range Format Date command to label the periods by month and year in column A. If you want, just use /Data Fill to number them in A13..A372.

Figure 6.2 shows the formulas used to create the worksheet in Figure 6.1. Don't be put off; they're only simple arithmetic and @Function calculations. The cell references (many of them absolute, as indicated by the $ signs) make them look more complicated than they are.

The formulas above the double line are really pretty simple. At the top of the worksheet, all of the entries except the Loan value and the Payment value are entered directly. The Loan value in B6 is simply the Price less the Down payment. The Payment calculation is the standard @PMT function, dividing Interest (E4) by Periods/Year (E6) to calculate the periodic interest rate.

The Start date is entered as a label that *looks* like a date. The label must be entered in a format 1-2-3 can recognize. Here, the entry is Apr-92. (Capitalization doesn't matter.) You could also enter '1-Apr-92, '1/4/92, or, if the current year is 1992, '1/4. Note the apostrophes designating labels in the last three examples. If you omit the day (e.g., Apr-92), 1-2-3 assumes you mean the first of the month. If you omit the year (e.g., '1/4), 1-2-3 assumes you mean the current year, based on the date on your computer's clock. (If your computer doesn't have a clock, 1-2-3 will use the date you entered when you started DOS.) In A12, we will use @DATEVALUE to convert this label into a date serial number. (See Chapter 9 for a full explanation of date @Functions.)

	A	B	C	D	E
1					
2	LOAN AMORTIZATION				
3					
4	Price	$150,000		Interest	11.23%
5					
6	Down	$20,000		Years	30
7	Loan	$130,000		Periods/Year	12
8	Payment	$1,260.67		Term	360
9				Start	Apr-92
10	==				
11	Date	Payment	Interest	Principal	Balance
12	Apr-92				$130,000.00
13	May-92	1,260.67	1,216.58	44.08	129,955.92
14	Jun-92	1,260.67	1,216.17	44.49	129,911.42
15	Jul-92	1,260.67	1,215.75	44.91	129,866.51
16	Aug-92	1,260.67	1,215.33	45.33	129,821.18
17	Sep-92	1,260.67	1,214.91	45.76	129,775.42
18	Oct-92	1,260.67	1,214.48	46.18	129,729.24
19	Nov-92	1,260.67	1,214.05	46.62	129,682.62
	**				
361	May-2021	1,260.67	133.32	1,127.34	13,119.24
362	Jun-2021	1,260.67	122.77	1,137.89	11,981.35
363	Jul-2021	1,260.67	112.13	1,148.54	10,832.81
364	Aug-2021	1,260.67	101.38	1,159.29	9,673.52
365	Sep-2021	1,260.67	90.53	1,170.14	8,503.39
366	Oct-2021	1,260.67	79.58	1,181.09	7,322.30
367	Nov-2021	1,260.67	68.52	1,192.14	6,130.16
368	Dec-2021	1,260.67	57.37	1,203.30	4,926.86
369	Jan-2022	1,260.67	46.11	1,214.56	3,712.30
370	Feb-2022	1,260.67	34.74	1,225.92	2,486.37
371	Mar-2022	1,260.67	23.27	1,237.40	1,248.98
372	Apr-2022	1,260.67	11.69	1,248.98	0.00

Figure 6.1. The early and late months of a 30-year mortgage.

Setting Up the Beginning Date and Beginning Balance

Beginning in A12, the model lists the payment periods, starting with the loan initiation date, when no payment is actually made. (Again, if you prefer, you can use /Data Fill to number the payments instead of entering dates.) In A12, the @DATEVALUE formula returns the numerical value

	A	B	C	D	E
1					
2	LOAN AMORTIZATION				
3					
4	Price	150000		Interest	0.1123
5	Down	20000		Years	30
6	Loan	+B4-B5		Periods/Year	12
7	Payment	@PMT(B6,#4/E6,E7)		Term	+E5*E6
8				Start	Apr-92
9					
10	===				
11	Date	Payment	Interest	Principal	Balance
12	@DATEVALUE(E8)+15				+B6
13	+A12+365/$E$6	+$B$7	+$E$4/$E$6*E12	+B13-C13	+E12-D13
14	+A13+365/$E$6	+$B$7	+$E$4/$E$6*E13	+B14-C14	+E13-D14
15	+A14+365/$E$6	+$B$7	+$E$4/$E$6*E14	+B15-C15	+E14-D15
16	+A15+365/$E$6	+$B$7	+$E$4/$E$6*E15	+B16-C16	+E15-D15
17	+A16+365/$E$6	+$B$7	+$E$4/$E$6*E16	+B17-C17	+E16-D17
18	+A17+365/$E$6	+$B$7	+$E$4/$E$6*E17	+B18-C18	+E17-D18
19	+A18+365/$E$6	+$B$7	+$E$4/$E$6*E18	+B19-C19	+E18-D19
20	+A19+365/$E$6	+$B$7	+$E$4/$E$6*E19	+B20-C20	+E19-D20

Figure 6.2. Formulas for a morgage amortization table.

> **Note:** You could also use @DATE to enter the Start date in this format: @DATE(92,4,1). Note that the format of the argument is YY,MM,11. If you use this method, you will initially get a date serial number, such as 33710. You can use the /Range Format Date 3 (MMM-YY) command to convert the display to Apr-92. If you take this option, you can simply enter +E8+15 in A12, rather than using @DATEVALUE.

of the date label entered in E8. This is the number of the date (January 1, 1900 = 1). Fifteen is added to the DATEVALUE to avoid skipping or repeating months. (Because the number of days in a month varies, and because of leap years, there is no average monthly interval that will avoid this problem over 30 years if you start with the first of the month.)

Initially, you will get a number like 33710, but when the model is finished, you can reformat the Date range to fix that. In order for this to work, Start in E8 must be entered in the MMM-YY format (e.g., Apr-92), and you must format A12..A372 with the /Range Format Date 3 (MMM-YY) command. The latter converts the DATEVALUES you have calculated to the MMM-YY format shown in Figure 6.1.

Note: Again, if you use @DATE to enter the Start date in E8, you can simply enter +E8+15 in A12. In this case, @DATEVALUE still works, but it is unnecessary.

The initial Balance is entered in E12 as a simple cell reference, +B6, which is the Loan amount. This simply sets up the worksheet so that all of the other formulas can be copied. The next step is to enter the formulas in row 13. After that, you can copy them down the rest of the worksheet.

Breaking Down the Payments

Row 13 contains formulas you can copy down the rest of the worksheet without modifications (hence, the absolute references indicated by $ signs). The result will be the correct Date, Payment, Interest, Principal, and Balance for each period, regardless of the term of the loan or the frequency of payments.

For the Date in A13, enter +A12+365/$E$6. A12 is the beginning DATEVALUE calculated in the cell above. The rest of the formula, 365/$E$6 divides the number of days in a year by the Periods/Year listed in E6. The reference to E6 is absolute, because it will remain constant down the column.

> **Note:** If you're only interested in loans with monthly payments, you can simplify this somewhat by entering +A12+365/12. This yields the DATEVALUE from the cell above plus the average number of days a month. However, if you change Periods/Year to anything other than 12, the Date column will be thrown haywire.

The Payment is already calculated in B7, so you can simply enter the absolute reference +$B$7 in B13.

In column C, the formula is +$E$4/$E$6*E12. The interest for the first period is the annual rate ($E$4) divided by Periods/Year ($E$6) times the last Balance (E12). Note that the first two cell references are absolute, but the last is relative.

The Principal (+B13-C13) is the difference between the Payment and the Interest; the new Balance (+E12-D13) is the old Balance less the Principal. Here, cell references are relative.

To complete the worksheet, copy the range A13..E13 down the length of the worksheet. The model makes the calculations automatically.

Tidying Up with @IF

If you change the Years in the model from 30 to 10, the Balance will reach 0 after 10 years instead of 30 (in this case, Apr-2002). Similarly, if you change Periods/Year from 12 to 4, the number of payments drops from 360 to 120, although the term of the loan in years does not change. In either case, the numbers after the loan has been paid off are meaningless. You can eliminate this data by deleting the remaining rows and saving under a new file name or by limiting the print range when you print. You can also quickly modify the model with @IF to display 0s all the way across after the Balance reaches 0.

@IF is entered in this format:

```
@IF(condition,x,y)
```

where the condition is a logical statement using any of 1-2-3's logic operators. If the logic statement is true, @IF returns *x*; if it is false, it returns *y*. Suppose, for example, that you enter @IF(C2,C3,1,2). If the value in C2 is greater than the one in C3, the function returns 1. If it is not, it returns 2.

In this case, we will use @IF to determine whether an outstanding balance remains on a loan. If the loan has been paid off, the model will return 0s for Payment, Interest, Principal, and Balance. If not, it will continue calculating.

To use the @IF option, go back to the first Payment formula, in B13. Enter @IF(E12>1,$B$7,0). This will return the Payment calculated above the double line if there is an outstanding balance, or 0 if the loan is paid off. (The value 1 is used in the argument instead of 0 to avoid rounding errors; otherwise, the model might include a payment for an extra month.)

Now, copy the formula in B13 down the column. Columns B–E will display 0s after the loan is paid off. You can still truncate the model by deleting rows or limiting the print range.

Now you have a tidy model that will neatly calculate the payments for principal and interest and the balance for each period of a loan. From this table, you can determine your balance at any point in a loan and add up the total interest for any range of payments. Often, however, you will want to analyze a loan, particularly interest payments, on an annual basis. The next section explains how to extract this information from the model you have just created.

Creating Annual Loan Summaries with @DSUM and @DMIN

It may be useful to analyze a loan payment for each period, as the model above does, but often you will want annual summaries for tax preparation, planning, and other purposes. Once you have set up your loan schedule, you could simply use @SUM to add up principal and interest for each year. You could calculate total payments for the year using either

@SUM or by multiplying the payment by the number of periods per year. And you could look up the ending balance for each year in the table. There are more elegant solutions. One is to use the database @Functions to extract annual information from the amortization schedule. (Later, we'll look at making annual calculations directly, without first setting up an amortization schedule.)

A Quick Introduction to Database @Functions

A 1-2-3 database is nothing more than a rectangular section of a worksheet that contains information recorded in an orderly format. In the case of the loan amortization schedule, Date, Payment, Interest, Principal, and Balance are arrayed across the columns, with varying values for each payment or period. Each period occupies a row, and is called a database record. Each column is called a field, representing a type of data each record has in common.

Database @Functions allow you to analyze data within a table that match certain criteria. All database @Functions use the same argument:

```
(input, offset, criterion)
```

where *input* is the range that defines the database, including column headings; *offset* is the number of columns to the right where the data to be analyzed are entered; and *criterion* is a range that defines the data to be analyzed.

The criterion consists of at least two cells, one above the other. It is not important exactly where these cells are located, but they should be in a portion of the worksheet that will not be affected if you add or change the database. The top cell must be a column heading from your database. Below the column heading, you can enter a label, a value, or a formula. Then when you enter the database @Function, 1-2-3 will calculate the result for all items in the table that match the criterion. For example, if you enter

Item
Mallets

as the criterion range, your @Function will make a calculation for all entries in your database where the entry in the Item column is Mallets.

Suppose you list an inventory with Item in the column A, Vendor in column B, and Cost in column C. You can use the /Range Name Create command to name your database Table and your criterion range Criterion. Then, the formula @DSUM(Table,2,Criterion) will return the total cost of mallets. In fields containing values, a single number can identify all matching records. For example, if you define a criterion range as

Cost
10

and name that range Criterion, then the formula @DSUM(Table,2,Criterion) will return the total cost of all items that cost exactly $10—no more and no less.

To use a formula in a criterion range, you must use a cell reference for the first value in a field, for example

Cost
+C2>10

In this case, the formula @DSUM(Table,2,Criterion) will return the total cost of all items that cost more than $10.

You can also use logical operators (#AND#, #NOT#, and #OR#) to set up a criterion. For example, you could enter

Cost
+C2>10#AND#C2<20

Now the formula @DSUM(Table,2,Criterion) returns the total cost of all items that cost between $10 and $20, omitting items that cost exactly those amounts.

You can also specify more than one factor in a criterion range. For example, if you enter

Item
Mallets
Hammers

the calculation will include all mallets and hammers. On the other hand, if you enter

Item	Vendor
Mallets	Good Guys

the calculation will include only mallets sold by Good Guys. And, if you enter

Item	Vendor
Mallets	Good Guys
Hammers	Ugly Guys

the calculation will include mallets sold by Good Guys and hammers sold by Ugly Guys, but not hammers sold by Good Guys or mallets sold by Ugly Guys.

In addition, you can use wildcards (? and *) in label criteria. The ? is a single character, while * is a wildcard for anything that matches the beginning of the entry. For example, Jo?n will identify John or Joan; Jo?? will identify John, Joan, and Joab. Jo* will identify John, Joan, Joab, Johannsen, and Johnson.

In the next sections, we will set up criterion ranges to identify data in the amortization schedule by calendar year.

Calculating Annual Summaries from a Loan Schedule

	A	B	C	D	E
1					
2	LOAN AMORTIZATION				
3					
4	Price	$150,000		Interest	11.23%
5	Down	$20,000		Years	30
6	Loan	$130,000		Periods/Year	12
7	Payment	$1,260.67		Term	360
8				Start	Apr-92
9					
10	==				
11					
12	Date	Payment	Interest	Principal	Balance
13	'92	10,085.33	9,720.90	364.43	129,635.57
14	'93	15,127.99	14,527.81	600.18	129,035.39
15	'94	15,127.99	14,456.83	671.16	128,364.22
16	'95	15,127.99	14,377.45	750.54	127,613.69
17	'96	15,127.99	14,288.69	839.30	126,774.38
18					
19	==				

Figure 6.3. Calculating annual totals from a loan amortization schedule.

At this point, you should already have set up the loan schedule described earlier. Now the objective is to calculate annual total Payments, Interest, Principal, and Balance using @DSUM and @DMIN, as shown in Figure 6.3. This is a straightforward procedure, but it requires several steps, as explained in the following sections.

Identifying Calendar Years

The first step in deriving annual totals from the amortization schedule is to use the /Worksheet Insert Row command to make space for your annual calculations between the basic loan information and the amortization schedule. Here, 10 rows are inserted beginning at row 11, and a

	F	G
21		Year
22		92 Date
23		@YEAR(A22)=92
24		93 Date
25		@YEAR(A22)=93
26		94 Date
27		@YEAR(A22)=94
28		95 Date
29		@YEAR(A22)=95
30		96 Date
31		@YEAR(A22)=96

Figure 6.4. Setting up criteria for each year.

second double line is entered in row 19. You can use the /Copy command to copy the column headings from the schedule to row 12.

You will need a separate criterion for each year you want to analyze. To set up the criteria, go to an out-of-the-way part of your worksheet and enter the formulas and labels shown in Figure 6.4. The information in column F is simply for reference. In column G, each criterion consists of two cells. The first contains the label Date, in reference to the heading for the left column of the database, which is column A. The cell below each label contains a formula specifying the @YEAR of the value in A22, the first value in the database.

> **Note:** You will have to devise different formulas if you numbered payment periods rather than using the @DATEVALUE approach. If there are nine payments in the first year, for example, you could enter +A22<=9 for the first year. This will identify periods 1 through 9. For the next year, you would enter +A22>9#AND#A22<=21, and so on.

Remember, the entries in column A were created by calculating the @DATEVALUE of the starting date of the loan. They are formatted with /Range Format Date 3 (MMM-YY). @YEAR returns a two-digit value for the year of a DATEVALUE—92 for a date that falls in 1992, for example. Since the @YEAR of A22 is 92, the formula in G23 returns the value 1, indicating that the formula is true. The other formulas return the value 0, indicating that they are false.

When you have completed the criteria, use /Range Name Create to label them. The name for the range G22..G23, for example, is '92; G24..G25 is '93; and so on. You must include the apostrophe, which makes the range name a label instead of a value. Although it is possible to use a value as a range name, you cannot use a value range name in a formula elsewhere. For example, if you assigned the value 92 to G22..G23, the formula +92 would simply return the value 92 rather than identifying the range.

Defining the Database

The next step is to assign a range name to the loan amortization schedule itself. In the example, the schedule now occupies the range A21..E382. In the formulas we are about to create, you could simply refer to the database that way, but it is easier to assign a range name. If your worksheet is different, the top left corner of the database is the label for the first column, in this case Date. The bottom right corner is the last balance, which should show the value 0.00.

Once you have identified the range of your loan schedule, use /Range Name Create to label it Table. Now you can simply enter Table for the input in a database @Function argument.

Writing the Formulas

At this point, you have set up a loan amortization schedule, made room for annual calculations in your worksheet, set up and named your criteria, and created a range name for the loan schedule, including the column headings. Now you can use @DSUM to calculate annual totals for Payment, Interest, and Principal, and @DMIN to calculate the Balance at the end of each year.

@DSUM and @DMIN are similar to @SUM and @MIN, only they make calculations based on database records that match certain criteria rather than on a simple range of numbers. Both take the standard database @Function argument (*input,offset,criterion*). In this case, we have defined the range G22..G23 as a criterion range for the year 1992, and named it '92. The loan amortization schedule, named Table, is the input range, with Payment one column to the right, Interest two, Principal three, and Balance four. Thus, @DSUM(Table,1,'92) provides total payments for the year; @DSUM(Table,2,'92) sums interest payments, and @DSUM(Table,3,'92) adds up the principal payments. @DMIN finds the smallest balance for the year, which, of course, is the ending balance.

The formulas in Figure 6.5 add a couple of twists to make it easier to copy them and to make calculations for different years without rewriting the formulas (you will still have to write new criterion ranges for additional years). Here's how the formulas work:

- In the Date column, the entries are '92, '93, '94, and so on. The double apostrophes are necessary because the actual names of the criterion ranges include apostrophes; the first apostrophe merely designates the entry as a label.

- $TABLE is an absolute reference to the range Table, which defines the loan schedule. The absolute reference simply allows you to copy the first @DSUM formula without changing the range.

- The numbers in the middle of each argument are column offsets: 1 for Payment, 2 for interest, 3 for Principal, and 4 for Balance.

- @@($A13), and so on, are indirect cell pointers referring to the labels in column A, which in turn identify the criterion ranges for each year. The reference to column A is absolute, so you can copy the formulas horizontally; the reference to row 13 is relative, so the row reference will be to the current row when you copy vertically. (For an explanation of @@, see Chapter 9, *A Guide to @Functions.*)

Once you have entered the first @DSUM formula in B13, you can copy it across row 13, and then edit the formulas to adjust the offsets and to

A	B	C	D	E
12 Date	Payment	Interest	Principal	Balance
13 '92	@DSUM($TABLE,1,@@($A13))	@DSUM($TABLE,2,@@($A13))	@DSUM($TABLE,3,@@($A13))	@DMIN($TABLE,4,@@($A13))
14 '93	@DSUM($TABLE,1,@@($A14))	@DSUM($TABLE,2,@@($A14))	@DSUM($TABLE,3,@@($A14))	@DMIN($TABLE,4,@@($A14))
15 '94	@DSUM($TABLE,1,@@($A15))	@DSUM($TABLE,2,@@($A15))	@DSUM($TABLE,3,@@($A15))	@DMIN($TABLE,4,@@($A15))
16 '95	@DSUM($TABLE,1,@@($A16))	@DSUM($TABLE,2,@@($A16))	@DSUM($TABLE,3,@@($A16))	@DMIN($TABLE,4,@@($A16))
17 '96	@DSUM($TABLE,1,@@($A17))	@DSUM($TABLE,2,@@($A17))	@DSUM($TABLE,3,@@($A17))	@DMIN($TABLE,4,@@($A17))

Figure 6.5. Calculating annual totals with @DSUM and @DMIN.

	A	B	C	D	E
12	Date	Payment	Interest	Principal	Balance
13	'92	10,085.33	9,720.90	364.43	129,635.57
14	'93	15,127.99	14,527.81	600.18	129,035.39
15	'94	15,127.99	14,456.83	671.16	128,364.22
16	'95	15,127.99	14,377.45	750.54	127,613.69
17	'96	15,127.99	14,288.69	839.30	126,774.38

Figure 6.6. Annual totals for monthly payments on a $130,000 loan for 30 years at 11.23% interest.

change the Balance calculation from @DSUM to @DMIN. Then, you can copy those formulas down as many rows as you like. The result is shown in Figure 6.6.

This is all very well, provided you need the amortization schedule itself, as well as the annual calculations. The next section explains how to calculate annual loan tables without setting up a schedule first.

Calculating Annual Loan Summaries Directly

The model just presented works fine, but it's cumbersome to calculate 360 payments for a 30-year loan if all you really want is annual totals for several years. The model shown in Figure 6.7 makes the annual calculations directly. It also figures the annual tax benefit from deducting the interest and the after-tax cash flow.

Once you have entered the basic loan information at the top of the worksheet and made the calculations for the first year, you can complete the model by copying row 14 down the length of the worksheet. Like the loan amortization schedule, this model returns meaningless numbers for any years after the loan is paid off. As before, we will tidy up with @IF. The following sections take you through the procedure for setting up the model one step at a time.

	A	B	C	D	E	F	G
1							
2	ANNUAL LOAN ANALYSIS						
3							
4	Price	$150,000		Interest	11.23%		
5	Down	$20,000		Years	30		
6	Loan	$130,000		Pds/Year	12		
7	Payment	$1,260.67		Term	360		
8	Tax Rate	35.00%		Start	Apr-92		
9							
10	========	========	========	========	========	========	========
11					Tax	Cash	Balance
12	Year	Payment	Interest	Principal	Benefit	Flow	
13	0						130,000
14	1	15,128	14,571	557	5,100	10,028	129,443
15	2	15,128	14,505	623	5,077	10,051	128,820
16	3	15,128	14,431	697	5,051	10,077	128,123
17	4	15,128	14,349	779	5,022	10,106	127,344
18	5	15,128	14,257	871	4,990	10,138	126,473
19	6	15,128	14,154	974	4,954	10,174	125,499
20	7	15,128	14,039	1,089	4,914	10,214	124,410
	**********	**********	**********	**********	**********	**********	**********
38	25	15,128	6,981	8,147	2,443	12,685	57,677
39	26	15,128	6,018	9,110	2,106	13,022	48,567
40	27	15,128	4,940	10,188	1,729	13,399	38,379
41	28	15,128	3,735	11,393	1,307	13,821	26,986
42	29	15,128	2,388	12,740	836	14,292	14,247
43	30	15,128	881	14,247	308	14,819	0

Figure 6.7. Calculating annual totals for a loan with monthly payments.

Entering the Loan Information

The top of the model is virtually identical to the top of the loan amortization schedule shown in Figure 6.1, except for the addition of the Tax Rate in B8. The Loan amount is the Price – Down (+B4-B5), and Term is Years × Pds/Year (+E5*E6). The Payment is @PMT(B6,E4/E6,E7), where B6 is the Loan amount, E4 is the annual Interest, E6 is Pds/Year, and E7 is Term. You can vary the other entries as you like to make calculations about different loans.

We are assuming here that the interest on the loan is tax deductible, as is the case with home mortgages and business loans. For other personal loans, 10% of the interest is deductible in 1990 and none thereafter. Your tax rate is your *marginal* tax rate, or the rate you pay on your last dollar of taxable income. If your interest deduction straddles a tax bracket, you may want to calculate the proportion that falls in each category to determine your actual tax savings.

You can add your state and/or local income tax rate to your federal rate. Note, however, that a state/local deduction actually increases your federal tax slightly because it reduces your federal deduction for those taxes. For example, suppose your federal tax rate is 28%, your state rate is 10%, and you have a $10,000 interest deduction. Your federal deduction for interest is worth $2,800 (28% of $10,000), and your state interest deduction is worth $1,000 (10% of $10,000). However, you also lose a $1,000 federal deduction because of your state tax deduction. That will cost you $280 on your federal taxes (28% of $1,000). Your actual tax saving looks like this:

Federal Deduction	$2,800
+ State Deduction	1,000
	======
	3,800
– Loss of State Tax Deduction	280
	======
Total	$3,520

Your marginal tax rate is 38%, the amount you would pay on additional earnings. But, because reducing state tax increases your federal liability, your overall tax savings on deductible interest is only 35.2%.

The general formula for making this calculation is:

```
Rate = (federal + state) - (federal X state)
```

Or, in this case:

```
Rate = (28%+10%)-(28%*10%) = 38%-2.8% = 35.2%
```

Now, you have completed the information on which your calculations are based. Once you have completed the model, you can freely change any of the information above the double line to analyze different loans.

Making Calculations for the First Year

Below the double line of the worksheet, the opening Balance for Year 0 (G13) is +B6, a simple cell reference to the Loan amount above the double line. This simply allows you to write a formula that can be easily copied one cell below, in G14. Once you have made the calculations for Year 1, you can copy them down the rest of the worksheet. The formulas for the first screen of the worksheet are shown in Figure 6.8.

The formulas beginning in row 14 are really quite simple. The absolute references make the formulas look more complicated than they are, but they are necessary if you want to copy the formulas. (See *A Note on Absolute and Relative Cell References* in Chapter 3 for a full explanation.)

The critical formula is the Balance calculation in G14. From Chapter 2, we know that the remaining balance of a loan is the present value of the remaining payments:

Balance = @PV(payment, interest, remaining payments)

In G14, this formula appears this way:

@PV($B$7, $E$4/$E$6, $E$7-$E$6*A14)

Let's break down the argument:

- $B$7 is the Payment calculated in B7. The reference is absolute because the payment remains the same for the life of the loan.

- $E$4/$E$6 is the periodic interest, calculated by dividing the annual Interest in E4 by Pds/Year in E6. Again, this is a constant, so the cell references are absolute.

	A	B	C	D	E	F	G
1							
2	ANNUAL LOAN ANALYSIS						
3							
4	Price	$150,000		Interest	11.23%		
5	Down	$20,000		Years	30		
6	Loan	$130,000		Pds/Year	12		
7	Payment	$1,260.67		Term	360		
8	Tax Rate	35.00%		Start	Apr-92		
9							
10							
11					Tax	Cash	
12	Year	Payments	Interest	Principal	Benefit	Flow	Balance
13	0						+B6
14	1	+$E$6*$B$7	+B14-D14	+G13-G14	+$B$8*C14	+B14-E14	@PV($B$7,$E$4/$E$6,$E$7-$E$6*A14)
15	2	+$E$6*$B$7	+B15-D15	+G14-G15	+$B$8*C15	+B15-E15	@PV($B$7,$E$4/$E$6,$E$7-$E$6*A15)
16	3	+$E$6*$B$7	+B16-D16	+G15-G16	+$B$8*C16	+B16-E16	@PV($B$7,$E$4/$E$6,$E$7-$E$6*A16)
17	4	+$E$6*$B$7	+B17-D17	+G16-G17	+$B$8*C17	+B17-E17	@PV($B$7,$E$4/$E$6,$E$7-$E$6*A17)
18	5	+$E$6*$B$7	+B18-D18	+G17-G18	+$B$8*C18	+B18-E18	@PV($B$7,$E$4/$E$6,$E$7-$E$6*A18)
19	6	+$E$6*$B$7	+B19-D19	+G18-G19	+$B$8*C19	+B19-E19	@PV($B$7,$E$4/$E$6,$E$7-$E$6*A19)
20	7	+$E$6*$B$7	+B20-D20	+G19-G20	+$B$8*C20	+B20-E20	@PV($B$7,$E$4/$E$6,$E$7-$E$6*A20)

Figure 6.8. Formulas for calculating annual loan summaries.

- $E$7-$E$6*A14 calculates the periods remaining at the end of the year. This is Term–(Pds/Year)×(Year). In this case, the Term (E7) is 360 months, Pds/Year is 12 (E6) and the Year is 1 (A14). Thus, the calculation is really just 360–(12*1) = 348. (The parentheses are not really necessary because 1-2-3 performs multiplication in a formula before subtraction.) The reference to A14 is relative, because we want the model to recalculate remaining periods each year, based on the values listed in the Year column.

The rest of the formulas for Year 1 are simple arithmetic:

- Principal, the amount by which the debt is reduced, is simply the previous Balance (+G13) minus the ending Balance (G14). References are relative, because this calculation changes each year.

- Payments are constant throughout the worksheet. Each year, the Payments equal the Payment (B7) times Pds/Year (E6).

- Interest is the difference between Payments (B14) and payments on Principal (D14). Again, cell references are relative because the calculation will change for each year.

- Tax Benefit is the Tax Rate (B8) times the current year's Interest (C14). The reference to $B$8 is absolute, because Tax Rate is fixed. The reference to C14 is relative, because Interest changes every year.

- Cash Flow is Payments (in column B) minus the Tax Benefit (column E). Cell references can be relative because Payments is already constant, and Tax Benefit varies each year.

If you want to simplify the worksheet and all you really want to know is the annual interest total, you can leave out the Tax Benefit and Cash Flow calculations because none of the other formulas depend on them. However, you must include all of the other calculations, because the formulas are interdependent. But remember that you only have to enter one formula for each column. Once you have entered the first-year formulas, you can complete the worksheet in a matter of seconds by copying them, as explained in the next section.

Completing the Worksheet

Once you have completed the first 14 rows of the worksheet, finishing the model consists of two easy steps. First use /Data Fill to fill in values for the remaining years of the loan, beginning in A15. You can fill in values for any number of years. The second step is to use /Copy to copy the calculations for the first year (B14..G14) down the rest of the worksheet. (For a 30-year schedule, the range to copy TO is B15..B43.)

Your worksheet should now look like the model in Figure 6.7. The model will automatically recalculate when you change any of the values in rows 4 through 8 above the double line.

Tidying Up with @IF

Like the Loan Amortization Schedule, the Annual Loan Analysis will return meaningless figures for years after the loan has been paid off. For example, if you set up a model for a 30-year mortgage, then change Years to 15 to analyze a shorter-term loan, then there are no Payments, Interest, Principal, Tax Benefit, Cash Flow, or Balance after the 15th year. Nevertheless, the Annual Loan Analysis will continue the calculations, even though the results mean nothing.

Again, you can remove the extraneous data with /Worksheet Delete Row command or by limiting the print range when you print. You can also use @IF to make the worksheet return 0s across all calculated columns after the loan is paid off.

To use the latter option, you simply need to tell the worksheet to stop calculating Payments and Balance when the Balance reaches 0. (The rest of the calculations will go to 0 automatically.) The formulas look long, but you can adjust your worksheet in a couple of minutes by copying.

First go to the Payments calculation for Year 1, which is in B14. The formula should read +$E$6*$B$7, which is Pds/Year times Payment. Edit the formula to read @IF(G13>1,$E$6*$B$7,0). G13 is a relative cell reference to the previous Balance. Now the formula will calculate the

Payments for the year if the previous Balance is greater than 1, or return a 0 if it is not. (The value 1 is used instead of 0 to avoid rounding errors.) Copy the formula in B14 down the length of column B, for as far as you have entered Year values in column A. (This will be B15..B43 if you have set up a 30-year table as shown in the model.)

The next step is to adapt the Principal calculations in column D. Go to the calculation for the first year, in D14. The formula should read +G13-G14. This is the previous Balance minus the year-end Balance, or the amount of principal paid off during the year. Edit the formula to read @IF(G13>1,G13-G14,0). If the previous Balance is greater than 1, the model continues to calculate as usual; otherwise, it returns a 0. Copy this formula down the length of column D. In the model the copy TO range is D15..D43.

Finally, go to G14. The formula should be @PV($B$7,$E$4/$E$6,$E$7-$E$6*A14). Edit it to read @IF(G13>1,@PV($B$7,$E$4/$E$6,$E$7-$E$6*A14),0). Again, this formula continues to calculate if the preceding balance is greater than 1; it returns 0 if the preceding balance is less than 1. Copy this formula down the length of column G.

To test the model, change Years in E5 from 30 to 10. If the model is working correctly, the Balance should be 0 in Year 10, and all of the columns should return 0s beginning in Year 11.

You now have a model that will provide an annual analysis of any loan with a few keystrokes. You can analyze a $10,000 loan for five years, a $10 million loan for three years, for that matter, a $100 loan for 25 years. Suppose you want to analyze just the principal, with no down payment. Simply enter 0 for Down in B5. The interest is not tax deductible? Just enter 0 for Tax Rate in B8. (The Tax Benefit column will be filled with 0s and the Cash Flow will be the same as Payments.) You can enter any annual percentage rate you like for Interest in E4 and any term for Years. And, although loan payments are almost always monthly, you are free to change Pds/Yr in E6 to 4 for quarterly payments, 2 for semiannual payments, or 1 for annual payments.

All of the loans, leases, and savings calculations we have discussed so far, both here and in Chapter 2, have been simple annuities—even series of payments. The examples in the rest of this chapter combine the lump-sum calculations from Chapter 1 with basic annuity calculations.

Dealing with Balloons, Beginning Balances, and Salvage Values

Financial life does not always consist of regular annuities, even when you are calculating a series of regular payments. You might, for example, want to calculate how much you need to save each month until your retirement in eight years to accumulate $1 million if you already have $500,000 invested. As interest rates rose in the early 1980s, some home buyers agreed to "creative financing" arrangements to increase their borrowing capacity or reduce monthly payments. One such arrangement was to pay off the loan with a lump sum, or balloon payment, after a few years in the hope that refinancing would be available on more favorable terms. Similarly, a lease may be calculated on the assumption that the asset will have a residual value or salvage value at the end of the lease. When you lease a car, for example, the end of the lease you usually have a choice between returning the car and buying it at a predetermined price. That price is the car's residual or salvage value at the end of the lease.

All of these calculations actually involve two problems: an annuity calculation and a calculation involving the time value of a lump sum. The trick, in each case, is to calculate either the present value or the future value of both the lump sum and the series of payments, then combine the results. For example, if you expect your $500,000 investment to earn 7.75% interest for the next eight years, you can calculate the future value of the lump sum, then figure how much you must add each year to reach your $1 million goal. Of course, if your goal is to accumulate $1 million in *today's* dollars, you will also have to calculate how much that will be in eight years, given an inflation rate of, say, 5%. The same basic tactics apply to both ordinary annuities and to annuities due.

There are too many possible variations to cover them all here, but the next sections provide a range of examples. They should allow you to set up a worksheet for most situations. We'll look first at balloon loans, then at individual savings, and finally at leases with residual values.

Making Calculations for Balloon Loans

Some loans carry balloon payments at the end; that is, the loan is repaid with a series of regular payments, followed by a large, lump-sum payment at the end. There are two ways of thinking about this arrangement, both of which actually come to the same thing.

One way is to calculate the payments for a loan with a longer term, understanding that the borrower will pay off the balance at a certain time. The payments on a balloon mortgage, for example, might be calculated as though the term were 30 years, even though the borrower agrees to pay off the balance at the end of five. This is the method used in *Finding the Amount of a Balloon Payment* below.

A second way of looking at a balloon loan is to break it down into two transactions. In the first, you borrow the principal less the present value of the balloon payment for the period until the balloon is due. In the second, you borrow the present value of the balloon payment and pay it back with interest at the end of the loan. See *Calculating Payments on a Balloon Loan*, below, for an example.

Again, both ways of making the calculations will yield the same results. The one you choose depends on which values are known and which ones you want to calculate.

As previously mentioned, balloon mortgages were often used as "creative financing" during the high-interest days of the early 1980s. Usually, such buyers hoped to refinance with more favorable terms when the balloon came due. As another example, a startup company might opt for a balloon loan to reduce payments in the short term with the expectation of paying off the loan when revenues increase or when the company plans to go public.

Balloon loans can reduce monthly payments temporarily—though not always by as much as you might expect—or increase the amount you can borrow. The risk, of course, is that future developments might make the balloon payment difficult—interest rates might go up instead of down, for example, or a startup company's revenues might not reach the goals in its business plan.

From the lender's point of view, a balloon loan provides the same rate of return as a longer mortgage, but the money is committed for a shorter period of time. Thus, some lenders might be willing to make a balloon loan on terms that would otherwise be unacceptable.

The following sections explain how to calculate the amount of a balloon payment at a certain time, given the terms of an ordinary loan; how to calculate the payments on a balloon loan; and how to determine the effect of a balloon payment on the amount you can borrow.

Finding the Amount of a Balloon Payment

We have already seen that a balloon loan is simply an ordinary loan, except that the borrower agrees to pay off the balance of the loan at a certain date. The amount of the balloon payment is simply the balance of the loan on the payoff date. The Annual Loan Analysis in Figure 6.7, for example, calculates annual totals for a 30-year mortgage for $130,000. At the end of the seventh year, the Balance is $124,410. Therefore, if this were a balloon loan with the balance due loan at that point, the borrower would make 84 monthly payments of $1,260.67, with a final payment of $124,410 at the end of the seventh year.

Thus, calculating the amount of a balloon payment is the same as calculating the balance of any ordinary loan. As explained earlier in this chapter and in Chapter 2, the balance of a loan is simply the present value of the remaining payments. That calculation is easy to make with @PV.

Suppose, for example, that *The Advent*, a new magazine, borrows $125,000 for typesetting equipment. The loan is for 10 years, with monthly payments, at an APR of 15%. The magazine's business plan calls for it to go public at the end of seven years, when it expects to pay off the loan. What is the balloon payment?

The magazine can first calculate the monthly payments, and then use @PV to determine the balance after seven years, when it will have made 84 payments out of 120, with 36 remaining (120 – 84).

To calculate the monthly payment, enter:

```
@PMT(125000,0.15/12,120)
```

where 125000 is the principal, 0.15/12 is the periodic interest rate, and 120 is the number of periods.

Answer: The monthly payment is $2,016.69.

Note: This calculation is subject to a small rounding error, depending on how the amortization of the actual loan is constructed. The problem is that the actual result of the @PMT calculation is $2,016.68696..., while the company is actually paying $2,016.69—a fraction of a cent more. This problem can arise in any annuity calculation. In real life, the final payment is sometimes higher or lower than the others. Sometimes the rounding error is ignored. The difference is only a few cents. If you calculate the payment, then include it in the @PV calculation as a cell reference, rather than entering the actual payment, the result will be $58,175.91—9 cents less.

	A	B
1	BALLOON TO PAY OFF A LOAN	
2		
3	Principal	125000
4	Annual Interest	0.15
5	Term	10
6	Periods/Year	12
7	Years to Balloon Payment	7
8	Payment	@ROUND(@PMT(B3,B18,B16),2)
9		
10	Balloon Payment	+B21
11		
12		
13	===	
14	Calculations	
15		
16	Total Periods	+B5*B6
17	Payments to Balloon	+B7*B6
18	Periodic Interest	+B4/B6
19	Present Value of Payments	@PV(B8,B18,B17)
20	Present Value of Balloon	+B3-B19
21	Future Value of Balloon	+B20*(1+B18)^B17

Figure 6.9. Calculating a balloon payment based on present value of payments made.

Using this value, you can calculate the present value, as of 84 months into the loan, of the remaining 36 payments:

@PV(2016.69,0.15/12,36)

Answer: $58,176.00.

	A	B
1	BALLOON TO PAY OFF A LOAN	
2		
3	Principal	$125,000.00
4	Annual Interest	15.00%
5	Term	10
6	Periods/Year	12
7	Years to Balloon Payment	7
8	Payment	$2,016.69
9		
10	Balloon Payment	$58,175.46
11		
12		
13	==	
14	Calculations	
15		
16	Total Periods	120
17	Payments to Balloon	84
18	Periodic Interest	1.25%
19	Present Value of Payments	$104,509.28
20	Present Value of Balloon	$20,490.72
21	Future Value of Balloon	$58,175.46

Figure 6.10. The results of the balloon payment calculations shown in the previous figure.

The model shown in Figure 6.9 takes the slightly longer approach of calculating the present value of payments already made, subtracting that from the original principal, and then calculating the future value to determine the balloon payment. Note that @ROUND is used to round the Payment to two decimal places; simply formatting the Payment entry to two decimal places would not affect the calculation, even though the value displayed would be the same. The results of the calculations are shown in Figure 6.10. The answer is now $58,175.46, so the range of possibilities for the three methods in this case is only 55 cents out of $54,000 plus.

Calculating Payments on a Balloon Loan

The terms of a balloon loan are sometimes negotiable, and you may need to modify the basic loan calculation to fit the circumstances. Here, we look at a very specific set of terms, which you can adapt to different situations.

	A	B
1	PAYMENTS WITH A BALLOON	
2		
3	Principal	20000
4	Annual Interest	0.12
5	Term	7
6	Periods/Year	12
7	Balloon Payment	10000
8		
9	Payment with Balloon	@PMT(B20,B18,B17)
10	Payment without Balloon	@PMT(B3,B18,B16)
11	Payment on 15 year 2nd mortgage	@PMT(B3,B18,15*12)
12		
13	===	
14	Calculations	
15		
16	Total Periods	+B5*B6
17	Regular Payments	+B16-1
18	Periodic Interest	+B4/B6
19	Present Value of Balloon	+B7/(1+B18)^B16
20	Present Value of Payments	+B3-B19

Figure 6.11. Calculating payments for a balloon loan.

Suppose, for example, that you are negotiating to buy a house. The seller agrees to accept a $20,000 second mortgage at 12% APR, compounded monthly, with a $10,000 balloon payment at the end of seven years. The proposition is to pay off a $20,000 debt with a series of monthly payments over seven years, plus a lump-sum payment at the end of the loan. You need to make several calculations to analyze this situation.

There will be 83 regular payments with the balloon constituting the 84th and final payment. What are the monthly payments? What are the monthly payments if you agree to pay off the loan as an ordinary annuity with 84 regular payments? What would the payment be for a regular second mortgage at 12% for 15 years?

The monthly payment calculation for the balloon mortgage, shown in Figure 6.11, consists of three steps:

1. Determine the present value of the balloon, discounted for seven years at the stated interest rate. This calculation, in B19, uses the familiar formula $PV = FV/(1+i)^n$. In this case, the future value is the amount of the balloon payment, $10,000 from B7. The periodic interest rate is .01, calculated in B18. And the number of payments is 180, calculated in B16.

2. Subtract the present value of the balloon from the amount of the loan, $20,000. This is the present value of the payments, calculated in B20.

	A	B
1	PAYMENTS WITH A BALLOON	
2		
3	Principal	$20,000.00
4	Annual Interest	12.00%
5	Term	7
6	Periods/Year	12
7	Balloon Payment	$10,000.00
8		
9	Payment with Balloon	$278.66
10	Payment without Balloon	$353.05
11	Payment on 15 year 2nd mortgage	$286.94
12		
13	==	
14	Calculations	
15		
16	Total Periods	84
17	Regular Payments	83
18	Periodic Interest	1.00%
19	Present Value of Balloon	$4,355.15
20	Present Value of Payments	$15,664.85

Figure 6.12. The outcome of payment calculations for a loan with a balloon payment.

3. Using the last figure as the first argument, use @PMT to calculate the regular payments, using a term of 83 months (not 84, since the last payment has already been accounted for). The @PMT formula appears in B9.

The 7-year and 15-year ordinary annuity calculations are straightforward @PMT problems. The calculations appear in B10 and B11, respectively.

The results of the calculations are shown in Figure 6.12. As you can see, the payment for the balloon mortgage, $278.66, is less than for a regular loan with the same term, $353.05. (The difference would decline for loans with longer terms, because the present value of the balloon payment would decrease.) However, the payment for a regular 15-year second mortgage would have a payment of $286.94, only slightly more than the payment for the balloon loan. Thus, a second mortgage might be the better option if it were available.

Comparing Borrowing Capacity for Two Loans

One reason to opt for a balloon loan is to maximize cash on hand without committing to payments you can't afford. A balloon loan will, in fact, reduce payments, and therefore increase the amount you can afford to borrow. The risk is whether you will be able to make the balloon payment when it comes due.

Suppose, for example, that you are renovating an historic property and want to borrow as much as you can with monthly payments of $1,000. You can get an 8-year loan at 11% APR with a balloon of $25,000 as the final payment. You can also take out a 15-year second mortgage at 12% APR. Which loan allows you to borrow more?

This problem is simply a matter of comparing the present values of the two loans. Finding the present value of the second mortgage is a straightforward @PV calculation. You could make it without setting up a model by entering @PV(1000,.12/12,12*15), where 1,000 is the payment, .12/12 is the periodic interest rate, and 12*15 is the term in months. To find the present value of the balloon loan you must find the present value

	A	B
1	AMOUNT YOU CAN BORROW WITH BALLOON	
2		
3	Affordable Payment	1000
4		
5	Balloon Mortgage	
6	Annual Interest	0.11
7	Term	8
8	Periods/Year	12
9	Balloon Payment	25000
10		
11	Second Mortgage	
12	Annual Interest	0.12
13	Term	15
14	Periods/Term	12
15		
16		
17	Capacity (Balloon)	+B27+B28
18	Capacity (Second Mortgage)	@PV(B3,B32,B31)
19		
20	===	
21	Calculations	
22		
23	Balloon Mortgage	
24	Total Periods	+B7*B8
25	Regular Payments	+B24-1
26	Periodic Interest	+B6/B8
27	Present Value of Balloon	+B9/(1+B26)^B24
28	Present Value of Payments	@PV(B3,B26,B25)
29		
30	Second Mortgage	
31	Periods	+B13*B14
32	Periodic Interest	+B12/B14

Figure 6.13. Comparing borrowing power with a balloon loan vs. a second mortgage.

of the loan payment and the present value of the 95 regular payments (8*12-1 = 95). The amount you can borrow is the sum of those two figures. Figure 6.13 is a model that allows you to change the variables for any two loans.

The critical calculations for the balloon mortgage are in B27 and B28, Present Value of Balloon and Present Value of Payments. Again the familiar compound interest formula is used: $PV = FV*(1+i)^n$. Here FV, or future value, is the amount of the balloon payment (B9). The periodic interest rate, i, is the value calculated in B26 by dividing APR (B6) by Periods/Year (B8). And n, the number of periods is the total term of the loan, calculated in B24 because balloon is the last payment of the loan.

The present value of the regular payments on the balloon loan is a straightforward @PV calculation in B28—@PV(*payment,interest,term*). Note, however, that the term is one period less than the full term of the loan (calculated in B25) because the balloon payment has already been accounted for.

	A	B
1	AMOUNT YOU CAN BORROW WITH BALLOON	
2		
3	Affordable Payment	$1000.00
4		
5	Balloon Mortgage	
6	Annual Interest	11.00%
7	Term	8
8	Periods/Year	12
9	Balloon Payment	$25,000.00
10		
11	Second Mortgage	
12	Annual Interest	12.00%
13	Term	15
14	Periods/Term	12
15		
16		
17	Capacity (Balloon)	$73,654.88
18	Capacity (Second Mortgage)	$83,321.66
19		
20	===	
21	Calculations	
22		
23	Balloon Mortgage	
24	Total Periods	96
25	Regular Payments	95
26	Periodic Interest	0.92%
27	Present Value of Balloon	$10,411.23
28	Present Value of Payments	$63,243.65
29		
30	Second Mortgage	
31	Periods	180
32	Periodic Interest	1.00%

Figure 6.14. A balloon loan does not necessarily increase borrowing capacity; in fact, it may have the opposite effect.

Once you have determined the present values of the balloon and of the remaining payments, all you have to do to determine the amount you can borrow is to add the two numbers. This is done in B17 with the formula +B27+B28.

For the regular second mortgage, finding your borrowing capacity is a straightforward @PV calculation, once you have calculated Periods in B31 and Periodic Interest in B32. The results are shown in Figure 6.14. Given these circumstances, you can borrow nearly $10,000 more with the ordinary second mortgage than with the balloon loan. Note, incidentally, that these are also the amounts that an investor would be willing to pay to purchase the two loans if he required a return of 11% or 12%, respectively.

Saving with a Beginning Balance

There are many times when people must plan regular savings to meet a goal, such as college educations, down payments on houses, retirement nest eggs; the purpose doesn't affect the calculations. Often there is a sum of cash on hand at the beginning of the savings program. You might want to know regular savings required to reach a goal, the future value of your investment after a certain period, or how long it will take to reach a goal with regular savings.

These calculations are similar to those for balloon loans, although some new wrinkles appear. Payments may be at the end of each period (ordinary annuity) or at the beginning (annuity due). The difference may not be large enough to make a difference for planning purposes if savings are scheduled on a monthly basis. However, the difference can be significant on an annual basis, particularly if the term is relatively short.

Calculating Payments to Reach a Goal (Ordinary Annuity)

Suppose you have already begun building a nest egg for retirement, the children's college expenses, or the down payment on a house. You have a fairly good idea of the goal you need to reach, but you need to determine

how much you must set aside on a regular basis to reach the goal. You
need to know two things: how much the nest egg will be worth when the
time comes, and how much you must set aside regularly to make up the
difference.

Consider this example. Your investments allocated for retirement total
$500,000, earning 7.75% APR, compounded monthly. How much must
you save each month to accumulate $1,000,000 when you retire in eight
years, assuming the same interest rate? Assume payments will be made
at the end of each month (ordinary annuity).

	A	B
1	PAYMENTS TO REACH A GOAL (ORDINARY ANNUITY)	
2		
3	Goal	1000000
4	Beginning Balance	500000
5	Payments/Year	12
6	Term	8
7	Annual Interest	0.0775
8		
9	Payment	@PMT(B18,B15,B14)
10		
11	===	
12	Calculations	
13		
14	Periods	+B5*B6
15	Periodic Interest	+B7/B5
16	Present Value of Goal	+B3/(1+B15)^B14
17	Less Beginning Balance	+B4
18	Present Value of Payments	+B16-B17

Figure 6.15. Calculating savings to reach a goal with a beginning balance.

The calculations are shown in Figure 6.15. Once again, the crux of the
calculation requires three steps:

1. Calculate the present value of the goal, again using the familiar
   formula $PV = FV/(1+i)^n$. This calculation appears in B16, the
   future value (*FV*) is the goal (B3), the periodic interest rate is
   calculated in B15, and the Periods (*n*) is calculated in B14.

	A	B
1	PAYMENTS TO REACH A GOAL (ORDINARY ANNUITY)	
2		
3	Goal	$1,000,000.00
4	Beginning Balance	$500,000.00
5	Payments/Year	12
6	Term	8
7	Annual Interest	7.75%
8		
9	Payment	$546.64
10		
11	==	
12	Calculations	
13		
14	Periods	96
15	Periodic Interest	0.65%
16	Present Value of Goal	$539,017.90
17	Less Beginning Balance	$500,000.00
18	Present Value of Payments	$39,017.90

Figure 6.16. Calculating end-of-month payments to reach a goal.

2. The present value of the beginning balance, of course, is the beginning balance. Subtract the beginning balance from the present value of the goal. Here that calculation is in B18.

3. Use @PMT(*PV,interest,term*) to calculate the payments required to match the present value of the figure calculated in step 2. Here, that calculation appears in B9. The present value is the Present Value of Payments, from B18. The periodic interest rate is calculated in B15. And the term is calculated in B14.

The results are shown in Figure 6.16. With a beginning balance of $500,000, you can accumulate $1,000,000 in eight years by saving $546.64 a month if all of your investments earn 7.75% per year. If your beginning balance earns a different interest rate than your payments, you would simply have to expand the model to accommodate a different interest rate for calculating the present value of the goal. Once that figure is established, the remainder of the calculation is the same.

Calculating Payments to Reach a Goal (Annuity Due)

Often, when you are setting up a savings or investment plan, you intend to make the payments (or deposits) at the beginning of each period, starting now. Now let's do the same calculation shown in Figure 6.16, assuming that payments will be made at the beginning of each month—starting today—rather than at the end. This simply requires you to adapt the payment formula in B9 for an annuity due. Otherwise the calculation is the same.

As we saw in Chapter 2, the format of an @PMT calculation for an annuity due is @PMT(*PV,interest,term*)/(1+*interest*). Thus, the calculation in B9 becomes @PMT(B18,B15,B14)/(1+B15), where B18 is Present Value of Payments, B15 is Periodic Interest, and B14 is Periods. Otherwise, the formulas in the model are identical to those in Figure 6.15.

This time, the required monthly payment is $543.13, only $3 and change less than for end-of-month payments. The only difference is that with an annuity due you earn interest for the first period, while with an ordinary annuity you do not, since the first payment is not made until the end of the first period.

How Long Will It Take?: Finding the Term for an Ordinary Annuity

When you set up a savings plan or investment program, it's not very useful to know that you would have to deposit $5,000 a month to reach a goal in five years if there is no way you could set aside anywhere near that amount. If you know how much you *can* set aside (the monthly payments), how much you already have (beginning balance), and the interest rate, you can figure out how long it will take you to reach your goal (the term). As we are about to see, the size of the beginning balance plays a very large role in the calculation.

Suppose, to continue the same example, you have a current balance of $500,000, earning 7.75% interest, but you can save only $50 a month. Now how long will it take you to reach your $1,000,000 goal?

Believe it or not, by saving $50 a month you will accumulate $1,000,000 only about 10 1/2 months later than if you save the $546.64 a month calculated in Figure 6.16 (8.87 years, compared with 8 years, to be exact). Be careful with this thought, however. The reason for the apparent incongruity is that we have deliberately set up a calculation where the future value of the beginning balance would approach the goal anyway. If the goal were larger, or the beginning balance lower, the swing in term would be much larger with varying monthly payments.

To check this out, try this formula:

```
@CTERM(0.0775/12,1000000,500000)/12
```

The answer is 8.97 years. That means that at 7.75% APR, compounded monthly, $500,000 will grow to $1,000,000 in 8.97 years without any additional deposits. @CTERM, you will recall, calculates the term required for a lump sum to reach a future value using this argument: (*interest,future value,present value*). In this case, the periodic interest rate is 0.0775/12, the future value is 1000000, and the present value is 500000. Dividing the whole calculation by 12 converts the @CTERM result from months to years.

There isn't any direct way to use @Functions to solve for term with a beginning balance and regular payments. The mathematical equation is not exactly easy, but it isn't hard to make the calculation if you break it down into its parts. It comes to this:

$$term \quad = \quad \frac{\ln\dfrac{(FV*i)+pmt}{(PV*i)+pmt}}{\ln(1+i)}$$

where *term* is the number of periods; ln is the natural logarithm; *FV* is the future value; *i* is the periodic interest rate; *pmt* is the periodic payment; and *PV* is the present value.

Here is the right side of the equation in 1-2-3 syntax:

```
@LN((FV*i+pmt)/(PV*i+pmt))/@LN(1+i)
```

And, here is the formula for calculating term to $1,000,000 with monthly payments of $50, a $500,000 beginning balance, and an APR of 7.75%, compounded monthly:

	A	B
1	TERM TO REACH A GOAL WITH BEGINNING BALANCE	
2		
3	Goal	1000000
4	Beginning Balance	500000
5	Payments/Year	12
6	Payment	50
7	Annual Interest	0.0775
8		
9	Term	+B28
10	Years	+B9/B5
11		
12	Future Value of Balance	+B4*(1+B23)^B9
13	Future Value of Payments	@FV(B6,B23,B9)
14		=========================
15	Total	+B12+B13
16		
17		
18	==	
19	Calculations	
20		
21	'@LN((FV*i+pmt)/(PV*i+pmt))/@LN(1+i)	
22		
23	Periodic Interest	+B7/B5
24	'(FV*i+pmt)	+B3*B23+B6
25	'(PV*i+pmt)	+B4*B23+B6
26	'@LN(FV*i+pmt)/(PV*i+pmt))	@LN(B24/B25)
27	'@LN(1+i)	@LN(1+B23)
28	Term	+B26/B27

Figure 6.17. A model for calculating the term for regular savings with a beginning balance.

```
@LN((1000000*0.0775/12+50)/(500000*0.0775/12+50))
    /@LN(1+0.0775/12)
```

Answer: 106.48 months. To convert that result to years, simply divide by 12. The answer is 8.87 years.

	A	B
1	TERM TO REACH A GOAL WITH BEGINNING BALANCE	
2		
3	Goal	$1,000,000.00
4	Beginning Balance	$500,000.00
5	Payments/Year	12
6	Payment	$50.00
7	Annual Interest	7.75%
8		
9	Term	106.48
10	Years	8.87
11		
12	Future Value of Balance	$992,376.11
13	Future Value of Payments	$7,623.89
14		================
15	Total	$1,000,000.00
16		
17		
18	==	
19	Calculations	
20		
21	@LN((FV*i+pmt)/(PV*i+pmt))/@LN(1+i)	
22		
23	Periodic Interest	0.65%
24	(FV*i+pmt)	6508.33
25	(PV*i+pmt)	3279.17
26	@LN(FV*i+pmt)/(PV*i+pmt))	0.685494082
27	@LN(1+i)	0.0064375677
28	Term	106.48

Figure 6.18. The results of the model for term to reach a goal shown in the previous figure.

Building a Model

That last formula is not one that you will want to enter very often, and it makes experimenting with different values difficult. The calculation is much easier if you break the formula down into its components. A model also helps ensure accuracy. While the full formula is fairly complex, the calculation within each pair of parentheses is relatively simple.

Figure 6.17 shows a model that breaks the calculation down into its components.

The result is shown in Figure 6.18. As you can see, it will take 106.48 months or 8.87 years to accumulate $1,000,000 under these terms. The next sections examine the formulas in more detail. The future value calculations in B13..B16 are not essential. They merely show that the future value of the balance plus the future value of the payments actually do equal the goal.

Entering the Variables

The raw data for calculating term for an annuity due with a beginning balance and regular payments are Goal, Beginning Balance, Payments/Year, Payment, and Annual Interest. You can enter these as you would in any other annuity model. No calculations are involved. Here, we have entered a Goal of $1,000,000, a Beginning Balance of $500,000, 12 Payments/Year, $50 for Payment, and 7.75% for the APR. Once you have completed the model, you can freely change any (or all) of these values to experiment with alternatives.

Breaking Down the Formulas

The calculations below the double line break the main formula down into its components. This facilitates the use of cell references, which allow you to vary the input values without changing formulas. Simply for reference, the entire formula is entered as a label in A21. Note that any label that begins with an @ sign or a parenthesis must be preceded by an apostrophe ('). Otherwise, 1-2-3 will assume you are trying to enter a value and will not let you complete the entry.

The formulas in B23..B28 should be self-explanatory when you compare the labels in column A with the main formula in A21. Periodic Interest is calculated in the usual way in B23, by dividing Annual Interest (B7) by Payments/Year (B5). This is i, or interest, in the formula. Here, i is 0.65% per month.

The formulas in B24 and B25 calculate values for the arguments in the first two pairs of parentheses in the main formula—$FV*i+pmt$ and $PV*i+pmt$. Here, FV is the Goal (B3), i is Periodic Interest (B23), pmt is Payment (B6), and PV is Beginning Balance (B4). These numbers do not mean much by themselves.

In B26, the formula calculates the natural logarithm of B24/B25. You have now completed the formula up to the last division. In other words, the value returned in B26 is @LN(($FV*i+pmt$)/($PV*i+pmt$)). Again, this is useless by itself. Two more steps are required to complete the main formula.

The final component of the main formula, @LN($1+i$) is calculated in B27. (We're almost there.) The formula @LN(1+B23) returns the natural log of 1 + Periodic Interest (B23).

Now you have all of the components of the main formula. All you have to do is make the final division in the main formula—the / before @LN($1+i$)—in B28. This is simply +B26/B27, which divides the first logarithm by the second. The value returned here is the number of periods (in this case, months) required to reach the Goal. In this case, it will take 106.48 months to reach the goal.

Getting Results

Now comes the payoff. Rows 9–15 summarize the results of your calculations. For Term, in B9 the formula +B28 recalls the final calculation below the double line. This will be the number of periods (in this case months) required to reach the goal. For Years, the formula +B9/B5 converts the number of periods just calculated to years. Here the Term is 106.48 months, which converts to 8.87 years.

The calculations in rows 12–15 are not necessary for the model to work, but they provide useful information. The formula in B12 calculates the future value of the beginning balance, as if no additional payments were added. In this case, the future value is $992,376.11. That explains why payments of only $50 a month are required to build $500,000 into $1,000,000 in 8.87 years. The calculation is the standard compound interest formula $FV = PV*(1+i)^n$. Here PV, or present value, is the Beginning Balance (B4); i, the periodic interest rate, is calculated in B23; and n, the number of periods, is the Term, from B19.

Future Value of Payments, calculated in B13, is a regular @Function calculation using @FV($payment,interest,term$). In this case, the future value of the payments is only $7,623.89, a tiny fraction of the $1,000,000 total. Again, you can see that the compound interest on the Beginning

Balance has done most of the work. Here *pmt* is the Payment entered in B6, *i* is the Periodic Interest calculated in B23, and term is the Term calculated in B9.

Finally, Total, in B15, is simply the sum of Future Value of Balance and Future Value of Payments. As you can see, the calculations you have made actually produce a future value of $1,000,000, the goal you set out to reach. This last calculation serves as an error check to make sure you have entered the formulas correctly. If the Total does not equal the Goal, you will need to recheck your work.

You now have a model that allows you to calculate how long it will take to reach a goal, given payments, beginning balance, and interest rate, provided payments are made at the *end* of each period. In the next section, we adapt the model for payments at the beginning of each period.

Calculating Time Required to Reach a Goal (Annuity Due)

Again, if you're planning a savings or investment plan, there's no point in putting off the first deposit. You can start earning interest immediately if you do it now, so why wait? The case for starting now is even more compelling in the case of IRAs and other investments that provide tax breaks. (The interest on IRAs is still tax-deferred, even though you can no longer deduct an IRA contribution unless neither you nor your spouse is covered by an employer-sponsored retirement plan.) If you plan to deposit $2,000 in an IRA, for example, there is no point in delaying the contribution and paying taxes on the interest you earn until the end of the year. If you make the deposit now, your tax savings start immediately. The same logic would apply to investments in municipal bonds, tax deferred annuities, Keogh plans, or any other investment that provides tax benefits.

To calculate term to reach a goal, with payments at the beginning of each period, you will need to adapt the model shown in Figures 6.17 and 6.18 for an annuity due. This is easily done. Shifting payments to the beginning of each period has the effect of adding an interest period to the payment calculations in the model. The main formula becomes:

$$term \quad = \quad \frac{\ln \dfrac{(FV*i)+pmt*(1+i)}{(PV*i)+pmt*(1+i)}}{\ln\,(1+i)}$$

Or, in 1-2-3 syntax, the right side of the equation is:

```
@LN(((FV*i+pmt*(1+i))/(PV*i+pmt*(1+i)))/@LN(1+i)
```

	F	G
13	Future Value of Payments	@FV(B22,B23,B9)
	**	
24	'(FV*i+pmt*(1+i))	+B3*B23+B22
25	'(PV*i+pmt*(1+i))	+B4*B23+B22

Figure 6.19. Revising the ordinary annuity model for annuities due.

Fortunately, this directly affects only three formulas in the model, and all can easily be changed with the same method. The formulas are those for Future Value of Payments in B13 and the partial equation calculations in B24 and B25. Cell references will carry the changes to other formulas as appropriate.

To make the change, edit the formula in A21 for reference, then find a blank row in which to calculate the value of $pmt*(1+i)$. We will use row 22, the blank row between the full formula and the beginning of the intermediate calculations. Enter the label $pmt*(1+i)$ in A22 to document the formula. In B22, enter this formula:

```
+B6*(1+B23)
```

where B6 is the Payment, entered above; and B23 is Periodic Interest, calculated in the cell below.

Now, all you have to do is to substitute B22 (the new calculation) as the cell reference wherever the reference B6 (Payment) appears and edit the labels in column A to reflect the changes. This affects only rows 13, 24, and 25. They should now look like Figure 6.19. (Be sure to label your new model to distinguish it from the one for ordinary annuities.)

	A	B
1	TERM TO REACH A GOAL WITH BEGINNING BALANCE (ANNUITY DUE)	
2		
3	Goal	$1,000,000.00
4	Beginning Balance	$500,000.00
5	Payments/Year	12
6	Payment	$50.00
7	Annual Interest	7.75%
8		
9	Term	106.48
10	Years	8.87
11		
12	Future Value of Balance	$992,327.63
13	Future Value of Payments	$7,672.37
14		================
15	Total	$1,000,000.00
16		
17		
18	==	
19	Calculations	
20		
21	@LN((FV*i+pmt*(1+i))/(PV*i+pmt*(1+i)))/@LN(1+i)	
22	pmt*(1+i)	50.32
23	Periodic Interest	0.65%
24	(FV*i+pmt*(1+i))	6508.66
25	(PV*i+(pmt*1+i))	3279.49
26	@LN((FV*i+pmt)/(PV*i+pmt))	0.6854452263
27	@LN(1+i)	0.0064375677
28		

Figure 6.20. Term to reach a future value for an annuity due with a beginning balance.

For the sake of comparison, we will continue to use the example for calculating the term of an ordinary annuity. Your goal is still $1,000,000, and you already have $500,000. You plan to deposit $50 *at the beginning of each month*, rather than at the end, and to earn annual interest (APR) of 7.75%. The calculation is shown in Figure 6.20.

If you compare the outcome with Figure 6.18, you will find that the Future Value of Balance and Future Value of Payments have shifted by about a dollar an a half, but that the term does not appear to have changed at all. (Actually, it has, but not enough to show up in two decimal places.) In situations where the Payment makes a much larger contribution to the Future Value, you will be able to see the difference, although it still may not be enough to make a difference for planning purposes.

Working with Leases with Residual or Salvage Value

Chapter 2 covered a variety of lease calculations. All assume that the asset will have no value at the end of the lease—that for the purposes of the lease calculation, at least, it will be discarded. Often, the lessee has a choice of buying the asset at the end of the lease or returning it to the lessor, who can then sell it. Most car leases work that way, for example. In such cases, the value of the asset—the amount you would have to pay to keep it or the amount you could sell it for at the end of the lease—is the asset's residual or salvage value.

Some leases, like car leases, take residual value into account; some do not. In the former case, lease payments are usually treated as simple expenses. Leases that do not account for residual value are sometimes called financing leases, and for accounting and tax purposes, you may have to treat such a lease almost like a purchase. (The accounting and tax rules are far too complex to go into here, but you should be aware of the difference.) A company might, for example, choose a financing lease over a purchase/loan arrangement to avoid drawing down its line of credit at a bank. The lender/lessor will make the options clear.

Calculations for a lease with a residual value are basically the same as for a lease based on the current value of the asset. The only difference is that you must discount the residual value to its present value in order to determine the present value of the lease. The procedure is similar to calculating payments for a loan with a balloon payment, except that leases are usually annuities due, while loans are ordinary annuities. Once you have made that calculation, you can treat the present value of the lease as you would the present value of a lease without a residual value.

In the following examples, we calculate the payments and residual value of two specific leases. Once you understand the way this works, you should be able to adapt any annuity due calculation in this book for a lease with residual value.

Calculating Lease Payments with a Residual Value

When you lease a car, the payments are based on an interest rate, a term, the price of the car, and the *present value* of the worth of the car at the end of the lease. Thus, the present value of the lease equals the price of the car, less the present value of its residual value. The present value of the lease also equals the present value of the lease payments plus the present value of the residual. Either way, you must discount the residual value of the car back to the present. The procedure is the same for any lease with residual value.

Suppose, for example, that Jane's Industrial Supply purchases scaffolding for $12,000 and immediately leases it to Dick's Construction Co. for three years. At the end of the lease, the scaffolding should have a market value of $7,500. With an APR of 18%, what are Dick's monthly payments?

	A	B
1	PAYMENTS FOR A LEASE WITH RESIDUAL VALUE	
2		
3	Present Value	12000
4	Annual Interest	0.18
5	Term	3
6	Periods/Year	12
7	Residual Value	7500
8		
9	Payment	@PMT(B17,B15,B14)/(1+B15)
10		
11	==	
12	Calculations	
13		
14	Total Periods	+B5*B6
15	Periodic Interest	+B4/B6
16	Present Value of Residual	+B7/(1+B15)^B14
17	Present Value of Payments	+B3-B16

Figure 6.21. Calculating payments for a lease with residual value.

As explained in Chapter 2, the @Function formula for calculating payments for an annuity due is:

$$@PMT(PV, i, term)/(1+i)$$

where *PV* is the present value; *i* is the periodic interest; and *term* is the number of periods.

In addition to the usual calculations for periods (in B14) and periodic interest (in B15), the model shown in Figure 6.21 breaks the basic problem into three steps:

1. Calculate the present value of the residual. The formula in B16 divides the residual value by the standard compound interest calculation, $PV = FV/(1+i)^n$.

2. Calculate the present value of the payments. This is simply the present value of the asset (B3) less the present value of the residual (B16).

3. Determine the payment, based on Present Value of Payments, calculated in B17 by subtracting the present value of the residual (B16) from the Present Value of the asset (B3).

The results are shown in Figure 6.22. Present value of the residual is $4,388.17, so the present value of payments must be $7,611.83. Dick's monthly payment is $271.12.

	A	B
1	PAYMENTS FOR A LEASE WITH RESIDUAL VALUE	
2		
3	Present Value	$12,000.00
4	Annual Interest	18.00%
5	Term	3
6	Periods/Year	12
7	Residual Value	$7,500.00
8		
9	Payment	$271.12
10		
11	===	
12	Calculations	
13		
14	Total Periods	36
15	Periodic Interest	1.50%
16	Present Value of Residual	$4,388.17
17	Present Value of Payments	$7,611.83

Figure 6.22. The results of the model shown in Figure 6.22.

This model allows you to calculate the payments for a lease with residual value for any asset, regardless of cost (present value), term, interest rate, residual value, or payment period. You can freely change any of these variables. Sometimes, however, the payment, rate, and term are given, but it may not be clear on what basis the residual value is determined. That is discussed in the next section.

Determining Residual Value

If you are the lessor, you can determine the residual value of an asset at the end of a lease in whatever way makes business sense. A Mercedes dealer, for example, probably has a good idea of how much one of its cars depreciates each year—or can make that calculation based on resale prices. If there is a purchase option at the end of a lease, the price and any other terms (such as mileage) will probably be stated in the lease agreement. If you lease an asset with no purchase option, however, it may

	A	B
1	RESIDUAL VALUE OF LEASE	
2		
3	Present Value	18537
4	Annual Interest	0.1497
5	Term	6
6	Periods/Year	12
7	Payment	280
8		
9	Residual Value	+B18
10		
11	==	
12	Calculations	
13		
14	Total Periods	+B5*B6
15	Periodic Interest	+B4/B6
16	Present Value of Payments	@PV(B7,B15,B14)*(1+B15)
17	Present Value of Residual	+B3-B16
18	Future Value of Residual	+B17*(1+B15)^B14

Figure 6.23. Calculating the residual value of a lease.

not be clear on what the residual value the lease is calculated. Or, as is the case in the following example, there may be a purchase option with no price stated. In any case, the problem is to determine the future value of the asset, given present value, interest rate, term, and payments.

This example is taken almost directly from a newspaper advertisement for a car lease. Bob's Auto World offers to sell a new car for $20,995 or to lease it for $280 a month for six years, with a purchase option at the "stated residual value." The small print indicates that a "capital cost reduction" (read "down payment") of $2,458 is required and that the APR is 14.97%, but the residual value is not stated in the ad. How much would you have to pay for the car at the end of the lease?

At the outset, you know that the present value of the lease is $18,537 ($20,995 – $2,458). You could calculate this within the model, but to avoid unnecessary complexity, the model shown in Figure 6.23 starts with the actual present value of the lease.

Once again, this is basically a three-step calculation, after you have calculated Total Periods (B14) and Periodic Interest (B15):

1. Determine the present value of payments. The formula in B16 uses the basic @PV calculation for an annuity due: @PV(pmt,i,term)*(1+i). Here, the payment is entered as a value in B7, i is Periodic Interest in B15, and term is Total Periods in B14.

2. Find the present value of the residual. The present value of the residual is Present Value of Payments (B16) less Present Value of the lease (B3).

3. Calculate the future value of the residual. This is the amount you will have to pay to buy the car at the end of the lease. The formula in B18 uses the basic compound interest formula: $FV = PV*(1+i)^n$. PV is the Present Value of the Residual (B17), i is Periodic Interest (B15), and n is Total Periods (B14). The Residual Value (B9) is entered in the upper part of the worksheet as a cell reference to Future Value of Residual (B18).

The results are shown in Figure 6.24. The Residual Value of the Lease—the amount you will pay to buy the car at the end of the lease—is

	A	B
1	RESIDUAL VALUE OF A LEASE	
2		
3	Present Value	$18,537.00
4	Annual Interest	14.97%
5	Term	6
6	Periods/Year	12
7	Payment	$280.00
8		
9	Residual Value	$12,499.84
10		
11	===	
12	Calculations	
13		
14	Total Periods	72
15	Periodic Interest	1.25%
16	Present Value of Payments	$13,417.42
17	Present Value of Residual	$5,119.58
18	Future Value of Residual	$12,499.84

Figure 6.24. The residual value of a lease.

$12,499.84. Allowing for rounding, it's a fairly safe bet that the dealer based the calculations for the advertisement on a residual value of $12,500.

Once you have set up the model, you can enter any values for Present Value, Annual Interest, Term, Periods/Year, and Payment. The model will calculate the residual value of the asset automatically.

Conclusion

In this chapter, you have learned to set up a loan amortization schedule, two ways to create an annual loan summary, and to perform a variety of calculations that combine lump-sum and annuity formulas. As it turns out, you can use many of these methods to evaluate stocks and bonds, as you will see in the next chapter. The next chapter also explains some more sophisticated business applications, using 1-2-3's statistical @Functions and regression analysis features.

7

Making Business Decisions

A fair percentage of business mathematics is quite simple. The *accounting* may befuddle a layman. But once the accounting is done, filling out a tax return, for example, or completing a balance sheet, requires only simple arithmetic.

Other problems you might find in a finance text are simple in concept, but may be difficult in practice. Suppose, for example, that Kopperklad Industries' fixed costs are $250,000 a year, variable costs are $75 per unit, and the price per unit is $100. It doesn't take much of a calculation to determine how many units the company must sell to break even:

$$Break\ Even = \frac{Fixed\ Cost}{Price\ -\ Variable\ Cost} = \frac{\$250,000}{\$25} = 10,000\ units$$

If the fixed cost includes $50,000 in depreciation, calculating the cash break even point is not much harder:

$$Cash\ Break\ Even = \frac{Fixed\ Cost\ -\ Depreciation}{Price\ -Variable\ Cost} = \frac{\$200,000}{\$25} = 8,000\ units$$

In real life, calculating Kopperklad's actual fixed costs, depreciation, and variable cost would require considerably more work, especially if the plant makes several different products.

The focus of this book is using 1-2-3 to make basic financial calculations, not the theory of accounting or finance. The beauty of the program, after all, is that you can adapt it to your own specific needs. This chapter continues to focus on calculations. First, it applies basic principles of calculating the time value of money to stocks and bonds. This will not help you forecast the market, but it does allow you to assess the returns you would get if your projections were accurate. (An exception is a bond's yield to maturity, which is mathematically fixed.) The second half of the chapter applies some of 1-2-3's statistics features to estimating risk (variance and standard deviation) and to making projections based on past experience (data regression). Again, your results are only as good as your assumptions.

Evaluating Securities

Analyzing the returns on investments in stocks and bonds is quite similar to analyzing balloon loans and leases with residual value (see Chapter 6). A stock provides a series of dividend payments (which may or may not be even), and you can sell it for a lump sum at a future date. A bond yields regular interest payments, and also can be sold at a future date or redeemed at face value at maturity. The calculations offered here are of no use in predicting the behavior of the markets, but you can use them to assess results once you have settled on your predictions. In the case of a bond held to maturity, the calculations are accurate, because both the interest payments and the redemption value are fixed.

Schematically, the calculation is this:

```
Present Value (investment) = present value (payments)
 + present value (sale price or redemption value)
```

If the payments are even, they constitute an annuity, and thus are subject to the calculations already discussed. If they are uneven, somewhat more elaborate calculations are required. The sale price or redemption value is the future value of a lump sum, and you can use the usual compound interest calculations.

Commissions and taxes are deliberately omitted in the following examples in order better to show the basic calculations. When you buy securities, commissions are added to the purchase price. When you sell, the IRS requires you to report commissions to them the same way your broker does on Form 1099-B. If the broker reports the *net* amount of the sale, after commissions, the final commission is deducted from the sales price. If the broker reports the *gross* amount of the sale, before commissions, the IRS requires you to report that figure as the sales price. The commission is added to the cost or basis, as if it were part of the original price of the stock. Tax will simply be your marginal tax rate times each cash flow and your marginal rate times the profit or loss when you sell. Adapting this chapter's models to these calculations is a matter of simple arithmetic. Even though commissions and taxes are not shown, you should have no trouble adapting the examples to your situation.

We start with preferred stock because that is the simplest example.

Analyzing Preferred Stock

Preferred stock is a perpetual annuity: once you purchase the stock, you receive fixed dividends forever. If market interest rates decline, the investment is a winner; you can either continue to collect the higher return or sell the stock at a premium. If market interest rates increase, however, you have a choice between accepting the lower return paid by the preferred stock and selling the stock for less than you paid for it.

The theoretical price of a preferred stock is simply d/i, where d is the periodic dividend and i is the periodic interest rate (the two periods must match). Suppose, for example, that you require a 10% annual return before taxes (or that 10% is the going rate for preferred stock in your selection's class), and a preferred stock pays an annual dividend of $10 a year. The price should be $10/0.10 = $100. If the required rate drops to 7.5%, the expected stock price increases to $133.33 ($10/0.075). If the required rate rises to 12.5%, the expected stock price drops to $80 ($10/0.125). If the interest rate does not change, in theory neither does the price of the stock.

Conversely, the return on preferred stock is d/p, where d is the periodic dividend, and p is the price. Thus, a preferred stock that costs $100 and pays $10 a year has a return of 10% ($10/$100). If the company pays semiannual dividends of $5, the semiannual return is 5% ($5/$100). You can experiment with other dividends and prices.

Suppose you buy Amalgamated preferred at $100 a share. The stock pays an annual dividend of $10, at the end of the year, a 10% return. Where will you stand if you sell after five years if (a) interest rates drop to 7.5%; (b) if interest rates hold steady at 10%; and (c) if the rate rises to 12.5%?

Figure 7.1 shows the results of the calculations. The sales prices at the end of five years are calculated as before (e.g., if the rate is 10% and the annual dividend is $10, the price is $10/0.10 = $100). The cash flows for year 0–4 are given. The purchase occurs at year 0 because the rest of the cash flows occurs at the end of the year. You can think of year 0 as the beginning of year 1. In other words, you pay $100 for the stock in year 0 (now), and receive a $10 at the end of each year for the next four years. At the end of the fifth year, you receive the dividend plus the sale price of the stock.

	A	B	C	D
1	PREFERRED STOCK ANALYSIS			
2				
3	Current Price	$100.00		
4	Dividend (Annual)	$10.00		
5	Return	10.00%		
6				
7	If Sold after 5 Years			
8	Sales Price			
9	(a) If interest rate = 7.5%	$133.33		
10	(b) If interest rate = 10%	$100.00		
11	(c) If interest rate = 12.5%	$80.00		
12				
13	Cash Flows			
14		Year	A	B	C
15		0	($100.00)	($100.00)	($100.00)
16		1	$10.00	$10.00	$10.00
17		2	$10.00	$10.00	$10.00
18		3	$10.00	$10.00	$10.00
19		4	$10.00	$10.00	$10.00
20		5	$143.33	$110.00	$90.00
21					
22					
23	Net Return		$83.33	$50.00	$30.00
24	Internal Rate of Return		14.95%	10.00%	6.49%
25	Net Present Value @ 10%		$120.70	$100.00	$87.58

Figure 7.1. Analyzing the return on a preferred stock.

The Net Return is the @SUM calculation for years 0–5. This is the gross profit. The Internal Rate of Return is the @IRR calculation for years 0–5. The syntax for @IRR, remember, is @IRR(guess,range). @IRR is discussed in detail in Chapters 4 and 9.

To include the purchase commission in the calculation, you would add it to the initial outflows in row 16. (*Do not* add the commission to the Current Price in B3, since it does not affect the Sales Prices figured in rows 10–12.) The sales commission would either be added to the initial outflow or subtracted from the last year's cash flow, as explained earlier. It depends on how your broker reports the sale on Form 1099-B.

This model uses two basic techniques. The first is to divide the return by the required interest rate (rows 10–12). The second is to use the basic @IRR and @NPV calculations described in Chapter 4 to analyze the stock's return. As we see in the next section, similar calculations apply to bonds.

Buying Bonds

Bonds are similar to preferred stock, except that the issuer promises to repay the face value of the bond at maturity. Thus, a bond is basically an annuity with a balloon, while preferred stock is a perpetual annuity. Bonds are usually sold in denominations of $1,000, with interest paid semiannually.

Pricing a Bond Bought on a Coupon Date

You are considering buying a bond on the date of an interest payment. How much should you be willing to pay? When bonds are traded between interest dates, the interest is divided between the seller and the buyer, as explained at the end of our discussion of bonds. For now, adding that calculation would only complicate the models unnecessarily. The interest payments are an annuity due, because the previous holder will be entitled to today's coupon payment. Thus, the appropriate price is the present value of the payments plus the present value of the par value, discounted at your required rate of return. The market tends to set the return at the rate paid by comparable bonds. When you make a purchase decision, however, the required rate is the minimum rate at which you would buy the bond. If the market price is lower than the price indicated by that calculation, you may buy the bond; if the market price is higher, you will not.

Suppose a Kopperklad Industries bond sells for $940, with a stated interest rate of 10%, paid semiannually. Twelve coupon payments remain after today's interest payment, so you can redeem the bond for $1,000 at the end of six years. You decide to buy the bond if the yield to maturity is better than 12%, compounded semiannually. What is the most you should pay for the bond?

The calculations for this proposition are shown in Figure 7.2, and the underlying formulas in Figure 7.3. The Present Value of Par is the Redemption Value, discounted for 12 semiannual periods at the Required Return of 12%, compounded semiannually. This formula appears in B15. The Present Value of Coupons is the present value of the remaining payments, discounted at the required rate of 12%, not the nominal rate of 10%. This calculation is shown in B16. The indicated Price, in B9, is simply the sum of the latter figures.

	A	B
1	PRICE OF A BOND BOUGHT ON A COUPON DATE	
2		
3	Redemption Value	$1,000.00
4	Nominal Interest Rate	10.00%
5	Semiannual Interest	$50.00
6	Periods Remaining	12
7	Required Return	12.00%
8		
9	Price	$916.16
10		
11	==	
12	Calculations	
13		
14	Required Periodic Rate	6.00%
15	Present Value of Par	$496.97
16	Present Value of Coupons	$419.19

Figure 7.2. Calculating the price of a bond at a required rate of return.

The yield to maturity would be 12%, compounded semiannually, if the bond sold for $916.16. Since the market price is $940, the yield is less.

	A	B
1	PRICE OF A BOND BOUGHT ON A COUPON DATE	
2		
3	Redemption Value	1000
4	Nominal Interest Rate	0.1
5	Semiannual Interest	+B3*B4/2
6	Periods Remaining	12
7	Required Return	0.12
8		
9	Price	+B15+B16
10		
11	===	
12	Calculations	
13		
14	Required Periodic Rate	+B7/2
15	Present Value of Par	+B3/(1+B14)^B6
16	Present Value of Coupons	@PV(B5,B14,B6)

Figure 7.3. Formulas for calculating a bond price at a required return.

As mentioned earlier, calculations for bonds bought between coupon dates are discussed at the end of this section. But first, let's develop a model for calculating the yield of a bond.

Finding the Yield of a Bond Bought on a Coupon Date

The yield to maturity for a bond is the interest rate at which *present value (payments)* + *the present value (redemption value)* = *current price*. There is no mathematical model for this calculation; you must solve for interest by trial and error, or, in mathematical terms, iteration. The @IRR function (internal rate of return) will perform this iteration, but it requires you to list each cash flow, including original cost, each coupon payment, and redemption value separately. Let's take the trial-and-error approach first.

A Trial-and-Error Model

One way of determining the yield on a bond is to guess at the return until it produces the actual current price. Building a model makes the trial-and-error process relatively painless.

The $1,000 Kopperklad bond in the last examples has a quoted price of $940, with semiannual interest payments of $50. Twelve periods remain, and the bond redemption is simultaneous with the final interest payment. We have already seen that a price of $916.16 would provide a 12% yield to maturity. What is the actual yield to maturity?

The model shown in Figure 7.4 is an adaptation of the one shown in Figures 7.2 and 7.3. The main difference is that the calculations below the double line are based on Yield (Guess) rather than on a Required Periodic Rate. The underlying formulas are shown in Figure 7.5. Periodic Interest is Yield (Guess)/2, since payments are semiannual. Present Value of Par is a basic present value calculation, based on the periods remaining and the guess. And Present Value of Coupons is an @PV calculation, based on Semiannual Interest, Periodic Interest, and Periods Remaining. The latter is an annuity due, with end-of-period payments.

	A	B
1	PRICE OF A BOND BOUGHT ON A COUPON DATE	
2		
3	Redemption Value	$1,000.00
4	Nominal Interest Rate	10.00%
5	Semiannual Interest	$50.00
6	Periods Remaining	12
7	Actual Price	$940.00
8		
9	Yield (Guess)	12.00%
10	Expected Price	$916.16
11		
12	==	
13	Calculations	
14		
15	Periodic Interest	6.00%
16	Present Value of Par	$496.97
17	Present Value of Coupons	$419.19

Figure 7.4. A trial-and-error model for calculating the yield of a bond.

As you can see in Figure 7.4, the Expected Price in B10 is less than the Actual Price in B7. That means that the actual yield is lower than the guess. Try entering 0.11 (11%) as the guess in B9. Now the Expected Price is $956.61, more than the Actual Price. So the actual yield is between 11% and 12%. Try 11.5%. The expected price is 936.25, so the actual yield is

	A	B
1	PRICE OF A BOND BOUGHT ON A COUPON DATE	
2		
3	Redemption Value	1000
4	Nominal Interest Rate	0.1
5	Semiannual Interest	+B3*B4/2
6	Periods Remaining	12
7	Actual Price	940
8		
9	Yield (Guess)	0.12
10	Expected Price	+B16+B17
11		
12	==	
13	Calculations	
14		
15	Periodic Interest	+B9/2
16	Present Value of Par	+B3/(1+B15)^B6
17	Present Value of Coupons	@PV(B5,B15,B6)

Figure 7.5. Formulas for estimating yield on a bond to its maturity date.

still a little lower. Try 11.4%. Now the Expected Price is $940.34, pennies away from the Actual Price, so 11.4% is pretty close to the actual yield. If you carry this procedure out to the end, you will find that the actual return is 11.4082%.

This method will give you a fairly accurate result, but, as is often the case, it would be somewhat awkward to go through the procedure very often.

An @IRR Model for Bond Yield

As you know, @IRR calculates the internal rate of return for a series of uneven payments at regular intervals. A bond fits this description neatly. The initial outflow is the purchase price, followed by a series of interest payments, and finally, the sale or redemption of the bond. Once you have built a model, you can use it to calculate the yield for any bond. Again, the assumption here is that the bond is bought on the date of an interest payment (which goes to the seller). The following section explains how to adapt the model for bonds bought between coupon dates.

If you hold the Kopperklad bond to maturity, there will be 13 cash flows. The first (today) is the purchase price of (minus) $940. This is followed by 11 semiannual interest payments of $50, then a final payment of $1,050 (the $1,000 redemption value plus the final $50 interest payment).

Figure 7.6 incorporates these cash flows in a model that allows you to vary nominal interest rates, remaining period, and actual price of a bond. The Semiannual Interest is simply the Nominal Interest divided by 2 times the Redemption Value. Below the double line, the Semiannual IRR is a straightforward @IRR calculation using 0.1 as a guess for the interest and the series of cash flows (B14..B26) for the range. The Annual Yield in B29 is double the Semiannual IRR. Finally, the Net Present Value calculation in B30 is a simple @NPV calculation for periods 1–12

	A	B
1	@IRR OF A BOND BOUGHT ON A COUPON DATE	
2		
3	Redemption Value	$1,000.00
4	Nominal Interest Rate	10.00%
5	Semiannual Interest	$50.00
6	Periods Remaining	12
7	Actual Price	$940.00
8		
9	Yield (APR)	11.41%
10		
11	==	
12	Cash Flows	
13	Period	
14	0	($940.00)
15	1	$50.00
16	2	$50.00
17	3	$50.00
18	4	$50.00
19	5	$50.00
20	6	$50.00
21	7	$50.00
22	8	$50.00
23	9	$50.00
24	10	$50.00
25	11	$50.00
26	12	$1,050.00
27		
28	Semiannual IRR	5.70%
29	Annual Yield (APR)	11.41%
30	Net Present Value	$940.00

Figure 7.6. Calculating the yield of a bond bought on a coupon date.

(B15..B26), using the Semiannual IRR as the interest rate. This confirms the previous calculations, since the NPV is the same as the Actual Price. The underlying formulas are shown in Figure 7.7.

	A	B
1	@IRR OF A BOND BOUGHT ON A COUPON DATE	
2		
3	Redemption Value	1000
4	Nominal Interest Rate	0.1
5	Semiannual Interest	+B3*B4/2
6	Periods Remaining	12
7	Actual Price	940
8		
9	Yield(APR)	+B29
10		
11	===	
12	Cash Flows	
13		Period
14		0 -B7
15		1 50
16		2 50
17		3 50
18		4 50
19		5 50
20		6 50
21		7 50
22		8 50
23		9 50
24		10 50
25		11 50
26		12 +B3+B5
27		
28	Semiannual IRR	@IRR(0.1,B14..B26)
29	Annual Yield (APR)	+B28*2
30	Net Present Value	@NPV(B28,B15..B26)

Figure 7.7. Formulas for calculating the internal rate of return for a bond.

This model calculates the yield of a bond to maturity. If you plan to sell the bond before it matures, simply substitute the expected sale price for the Redemption Value in B26. You might want to add a line for Sale Price above the double line, and refer to that value as a cell reference. If you insert a Sale Price line in row 4, for example, the formula in B26 becomes

+B4+B6, where B4 is the Sale Price and B6 is the Nominal Interest Rate, which has now moved down a row. However, do not substitute the sale price for the Redemption Value in B3. That would throw off your calculations of interest payments.

This model may be accurate enough for many purposes, especially if you intend to hold a bond for a long time. Still, you can refine the calculations to determine the yield for a bond. The next section explains how to adapt the model for bonds bought between coupon dates.

Buying Bonds between Coupon Dates

When you buy a bond between coupon payments, a portion of the next payment goes to the previous owner. Simply enter Periods Remaining as a decimal. For example, to determine the maximum acceptable price if you buy the Kopperklad bond three months before there are 12 coupons remaining, in Figure 7.2 you would enter 12.5 for Periods Remaining in B6. The Price will be $913.78.

You can make a reasonable approximation of a partial period using a 360-day year with 30-day months. For example, if you buy a bond on March 15 with a semiannual payment due on July 1, you can figure that the relevant portion of the period to the next payment is 75/180, or 0.42.

Evaluating Common Stock

Evaluating a common stock is similar to assessing a bond, except that the variables—dividends and future value—are harder to predict. While bond interest is fixed, stock dividends may change over time. And, although the market price of a bond may vary in the interim, the redemption value at maturity is known. The price of a common stock will rise and fall indefinitely. The calculations given here will not help predict the performance of a stock. But once you have made estimates of dividend growth and the future value of the stock, you can determine the present value or rate of return.

If a stock does not pay dividends, the calculations are simple. Suppose you buy a stock for $100 and sell it after three years for $150. The return is simply @RATE(*future value,present value,term*). Here, the calculation is @RATE(150,100,3) = 14.47%. If you expect a stock to sell for $150 at the end of three years and require an annual return of 15%, you can use the basic formula for the present value of a lump sum: $PV = FV/(1+i)^n$. In this case, the calculation is $150/(1+0.15)^3 = \$98.63$. So the present value of the stock is slightly less than $100, and if you bought it at that price, you wouldn't quite make your 15% return.

Most stocks do pay dividends, however, and the dividends may change. For dividend-paying stocks the basic calculations turn on the schematic equation:

Present Value = Present Value (Dividends) + Present Value (Future Price)

This calculation reduces to simple formulas if dividends are constant or grow at a steady rate. However, if dividends vary, or if you want to calculate rate of return, you will have to look at cash flows individually. The easier example comes first.

Price of a Stock with Constant Dividends

Kopperklad common stock currently sells for $85 a share and pays quarterly dividends of $1.15. You expect the price to rise to $120 at the end of three years, but management has said that dividends will remain constant. If you require a 15% annual return, should you buy the stock? Once you build a model for this calculation, you can calculate the price of any stock with regular dividends.

The calculations are shown in Figure 7.8, and the underlying formulas in Figure 7.9. To break down the formulas:

- Number of Dividends (B13) is 4*Term (B5), and the Required Periodic Rate (B14) is Required Return divided by 4 (+B6/4).

- Present Value of Dividends (B15) is a straightforward @PV calculation—@PV(*payment,interest,term*). Quarterly Dividend (B3) is

	A	B
1	PRICE OF A STOCK WITH CONSTANT DIVIDENDS	
2		
3	Quarterly Dividend	$1.15
4	Future Value	$120.00
5	Term	3
6	Required Return	15.00%
7		
8	Price	$88.10
9		
10	===	
11	Calculations	
12		
13	Number of Dividends	12
14	Required Periodic Rate	3.75%
15	Present Value of Dividends	$10.95
16	Present Value of Future Sale	$77.15

Figure 7.8. Calculating the price you would pay, given constant dividends, a future value, and a required return.

	A	B
1	PRICE OF A STOCK WITH CONSTANT DIVIDENDS	
2		
3	Quarterly Dividend	1.15
4	Future Value	120
5	Term	3
6	Required Return	0.15
7		
8	Price	+B15+B16
9		
10	===	
11	Calculations	
12		
13	Number of Dividends	+B5*4
14	Required Periodic Rate	+B6/4
15	Present Value of Dividends	@PV(B3,B14,B13)
16	Present Value of Future Sale	+B4/(1+B14)^B13

Figure 7.9. The underlying formulas for the calculations shown in Figure 7.8.

the payment, Required Periodic Rate (B14) is interest, and Number of Dividends (B13) is the term.

- Present Value of Future Sale (B16) is a simple calculation of the present value of a lump sum: $PV = FV/(1+i)^n$ where FV is the Future Value (B4), i is the Required Periodic Rate (B14), and n is Number of Dividends (B13).

The indicated Price (B8) is $88.10, so if you buy the stock at $85 and your predictions hold, you will earn slightly more than your required rate of 15%. You can calculate the price you would be willing to pay for any stock. Of course you might hope for dividends to increase. That adds some new wrinkles, as we see in the next section.

Pricing a Stock with Dividend Growth

Suppose you expect Kopperklad dividends to increase by 5% per year, rather than remaining constant at the current level of $4.60. (To simplify the calculations, we switch to an annual analysis here). Now what is the present value of the stock?

You can use this formula to price any stock with constant dividend growth:

$$PV = \frac{D_1}{(RR-g)}$$

where PV is the present value; D_1 is the *next* dividend; RR is the Required rate of return; and g is the growth rate.

In the Kopperklad example, $D_1 = \$4.60*1.05 = \$4.83$, the dividend at the end of the first growth period. The required return is still 15%, and the growth rate is 5%. Thus, the price of the stock = $4.83/(0.15-0.05) = $4.83/0.10 = $48.30.

The basic formula can be converted to calculate the required return instead:

$$RR = \frac{D_1}{PV} + g$$

Thus, for Kopperklad, RR = \$4.83/\$48.30+0.05 = 0.10+0.05 = 0.15 = 15%. The answer is not surprising, since we calculated the price based on a required return of 15% in the first place.

This calculation is simple enough where dividend growth is constant. About the only constant in the stock market, however, is that nothing is constant. In the next section, we begin developing the formulas for a model that can take a variety of variables into account.

Analyzing Supergrowth Stocks with Other Variables

Now we are going to build a model that allows you to tinker with present and future growth rates, varying terms, and present and future required rates of return. You can also use it to calculate the present value of a stock with constant dividend growth that you plan to sell after a certain term.

Sometimes a stock experiences "supergrowth" dividends for a period, then returns to a normal rate of growth. For example, suppose that Steamroller Industrial Equipment currently pays an annual dividend of \$5. You expect the dividend to grow at an annual rate of 20% a year for the next five years, and then return to a normal growth level of 6%. You require a return of 12%. What is the maximum you should pay for the stock?

If you wrote out the mathematical formula for this calculation it would look horrendous. In fact, however, we have already covered almost everything you need to solve it; when you break the problem down into steps, there's nothing mysterious about it. (We stick with annual calculations here to avoid cluttering up the formulas. Once you have built the basic model, it's relatively easy to adapt it to quarterly dividends using the conversions that have been used throughout this book.)

In simple terms:

price = *present value (dividends)* + *present value (future price)*

Here, *present value (dividends)* represents the present value of dividends during the first growth period. In the Steamroller example, the company now pays an annual dividend that will grow at an annual rate of 20% for five years. So *present value (dividends)* is the present value of the dividends for the first five years, after which the growth rate drops back to a normal 6%.

Now we come to the second part of the right side of the equation: *present value (future price)*. We have already used the basic methods we need. All you have to do is to calculate the price after dividend growth drops back to normal—in the sixth year, in the case of Steamroller—and then discount the future price back to the present. But there's a new wrinkle. As of the beginning of the sixth year, Steamroller stock will have normal dividend growth, and we have just seen how to make that calculation. However, we do not yet know the dividend for year six, so we will have to add that factor to the calculation.

We will need one new concept to calculate *present value (dividends)* for the first growth period. Once we have that, we can easily break the entire calculation down into steps.

In the Steamroller example, the company now pays an annual dividend of $5, which will grow at an annual rate of five years. *Present value (dividends)* is the present value of the first five annual dividends. The flow of dividends is not an annuity, because the dividends increase at a constant rate, rather than remaining the same. The solution is to calculate an equivalent interest rate. Then you can plug the result into a normal @PV calculation to find the present value of the dividends. The equation is simple:

$$equivalent\ rate\ =\ \frac{1\ +\ RR}{1\ +\ g}\ -\ 1$$

where *RR* is the required return; and *g* is the growth rate.

In the Steamroller example, the required return is 12%, and the growth rate for the initial period is 20%, so the calculation is: $(1+0.12)/(1+0.2)-1 = -6.67\%$. To determine the present value, just plug the effective rate into a normal @PV formula: @PV(5,–0.067,5) = $30.90. This formula assumes that the first dividend you actually receive—the one at the end of the first year—is $6 ($5 + 20%). However, you base the calculation on the current dividend, even though you will not actually receive a $5 dividend.

Now that we know how to determine present value (dividends) for the first growth period, we can follow a series of relatively simple steps to determine the present value, or price, of the Steamroller stock:

1. Calculate the present value of the dividends for the growth period. The current dividend is $5, the equivalent rate is –6.67%, and the term is five years. As we have just seen, you can plug this information into a straightforward @PV calculation: @PV(5,–0.067,5) = $30.90. You now have the present value of dividends for the next five years. Next, you need to find the present value of the future price.

2. Calculate the first dividend for the second growth period. In the Steamroller example, we figure that the $5 dividend will increase by 20% a year for five years, and then drop to a growth rate of 6%. Calculating the fifth dividend is a simple compound interest problem: $5*(1+0.2)\wedge5 = \$12.44$. To calculate the sixth (or n^{th}) dividend, when the increase drops to 6%, simply multiply by 1.06: $5*(1+0.2)\wedge5*(1+0.06) = \$13.19$. With this information, you can determine the future price.

3. Calculate the future price. To make this calculation, mentally move forward to the end of the first growth period, the end of the fifth year in the Steamroller example. Now the calculation is the same as the one we made in Pricing a Stock with Dividend Growth:

$$future\ price\ =\ \frac{D_n}{(RR\ -\ g)}$$

The nth dividend is $13.19, the required return is 12%, and the future growth rate is 6%, so the calculation looks like this: $13.19/(0.12–0.06) = \$219.80$.

4. Calculate the present value of the future price. This is another easy compound interest problem: $PV = FV/(1+RR)^{n}$ or $219.80/(1+0.12)\wedge5 = \$124.72$.

5. Finally, add the present value (dividends) to present value (future price): 30.90+124.72 = $155.62.

The present value of the Steamroller stock is $155.62. If you can buy it for less, and your assumptions are right, you will earn more than your required rate of 12%. If it costs more, the return will be lower.

But you don't have to go through all of this over and over. Next we build a general-purpose model for evaluating stocks.

Building a Model for Stocks with Dividend Growth

Obviously, the last calculations will get a little tedious if you do them often. Setting up a model worksheet removes the drudgery, and isn't much more difficult than doing the calculation once.

The model shown in Figure 7.10 calculates the current and future prices of either a supergrowth stock or a stock with constantly growing dividends. For constant growth, just enter the same value for Present Growth Rate and Future Growth Rate. You can also enter a prediction for Future Required Rate. If interest rates go down, the Future Required Rate might be lower; if they go up, it might be higher.

	A	B
1	PRICE OF A STOCK WITH GROWING DIVIDENDS	
2		
3	Dividend	$5.00
4	Present Growth Rate	20.00%
5	Future Growth Rate	6.00%
6	Present Required Rate	12.00%
7	Future Required Rate	12.00%
8	Term	5
9		
10	Present Price	$155.62
11	Future Price	$219.80
12		
13	===	
14	Calculations	
15		
16	Equivalent Present Rate	-6.67%
17	PV Dividends for Term	$30.90
18	Nth Dividend	$13.19
19	Future Price	$219.80
20	Present Value (Future Price)	$124.72
21	Present Price	$155.62

Figure 7.10. Calculating the price of a stock with super dividend growth.

The calculation shown is for the Steamroller example. The current annual Dividend is $5; the Present Growth Rate in dividends is 20%, expected to drop to 6% after five years; and the required rate of return remains constant at 12%. The term of the analysis is five years. It doesn't matter whether you actually sell the stock at the end of the term; the present value of future dividends at that point by definition equals the Future Price.

The underlying formulas are shown in Figure 7.11. The calculations in rows 16–21 directly follow the steps outlined above. Finally, the Present Price and Future Price are entered above the double line as cell references to the calculations below.

	A	B
1	PRICE OF A STOCK WITH GROWING DIVIDENDS	
2		
3	Dividend	5
4	Present Growth Rate	0.2
5	Future Growth Rate	0.06
6	Present Required Rate	0.12
7	Future Required Rate	0.12
8	Term	5
9		
10	Present Price	+B21
11	Future Price	+B19
12		
13	==	
14	Calculations	
15		
16	Equivalent Present Rate	(1+B6)/(1+B4)-1
17	PV Dividends for Term	@PV(B3,B16,B8)
18	Nth Dividend	+B3*(1+B4)^B8*(1+B5)
19	Future Price	+B18/(B7-B5)
20	Present Value (Future Price)	+B19/(1+B6)^B8
21	Present Price	+B17+B20

Figure 7.11. Formulas for calculating the price of a stock with growing dividends.

The first part of this chapter has dealt with securities—preferred stock, bonds, and common stock. You should be able to adapt the models and examples to many more securities calculations. These calculations are useful to investors or businesses that issue securities, but they have little to do with the most important operational calculations a business must make. Next, we turn to management finance.

Managing Your Business

As noted at the beginning of this chapter, many calculations required to manage a business are simple arithmetic. If you understand the accounting, or the business aspect of the problem, there's no trick to doing the arithmetic with 1-2-3. Since the focus of this book is on business *calculations*, it omits many of the problems you will encounter in any basic finance text, such as running up balance sheets and profit and loss statements.

However, 1-2-3's statistical capabilities warrant serious consideration, and their applications may not always be so obvious. That's the topic of the rest of this chapter. First, we look at forecasting cash flow, using variance and standard deviation to estimate risk and forecast results, and comparing competing projects with simple statistics. The latter part of the chapter explores using the /Data Regression command to forecast business outcomes based on past experience.

Determining Expected Cash Flow

Businesses constantly weigh options. Should you expand your current store or open a second? If you open a second, should it be in Miami or Fort Lauderdale? Should you introduce a new product or expand production of current models? The problem is, you never know the exact outcome of each option. One simple method of comparison is to project cash flow, based on the probabilities of various possible results.

Suppose Alias Smith & Jones is considering two projects. The initial cost of both is $150,000 (assume all numbers are net figures). Both will last for five years. After analyzing the projects, management judges that the probabilities of annual cash flows on Project A are as follows:

$ 7,500	20%
$25,000	60%
$37,500	20%

Management's analysis of the probable annual cash flows for Project B looks like this:

$ 6,000	25%
$22,500	50%
$45,000	25%

Just looking at the numbers, you can see that the most likely result—the middle figure—is higher for Project A. Project B has the higher potential return, but also the greater risk. Which option should AS&J choose?

AS&J can refine that observation by calculating the expected return, based on management's judgment of the probability of each possible result. This is simply the weighted average of the projections, as shown in Figure 7.12. In 100 trials, according to the estimates, Project A would

	A	B	C
1	Project A		
2			
3	Cash Flow	Probability	CF*P
4	$7,500	20%	$1,500
5	$25,000	60%	$15,000
6	$37,500	20%	$7,500
7			
8		100%	
9	Expected Return		$24,000
10			
11	Project B		
12			
13	Cash Flow	Probability	CF*P
14	$6,000	25%	$1,500
15	$22,500	50%	$11,250
16	$45,000	25%	$11,250
17			
18		100%	
19	Expected Return		$24,000
20			

Figure 7.12. Expected returns for two different projects.

return $7,500 20 times, $25,000 60 times, and $37,500 20 times. In the example, the Expected Return for each Cash Flow is simply the Cash Flow (column A) times the Probability (column B). The formula in C4, for example, is +A4*B4.

The two projects have the same expected return. (The example is deliberately contrived.) But a glance at the numbers shows that Project B is riskier than project A. The upside is higher, but the downside is lower, and the odds of coming out somewhere in the middle are lower, as well. Management may want to quantify that risk. Several calculations are suggested in the following sections.

Estimating Risk

At this point, the management of Alias Smith & Jones might decide to take the more conservative course and select Project A, or it might put on its gambling shoes and try to improve the upside odds for Project B.

Often, however, an expected return calculation will not be so easy to assess intuitively. In such cases, you can use statistical calculations of variance and standard deviation to measure the degree to which observations vary from the expected return or mean. This is called dispersion, and in business it can be used to approximate risk. Bear in mind, however, that the apparent precision of the calculations may misleading. Statistically, the calculations *are* precise, but the entire calculation still turns on the probability estimates you start with; the outcome cannot be more accurate than the original estimates.

To be valid, variance and standard deviation require a *normal* distribution of the data being analyzed. This means that the observations are evenly distributed around the mean, with a concentration in the center— the familiar bell curve. Statisticians will go to great lengths to analyze the distribution of data. In business, the distribution is often assumed to be normal. Variance and standard deviation can be meaningful, if not statistically perfect, as long as observations are generally concentrated around the mean—in other words, if the graph of the distribution is more or less hump shaped. This is the case in the examples above. However, the calculations will not be useful if the data are strongly skewed. This caveat would apply, for example, if management believed that there was an 80% chance that a project would yield $15,000 a year, a 15% chance that it would return $20,000, and a 5% chance that the return would be $25,000. Intermediate cases may require more sophisticated analysis than can be provided here.

By assigning probabilities to three possible outcomes for Project A, AS&J management has concluded that in 100 trials, it would get a return of $7,500 20 times, $25,000 60 times, and $37,500 20 times. 1-2-3 provides @Functions (@VAR and @STD) for calculating variance and standard deviation. You could use these functions if you set up a column that listed $7,500 20 times, and so on. It's easier to make the variance and standard deviation calculations directly, as explained below.

A further note about @VAR and @STD: The formulas 1-2-3 uses for @VAR and @STD assume that the *entire* population is included in the data. This is called a census. For example, the Census Bureau might survey *every* household in a county. Here, the @Functions would be appropriate. A pollster, on the other hand, would survey a randomly selected *sample* of households. A slightly different calculation is required to determine sample variance and sample standard deviation, although the difference is small when the number of observations is more than 30. 1-2-3 Release 3 provides @Functions for these sample calculations (@VARS and @STDS), but earlier versions do not. Sample variance and sample standard deviation are discussed in more detail later. For additional discussion of @VAR and @STD, see Chapter 9.

Calculating Variance and Standard Deviation

For Alias Smith & Jones, Project A and Project B have the same expected return, $24,000 a year for five years. Project B is clearly riskier. But how much riskier is it?

One way of calculating risk might be to determine how much the possible outcomes differ from the mean, or average. However, by definition, the average difference between each observation and the mean will always be 0. For example, the mean of 2, 4, and 6 is 4 (2+4+6=12; 12/3=4). The differences between each number and the mean are -2, 0, and 2

(2-4=-2; 4-4=0; and 6-4=2). The average difference is 0 (-2+0+2=0; 0/3=0). You can make up more complicated examples, but the result will always be the same.

Statisticians have found that the best way to overcome this problem is to average the *squares* of the difference between each observation and the mean. This is the variance. In our simple example, the mean is 4, and the observations are 2, 4, and 6. The variance is 2.6666.... You can calculate it this way:

Value	Mean	Difference	Difference^2
2	4	-2	4
4	4	0	0
6	4	2	4
			==========
Total			8
Variance (total/observations = 8/3)			2.66666...

You can get the same result with @VAR(2,4,6) or with @VAR (range), where the range is three cells where the values 2, 4, and 6 are entered.

A variance means little by itself, but when one population is compared with another, the one with the larger variance is more dispersed, or, in business terms, riskier. For example, the values 1, 4, and 7 also have a mean of 4, but the variance is larger than in the last example:

Value	Mean	Difference	Difference^2
1	4	-3	9
4	4	0	0
7	4	3	9
			==========
Total			18
Variance (total/observations = 18/3)			6

Since the variance of the second example is larger than the first, you know that the observations are more widely dispersed. That is, in the second example, the next observation is more likely to be farther from the mean than in the first. But what does that mean, exactly?

Calculating the standard deviation helps make more sense out of these results. The standard deviation is simply the square root of the variance, but there are some rules of thumb that help you predict the likelihood that the outcome will fall within certain ranges. In general, for a normal distribution:

- About two-thirds of all observations will fall within one standard deviation of the mean.

- About 95% of all observations will fall within two standard deviations of the mean.

- Nearly all observations will fall within three standard deviations of the mean.

The standard deviation of 2, 4, and 6 is approximately 1.63: @SQRT(2.666666)=1.632992. The mean, remember, is 4. With a larger set of observations (three is not very meaningful), you could conclude:

- There is about a 67% chance that the actual outcome will fall between 2.37 (4-1.63) and 5.63 (4+1.63).

- There is about a 95% chance that the outcome will be between 0.74 (4-3.26) and 7.26 (4+3.26).

- It is virtually certain that the outcome will between -0.89 (4–4.89) and 8.89 (4+4.89).

For 1, 4, and 7, the standard deviation is about 2.45. The ranges of the probable outcomes are broader, but the calculations are the same.

These calculations are schematic (and useless, for practical purposes). *Comparing Projects*, below, applies the principles to the probability models set up earlier. First, let's look at one more measure of dispersion or variation: the coefficient of variation.

Measuring Risk with the Coefficient of Variation

Standard deviation is a good measure of the range in which outcomes are likely to fall, but it doesn't tell you much about the variability of a population in absolute terms. A standard deviation of 10, for example, is large if the mean of the sample is 5, but insignificant almost to the vanishing point if the mean is 10,000. We have already seen that about two-thirds of a population will fall within two standard deviations of the mean. If the mean is 5 and the standard deviation 10, that means that two-thirds of the group will fall between -15 and 25—a swing so large that it will probably be practically meaningless. However, if the mean is 10,000, two thirds of the group should fall between 9,980 and 10,020, which might look pretty precise in real life.

The coefficient of variation allows you to compare the variability of groups with different means. It is simply the standard deviation divided by the mean. In the last section, we saw that the standard deviation of 2, 4, and 6 is about 1.63. Thus, the coefficient of variation is about 0.41 (1.63/4). The standard deviation of 1, 4, and 7 is 2.45, so the coefficient of variation is about 0.61 (2.45/4). In this case, the calculation merely confirms the obvious fact that the second series is more variable than the first, but in practical applications that difference may not be so obvious.

Comparing Projects

Alias Smith & Jones has calculated the probable outcomes of Project A and Project B, shown in Figure 7.13. To the extent the probabilities are accurate, the variance, standard deviation, and coefficient of variation for each calculation will tell the company more about the likely outcomes.

As noted earlier, by assigning probabilities to three scenarios for each project, AS&J has essentially set up a table of 100 possible outcomes. Thus, to use @VAR and @STD to calculate the variance and standard deviation for Project A, you would have to set up a column listing $7,500 20 times, $25,000 60 times, and $37,500 20 times. It's much easier just to make the mathematical calculations on the worksheet.

	A	B	C	D
1	RISK ANALYSIS			
2				
3	Project A			
4				
5	Cash Flow	Probability	CF*P	(CR-ER)^2*P
6	$7,500	20%	$1,500	$54,450,000
7	$25,000	60%	$15,000	$600,000
8	$37,500	20%	$7,500	$36,450,000
9		===============		
10		100%		
11	Expected Return		$24,000	
12	Variance			$91,500,000
13	Standard Deviation			$9,566
14	Coefficient of Variation			0.40
15				
16				
17	Project B			
18				
19	Cash Flow	Probability	CF*P	(CF-ER)^2*P
20	$6,000	25%	$1,500	$81,000,000
21	$22,500	50%	$11,250	$1,125,000
22	$45,000	25%	$11,250	$110,250,000
23		===============		
24		100%		
25	Expected Return		$24,000	
26	Variance			$192,375,000
27	Standard Deviation			$13,870
28	Coefficient of Variation			0.58

Figure 7.13. Assessing the risk of two projects.

Variance, remember, is the average of the squares of the differences between each observation and the mean:

$$\frac{(o_1 - m)^2 + (o_2 - m)^2 \ldots (o_n - m)^2}{n}$$

where o represents each observation; m is the mean; and n is the number of observations.

The standard deviation is the square root of the variance, and the coefficient of variation is the standard deviation divided by the mean.

We have already seen that the expected return is $24,000 a year for both Project A and Project B. The worksheet in Figure 7.13 adds calculations for variance, standard deviation, and coefficient of variation. The calculation in column D is simply (*cash flow – expected return*)^2 × (*probability*). Because multiplying by probability has the effect of averaging the results, the variance is the sum of the calculations in column D. The standard deviation is the square root of that sum. And the coefficient of variation is the standard deviation divided by the expected return. The formulas for the worksheet are shown in Figure 7.14. The absolute references (indicated by $ signs) in column D are necessary only for copying the formulas.

	A	B	C	D
1	RISK ANALYSIS			
2				
3	Project A			
4				
5	Cash Flow	Probability	CF*P	(CR-ER)^2*P
6		7500	0.2	+A6*B6	(+A6-$C$11)^2*B6
7		25000	0.6	+A7*B7	(+A7-$C$11)^2*B7
8		37500	0.2	+A8*B8	(+A8-$C$11)^2*B8
9		===============		
10		@SUM(B6..B8)		
11	Expected Return		@SUM(C6..C8)	
12	Variance			@SUM(D6..D8)
13	Standard Deviation			@SQRT(D12)
14	Coefficient of Variation			+D13/C11
15				
16				
17	Project B			
18				
19	Cash Flow	Probability	CF*P	(CF-ER)^2*P
20		6000	0.25	+A20*B20
21		22500	0.5	+A21*B21
22		45000	0.25	+A22*B22
23		===============		
24		@SUM(B20..B22)		
25	Expected Return		@SUM(C20..C22)	
26	Variance			@SUM(D20..D22)
27	Standard Deviation			@SQRT(D26)
28	Coefficient of Variation			+D27/C25

Figure 7.14. The formulas for calculating variance, standard deviation, and coefficient of variation.

As we already knew, Project B is the riskier of the two; even though the expected return is the same for both projects, B has a higher variance, standard deviation, and coefficient of variation.

To the extent its assessment of the probabilities is accurate, Alias Smith & Jones can now predict the likelihood of annual cash flows as shown in Figure 7.15. The ranges are pretty broad. And again, to the extent the probabilities are guesses, AS&J is still flying by the seat of its pants, despite the mathematical precision of the calculations. Nevertheless, these calculations can be quite useful when the probability estimates are well grounded.

	A	B	C	D	E
1	LIKELY OUTCOMES				
2					
3	Project A			Range	
4	67% (+/- one standard deviation)			$14,434	$33,566
5	95% (+/- two standard deviations)			$4,869	$43,131
6	99% (+/- three standard deviations)			($4,697)	$52,697
7					
8	Project B			Range	
9	67% (+/- one standard deviation)			$10,130	$37,870
10	95% (+/- two standard deviations)			($3,740)	$51,740
11	99% (+/- three standard deviations)			($17,610)	$65,610

Figure 7.15. Projecting probable outcomes of two projects.

Comparing Projects with Sample Variance and Sample Standard Deviation

In business, it is often not practical to calculate the variance and standard deviation of an entire population. Instead, you may want to take a sample of the possible results and base your calculations on that.

Statisticians have found that, on average, the @VAR and @STD calculations of variance and standard deviation of a sample will give too low an estimate, compared with the comparable calculations for a census of a population. Put another way, there is likely to be less variation in a small sample than in a population as a whole. Variance, remember, is the square of the difference between each observation and the mean for the population, where the number of observations is n. The sample variance is similar, only the sum of the squares is divided by $n-1$ to offset the downward bias of the sample calculation. The sample standard deviation is the square root of the sample variance. The difference between the biased method and the $n-1$ method is small when the sample is more than 30 observations.

Release 3 of 1-2-3 provides @Functions for calculating sample variance and sample standard deviation. To use @VARS to calculate variance, simply list the sample observations, and then enter @VARS(*range*) to make the computation, where *range* is the range of cells where the samples are entered. @STDS calculates the standard deviation, using the same format. For example, if your sample observations are listed in B4..B19, @VARS(B4..B19) returns the variance and @STDS(B4..B19) returns the standard deviation.

Earlier versions of 1-2-3 do not have the @VARS and @STDS @Functions, but you can adapt @VAR and @STD to make sample calculations. The formulas are:

```
@VAR(range)*@COUNT(range)/(@COUNT(range)-1)
```

and

```
@STD(range)*@SQRT(@COUNT(range)/(@COUNT(range)-1)
```

Suppose, for example, that Peter Piper Pickled Pepper Packers has a new packing machine, and wants to pack 100 peppers in every peck. The machine is fairly accurate, but there is some variation in the number of peppers in each peck. Piper wants to make sure that there are at least 100 peppers in 95% of the pecks. He concludes that if he sets the machine to pack two standard deviations more than 100, 95% of the pecks should meet the criterion. So the question is, when Peter Piper packs a peck of pickled peppers, how many pickled peppers should Peter Piper pack?

Piper can't count the peppers in every peck, so he decides to take 15 random samples out of a production run. In Figure 7.16, Piper calculates the variance and standard deviation three different ways. (@VARS and @STDS, remember, are available only in Release 3.) Piper has listed the observations in B4..B18 and calculated the average in B20, using the formula @AVG(B4..B18). In column C, he has subtracted the average from each observation and squared the result. In C21, he has divided the sum of the squares by 14 (n-1) to determine the variance. The standard deviation in C22 is simply the square root of the variance. In C23 and C24, Piper has made the same calculations using the formulas given above. The answers, of course, are the same, and if you use the second method, you don't have to calculate the squares of the deviations. The underlying formulas are shown in Figure 7.17.

	A	B
1	SAMPLES FROM PETER PIPER'S PRODUCTION RUN	
2		
3	Sample (S)	(S-AVG)^2
4	85	225
5	105	25
6	115	225
7	89	121
8	99	1
9	109	81
10	96	16
11	105	25
12	106	36
13	95	25
14	92	64
15	109	81
16	105	25
17	103	9
18	87	169
19		=======================
20	Average	100
21	Variance (@SUM method)	80.57142
22	Standard Deviation (@SQRT method)	8.976158
23	Variance (@VAR method)	80.57142
24	Standard Deviation (@STD method)	8.976158
25	Variance (@VARS method)*	80.57142
26	Standard Deviation (@STDS method)*	8.976158

*Release 3 only

Figure 7.16. Three methods of calculating sample variance and sample standard deviation.

The standard deviation is about 9. Sure enough, about one-third of the observations fall within one standard deviation of the average. (We made up this example, but it works anyway.) All of the sample observations fall

	A	B	
1			
	SAMPLES FROM PETER PIPER'S PRODUCTION RUN		
2			
3		Sample (S)	(S-AVG)^2
4		85	(B4-$B$20)^2
5		105	(B5-$B$20)^2
6		115	(B6-$B$20)^2
7		89	(B7-$B$20)^2
8		99	(B8-$B$20)^2
9		109	(B9-$B$20)^2
10		96	(B10-$B$20)^2
11		105	(B11-$B$20)^2
12		106	(B12-$B$20)^2
13		95	(B13-$B$20)^2
14		92	(B14-$B$20)^2
15		109	(B15-$B$20)^2
16		105	(B16-$B$20)^2
17		103	(B17-$B$20)^2
18		87	(B18-$B$20)^2
19			
20	Average	@AVG(B4..B18)	
21	Variance (@SUM method)	@SUM(C4..C18)/(@COUNT(C4..C18)-1)	
22	Standard Deviation (@SQRT method)	@SQRT(C21)	
23	Variance (@VAR method)	@VAR(B4..B18)*@COUNT(B4..B18)/(@COUNT(B4..B18)-1)	
24	Standard Deviation (@STD method)	@STD(B4..B18)*@SQRT(@COUNT(B4..B18)/(@COUNT(B4..B18)-1))	
25	Variance (@VARS method)*	@VARS(B4..B18)	
26	Standard Deviation (@STDS method)*	@STDS(B4..B18)	

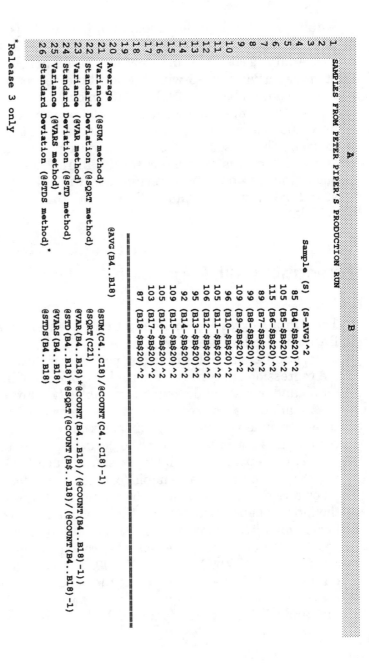

Figure 7.17. Formulas for calculating variance and standard deviation of a sample.

*Release 3 only

within two standard deviations. So, if Peter Piper wants at least 100 pickled peppers in every peck, he will have to set the machine to pack 118. Adding a constant (in this case, 18) will not change the variance and standard deviation, so with the machine set at 118, 95% of the pecks should contain between 100 and 136 pickled peppers.

Now, Piper might not want to put 136 peppers in a peck and charge for only 100. He might, for example, decide to start packing by weight instead. The reason the standard deviation is so high might also be the way the fictitious example is set up. In real life calculations, however, such standard deviation calculations will often yield a much smaller standard deviation that allows you to fine-tune your business calculations.

Forecasting with Regression Analysis

The /**D**ata **R**egression command first appeared in Release 2.0 of 1-2-3. Businesses often use regression analysis to predict sales, production costs, or other variables based on past experience.

A regression analysis requires at least one set of independent variables (or X) and one set of dependent variables (Y). For example, to estimate next year's sales, you could analyze the sales for the last 10 years. In this case, the independent or X variables are years 1–10. (For reasons of scaling, it is better to number the periods than to use the actual years.) The Y, or dependent variable, is sales. Once you have completed the regression, you can use a simple formula to project the next year's sales.

For a regression analysis to be meaningful, the relationship between the independent variables and the dependent variables must be *linear*. For example, if current sales are $100,000 and increase by $20,000 a year, you can estimate sales five years hence with the formula Sales (Year 5) = $100,000 + $20,000 $\times$ 5 = $200,000. The general formula for a linear regression is $y = a + bx$, where y is the dependent variable calculated by the regression, a is a constant (called the y intercept), b is the *slope* of the line, and x is the independent variable.

In many situations, a series of data does not plot a straight line. If you graph sales at an increase by 20% a year, for example, the plot will be a curve. (This is the basic compound interest calculation, so projected sales n years ahead is $x(1+0.20)^n$, where x is the current year's sales.) In such situations /Data Regression does not offer an appropriate solution.

You can, however, use /Data Regression with more than one independent variable. This is called a multiple regression analysis. A ski resort's revenues, for example, might vary according to snowfall, average temperature, prices, and the federal government's index of leading economic indicators.

With 1-2-3, you can use as many as 16 independent variables, with as many as 8,192 observations or data points. However, the number of observations must be the same for all. For example, you cannot have 50 observations for one variable and only 25 for another. When there are two independent variables (perhaps snowfall and prices in the ski resort example), the regression results describe a slanted plane. Think of lifting a corner of a chess board up from a table. With more than two variables, you can't describe the results geometrically, but the relationship between *each* independent variable and the dependent variable still must be linear.

Two additional caveats. First, the number of independent variables must be significantly smaller than the number of observations. If a store chain has five stores, for example, it would be pointless to attempt to forecast sales of a new store based on four independent variables. Second, the independent variables must not be directly related to each other. For example, if the store chain bases the size of each store on the number of people who live within five miles, it should not base sales estimates on *both* store size and population; pick the one that shows the highest correlation in a regression analysis.

Statisticians go to considerable lengths to determine the validity of regression analyses. You can find a lengthy discussion in any statistics book. (A book on business statistics will probably give you more practical, less theoretical information.) Nevertheless, with a little common sense and the information generated by /Data Regression, it's not at all difficult to put /Data Regression to work.

Forecasting with One Variable

Suppose that Mountaintop Outfitters operates eight stores and plans to open a ninth. Management might guess that sales at the new store should be about equal to the average for the others. But the company believes that monthly sales in its existing stores are related to household income in the surrounding areas. A linear regression might yield a more accurate projection.

First, Mountaintop lists monthly sales and household incomes for its existing stores, as shown in Figure 7.18. To make the calculation, first enter /Data Regression. When the regression menu appears at the top of the screen, select X-Range. Here, Household Income is the independent, or *X*, variable, so use the cursor as a pointer to identify C5..C12 as the X-Range, then press Enter. Next select Y-Range from the menu and define the Y-Range as B5..B12, where Monthly Sales is entered for each store. Finally, select Output Range from the menu, and then move the cursor to the top right corner of the range where you want the regression results to be displayed. (The area must be at least four columns by nine rows; anything in the way will be overwritten.) Finally, select GO to complete the regression analysis.

> **Note:** The Intercept is the point at which the regression line crosses the Y axis (the vertical one). In other words, this is the value of the dependent variable if the independent variable is zero. The normal setting is Compute, which tells 1-2-3 to calculate the Y intercept. You can change the setting to Zero, but don't unless the dependent variable must be zero if the independent variable (or all independent variables in a multiple regression) is zero. For example, a store's daily sales might be related to the number of hours it is open, but necessarily zero if it is closed all day. Using the Zero option will probably change the slope of the regression line slightly.

	A	B	C
1	MOUNTAINTOP OUTFITTERS		
2			
3		Monthly	Household
4	Store	Sales	Income
5		1	$13,500	$31,000
6		2	$17,500	$43,000
7		3	$20,500	$53,000
8		4	$21,000	$63,000
9		5	$11,000	$25,000
10		6	$25,000	$67,000
11		7	$21,500	$58,000
12		8	$12,500	$42,000

Figure 7.18. Average monthly sales and household income for Mountaintop Outfitters' eight stores.

Using the Results

The result of Mountaintop's calculation is shown in Figure 7.19. The first two figures to look at are the Constant and the X Coefficient. The Constant is the intercept, or the predicted value of y when x is 0. In other words, the predicted sales of the new Mountaintop store would be about $2,848 in the unlikely event that the household income in its area were $0. The X Coefficient is the *slope* of the regression line. In other words, Mountaintop can expect a 31-cent increase in sales for each additional dollar of average household income.

	A	B	C
19	Regression Output:		
20	Constant		2848.379
21	Std Err of Y Est		1819.523
22	R Squared		0.887116
23	No. of Observations		8
24	Degrees of Freedom		6
25			
26	X Coefficient(s)	0.313384	
27	Std Err of Coef.	0.045638	

Figure 7.19. The result of Mountaintop's regression analysis.

From this information, you can construct a formula that both describes the fitted line of the regression and allows you to predict the outcome (y) for any x (here, household income):

```
y = Constant + X Coefficient * x
```

Suppose that Mountaintop's marketing consultant finds that the average household income in the new store's marketing area is $55,000. Now, the company can make a sales projection:

```
Sales = $2,848.379 + 0.313384 * $55,000 = $20,084.53
```

You can do this on your worksheet using cell references to the Constant and X Coefficient. Mountaintop could also do a multiple regression analysis to refine the forecast, based on several independent variables, such as store size, advertising expenditures, or whatever else management believes affects sales. An example of a two-variable regression is given below. But first, let's take a look at how good Mountaintop's forecast is with one variable.

How Reliable Is the Regression?

Obviously, it would be silly to think that Mountaintop's sales projection for its new store is accurate to the penny, but is the calculation in the right ballpark?

Some of the values in the Regression Output were not discussed in the last section. They have technical statistical significance; to understand them fully, you will need to refer to a statistics text. However, there are several easy observations you can make that will give you some sense of how valid your calculation is.

The first is R Squared. This calculation is a measure of the degree to which variations in the sample are explained by the regression calculation. R Squared can be any value between 0 and 1. If there is a nearly perfect fit, R Squared will be close to 1, meaning that there is a very strong correlation between the independent (x) variables and the dependent (y) variables. If there were no correlation at all, R Squared would be 0. (This is not likely to occur except in contrived examples.) Mountaintop's R

Squared is 0.887116, well toward the upper end of the range. It looks as if the company is on the right track.

The Std Err of Y Est is the standard error of the y estimate. This is the standard deviation of the observations (here actual sales) around the regression line. This gives Mountaintop some idea of the range in which actual sales at the new store are likely to fall. (See the discussion of standard deviation earlier.)

Another important measure is the t-value of the slope or X Coefficient. The Regression Output does not provide this directly, but the calculation is simple:

```
t = X Coefficient/Std Err of Coef.
```

This is a measure of *how much* the y variable tends to be affected by x. It is possible for there to be a high R Squared but for x still not to be very useful as a predictor. We have seen that Mountaintop can, on average, expect a 31-cent increase in sales for each additional dollar of household income. If that figure were 1 cent, household income would not be a very valuable predictor, even if the calculation returned a high value for R Squared. The rule of thumb is that a regression is likely to be useful if t is greater than 2 for a moderate sample size. In Mountaintop's case, t is 6.866737 (0.313384/0.045638 or +B26/B27). So the regression continues to look useful.

A final figure to watch is Degrees of Freedom. This is defined as the number of observations – the number of independent variables – 1. Degrees of Freedom may not seem very meaningful by itself, but it is used in calculating other values, including standard error. As mentioned earlier, the number of independent (x) variables should be significantly smaller than the number of observations. Mountaintop's degrees of freedom is 6. If the company had attempted to perform a regression with five independent variables, the degrees of freedom would be 2, and the calculation probably wouldn't mean much.

Again, consult a statistics text if you have any doubts about the significance of a regression.

Graphing the Regression Line

A graph of a regression line provides a visual representation of what the calculation means and a common sense check on the validity of the calculation. The regression line calculated by /Data Regression is, by definition, straight. The actual observations should be clustered around the line, but not necessarily on it.

The first step is to calculate the fitted y coordinate for each observation—in Mountaintop's case, the predicted sales for each existing store. (Actually you could get by with calculating fitted y for the highest and lowest x variable, since two points define a line. However, it's not any more trouble to calculate all of the fitted y's, because you can copy the formula.)

As we have already seen, the formula for calculating the fitted y coordinate is Constant + X Coefficient * x. In Mountaintop's case, x is the Household Income for each store's area, listed in column C of Figure 7.18. The regression constant is in D20 of Figure 7.19, and the X Coefficient is in C26. Thus, the fitted y for Store 1 is +D20+C5*C26 = $12,563. By making the references to D20 and C26 absolute (+$D$20+C5*$C$26), you can set up a formula you can copy down a column to calculate the fitted y for all of the stores. The result is shown in Figure 7.20. (Mountaintop is leaving column D open for the next calculations.)

	A	B	C	D	E
1	MOUNTAINTOP OUTFITTERS				
2					
3		Monthly	Household		
4	Store	Sales	Income		Fitted Y
5		1	$13,500	$31,000		$12,563
6		2	$17,500	$43,000		$16,324
7		3	$20,500	$53,000		$19,458
8		4	$21,000	$63,000		$22,592
9		5	$11,000	$25,000		$10,683
10		6	$25,000	$67,000		$23,845
11		7	$21,500	$58,000		$21,025
12		8	$12,500	$42,000		$16,011

Figure 7.20. Calculating the fitted y for each observation of a regression.

Now Mountaintop can create an XY graph showing actual monthly sales for each store and a line straight line representing the regression calculations. (A line graph won't do because the coordinates on the X axis will be unevenly spaced, making the regression line look crooked.) The graph is shown in Figure 7.21.

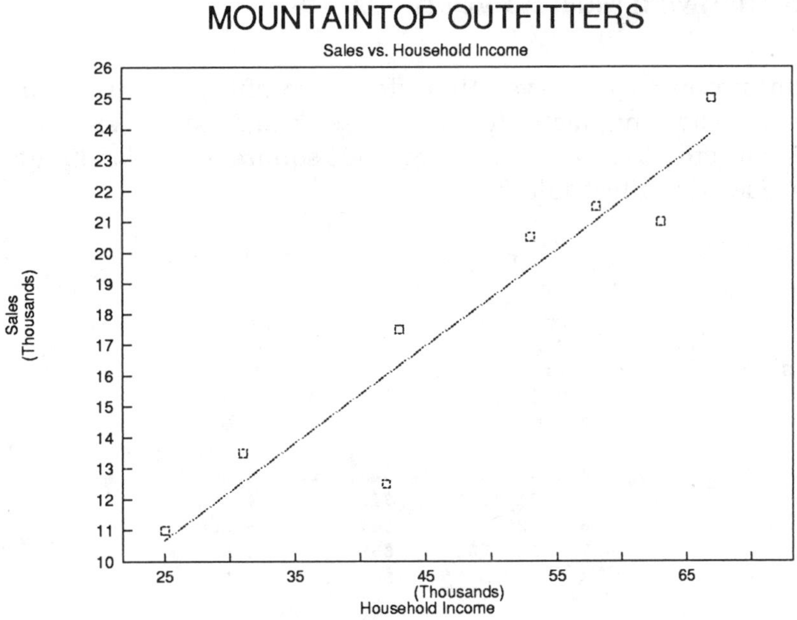

MOUNTAINTOP OUTFITTERS

Sales vs. Household Income

Figure 7.21. Plotting a regression line against a scatter graph of actual observations.

To create the graph, enter /Graph **T**ype **X**Y to specify an XY graph. Now specify the X range, in this case C5..C12, the household incomes for each store's area. The A range is B5..B12, the actual monthly sales for each store. And the B range is E5..E12, the fitted *y* calculations for each store.

Now use the **O**ptions command to enter the titles and formats for ranges A and B. The format for A (the actual observations) should be Symbols. (If you try to connect the observations with lines, you will get a spider web unless you use /**D**ata **S**ort to sort the stores by household income, the *x* variable.) The format for B, the fitted *y* calculations, should be Lines. Finally, simply press **V**iew to see the graph.

Mountaintop can now see that actual sales are clustered around the regression line. It can also see that two stores' sales are below the fitted y prediction. To the extent Mountaintop believes that household income drives sales, the two stores below the line might warrant some attention.

Forecasting with Multiple Variables

Mountaintop also believes that store size affects monthly sales, so it decides to add that factor to the regression analysis, as shown in Figure 7.22. The stores range is size from 4,500 square feet to 6,500 square feet. How does size affect sales?

	A	B	C	D
1	MOUNTAINTOP OUTFITTERS			
2				
3		Monthly	Household	
4	Store	Sales	Income	Size
5		1 $13,500	$31,000	4,750
6		2 $17,500	$43,000	5,500
7		3 $20,500	$53,000	6,250
8		4 $21,000	$63,000	5,500
9		5 $11,000	$25,000	4,500
10		6 $25,000	$67,000	6,000
11		7 $21,500	$58,000	6,500
12		8 $12,500	$42,000	4,500

Figure 7.22. Adding store size to the Mountaintop example.

Mountaintop does a new regression analysis, using the /Data Regression command. This time, the X-Range is C5..D12, including Household Income and Size. The company also calculates the t-value for each calculation by dividing the X Coefficient by the Std Err of Coef. The result is shown in Figure 7.23.

R Squared has risen from 0.887116 to 0.949809, and the t-value for both X Coefficients is more than 2, so it looks like Mountaintop may be onto something. (However, adding a second variable to a regression analysis will almost always increase R Squared, whether the calculation is valid or not.)

	A	B	C	D
30	Income and Size			
31				
32		Regression Output:		
33	Constant			-6049.36
34	Std Err of Y Est			1329.053
35	R Squared			0.949809
36	No. of Observations			8
37	Degrees of Freedom			5
38				
39	X Coefficient(s)		0.209285	2.550521
40	Std Err of Coef.		0.053351	1.020570
41	t-value		3.922786	2.499113

Figure 7.23. Mountaintop's regression output based on Household Income and Store Size.

To project sales at the new store, Mountaintop can use this formula:

```
Constant + (X Coefficient1 * x1) + (X Coefficient2 * x2)
```

You can use this formula for any number of x variables; just keep multiplying the X Coefficient by the x value. The household income in the area of Mountaintop's new store's area is $55,000 and the new store will have 6,500 square feet, so Mountaintop can project sales this way:

```
-6049.36 + $55,000 * 0.209285 + 6,500 * 2.550521 = $22,039.75
```

The projected monthly sales is a couple of thousand dollars higher than the earlier calculation. This makes sense because the new store will be one of Mountaintop's largest. However, it might turn out that Mountaintop has put its largest stores in areas where household income is highest, and that would suggest that Mountaintop shouldn't use both household income and store size as x variables in its regression analysis. To determine whether that is the case, Mountaintop could run a regression using household income as the X Range and store size as the Y Range. In this case, it turns out that there does seem to be a correlation between household income and store size, so the company might elect to use the linear regression described earlier to forecast the new store's sales. (R Squared is higher for the income-based calculation than for a regression based on store size.) Again, when in doubt about the validity of a regression analysis, consult a statistics book or an expert.

Measuring Stock Volatility with the Capital Asset Pricing Model

One use of regression analysis is to determine the beta, or volatility, of stocks. Beta is the slope, or X Coefficient of the regression analysis of a stock's total return (capital gains and dividends) vs. the return of the market as a whole. Beta can also be calculated by determining the covariance of the return of an individual stock with the return of the market. That, however, is another exercise, and it yields the same number. In fact, you don't have to calculate stock betas at all, because various financial services regularly publish them. The services use slightly different methods, but, in basic terms, beta is simply a standardized measure of the risk posed by a particular security in relation to the market.

By definition, the market has a beta of 1, meaning that there is no variation between the market return and itself. A security with a beta of 2 rises or falls by twice as much as the market as a whole, and thus is relatively risky. A security with a beta of 0.5 is less volatile than the market, and thus is less risky.

The Capital Asset Pricing Model (CAPM) calculates the required return of an investment, based on its riskiness compared with that of comparable investments as a group. Although CAPM is usually used for evaluating securities, it can be applied to other business risks where a marketwide return can be calculated. Here, CAPM is applied to common stocks.

CAPM gauges the required return for a particular stock against the return on a risk-free investment (usually U.S. Treasury bills) and the market as a whole. The formula is:

$$RR = RF + \text{beta} \ \times \ (RM - RF)$$

where *RR* is the required return for the stock; *RF* is the risk-free rate (e.g., T-bills); beta is the beta of the stock; and *RM* is the expected market return (usually based on a stock index).

Suppose, for example, that a stock has a beta of 0.50, meaning that tends to move it up and down less than the market; the expected market return is 12%, and that the T-bill rate is 7.5%. The required return for the stock is:

$$RR = 0.075+0.50*(0.12-0.075) = 0.0975 = 9.75\%$$

The stock is less risky than the market as a whole, so an investor should be willing to take a lower return than the market average.

Figure 7.24 calculates the required returns for four stocks with betas ranging from 0.60 to 2.00. The market return and risk-free rates are entered as decimals in B3 and B4, and the betas are entered in B9..B12.

	A	B	C
1	CAPITAL ASSET PRICING MODEL		
2			
3	Market Return	12.00%	
4	Risk-Free Rate	7.50%	
5			
6	==		
7			Required
8		Beta	Return
9	Stock A	0.60	10.20%
10	Stock B	1.00	12.00%
11	Stock C	1.50	14.25%
12	Stock D	2.00	16.50%

Figure 7.24. Calculating required returns for stocks with CAPM.

The formula in C9 is:

```
+$B$4+B9*($B$3-$B$4)
```

where $B$4 is an absolute reference to Risk-Free Rate; B9 is a relative reference to the beta for the stock; and $B$3 is an absolute reference to Market Return. Once you have entered this formula, you can copy it down column C for as many stocks as you like. Not surprisingly, there is a direct correlation between beta and the required return.

You have now seen three examples of ways to use /Data Regression. First Mountaintop Outfitters forecast sales for a new store using a single independent variable, average family income. Next, Mountaintop experimented with a multiple regression analysis, basing the sales forecast for the new store on family income and store size. But it appeared that those to variables were related, so Mountaintop retreated to the first calculation. Finally, we looked at beta, a measure of the volatility of stocks that you can calculate with /Data Regression. Once you understand the principle, it is easy to adapt /Data Regression to your particular circumstances. The trick is to find the important variables.

Footnote: Economic Order Quantity

Economic order quantity (EOQ) is a standard model for minimizing inventory cost that appears in many finance texts. It is included here because it is mathematically elegant and gives you another chance to try out the @SQRT function.

The EOQ model makes three key assumptions: (1) sales (and thus inventory depletion) are constant; (2) cost per order remains the same; and (3) just-in-time delivery allows the company to place orders so that new orders arrive when inventory reaches 0. The mathematical formula for EOQ is:

$$\sqrt{\frac{2SO}{C}}$$

where S is the annual sales (units); O is the cost per order; and C is the annual carrying cost per unit. In 1-2-3 syntax, this calculation translates to:

```
@SQRT(2*S*O/C)
```

Suppose, for example, that the Square Deal Electronics Company installs 10,000 power supplies in computers each year. The cost per order is $200, and the annual carrying cost per unit is $10. What is the economic order quantity? How often must Square Deal place orders?

The calculation is shown in Figure 7.25. In B7, the formula for EOQ is @SQRT(2*B3*B4/B5). Orders per Year is simply Sales/EOQ (+B3/B7). And Weeks between Orders is 52/Orders per Year (52/B8). Square Deal should probably order about 650 units about every three weeks.

	A	B
1	ECONOMIC ORDER QUANTITY	
2		
3	Sales (units)	10,000
4	Cost per Order	$200.00
5	Carrying Cost per Unit	$10.00
6		
7	Economic Order Quantity	632
8	Orders per Year	16
9	Weeks between Orders	3.29

Figure 7.25. Economic Order Quantity, given sales, cost per order, and carrying cost per unit.

Conclusion

This chapter is divided into two main parts. In the first, calculations for the time value of money are applied to securities, including preferred stock, bonds, and common stock. The second part applies 1-2-3's statistical capabilities to several common business problems, such as assessing risk and evaluating projects on the basis of variance and standard deviation, and forecasting sales with /Data Regression. Finally, a regression analysis was used to determine beta to analyze stocks.

This is hardly a comprehensive treatment of business finance calculations. (An introductory finance text, after all, is as large as this entire book.) However, as noted at the outset, many business calculations are simple arithmetic if you understand the problem. This chapter, along with the calculations discussed in earlier chapters, should take you a long way toward making the calculations you need to run your business. Next, we turn to one of the only two inevitable things in life: income taxes.

8

Personal Income Tax

Until now, this book has focused on specific calculations. These are the building blocks of the extended worksheets that are the power of 1-2-3. The greatest strength of 1-2-3 is that it allows you to build models that do exactly what you want them to do, rather than trying to fit your needs into a program written by someone else. This chapter goes beyond individual calculations. There are two objectives: the first, of course, is to show you how to do your taxes with 1-2-3; the second is to show you how to build a larger worksheet a step at a time.

Completing a federal income tax form doesn't require advanced mathematics. Most of the calculations are simple arithmetic, and 1-2-3 makes the job considerably easier. Using cell references and range names helps avoid copying errors and miscalculations. The model provided here also automatically calculates your tax and shows the total and amount you owe as a title at the top of the screen while you work. This is particularly helpful for tax planning because you can see the results of "what if" calculations immediately without having to move around the worksheet.

The IRS forms usually don't change very much from year to year unless Congress makes significant changes in the tax law. However, the tax brackets, the standard deduction, and the personal exemption are now indexed to inflation, so you will have to update your model every year. The model here is based on the 1990 tax schedules (Figure 8.1). The rate schedules are available on Form 1040-ES, for filing quarterly estimated taxes, long before the other tax forms are published. You can get a copy at most libraries. The actual tax forms are based on the 1989 Form 1040 and its accompanying schedules. The line numbers are likely to change, but the model should be easily adaptable, barring major changes by Congress.

The model developed on the next few pages is by far the largest in this book, but it is a good exercise in building a model. You can save time by eliminating lines on the federal forms that do not apply to you. If you don't pay alimony or make a deductible IRA contribution, for example, there is no point in including those lines in your model. (IRA contributions are no longer deductible unless neither you nor your spouse is covered by an employer retirement program or fall below certain income limits although taxes are still deferred for IRA interest.) Further, the final version of the model uses an @VLOOKUP formula to compute the tax, and there is no need to include any parts of the lookup tables that don't apply to you. If you're single, for example,

1990 Tax Rate Schedules

Caution: *Do not use these Tax Rate Schedules to figure your 1989 taxes. Use only to figure your 1990 estimated taxes.*

Schedule X—Single

If line 5 is: Over—	But not over—	The tax is:	of the amount over—
$0	$19,450	......15%	$0
19,450	47,050	$2,917.50 + 28%	19,450
47,050	97,620	10,645.50 + 33%	47,050
97,620	....	Use **Worksheet** below to figure your tax.	

Schedule Z— Head of household

If line 5 is: Over—	But not over—	The tax is:	of the amount over—
$0	$26,050	......15%	$0
26,050	67,200	$3,907.50+ 28%	26,050
67,200	134,930	15,429.50 + 33%	67,200
134,930	....	Use **Worksheet** below to figure your tax.	

Schedule Y-1—Married filing jointly or Qualifying widow(er)

If line 5 is: Over—	But not over—	The tax is:	of the amount over—
$0	$32,450	......15%	$0
32,450	78,400	$4,867.50 + 28%	32,450
78,400	162,770	17,733.50 + 33%	78,400
162,770	....	Use **Worksheet** below to figure your tax.	

Schedule Y-2— Married filing separately

If line 5 is: Over—	But not over—	The tax is:	of the amount over—
$0	$16,225	......15%	$0
16,225	39,200	$2,433.75 + 28%	16,225
39,200	123,570	8,866.75 + 33%	39,200
123,570	....	Use **Worksheet** below to figure your tax.	

Worksheet (Keep for your records)

1. If your filing status is:
   - Single, enter $27,333.60
   - Head of household, enter $37,780.40
   - Married filing jointly or Qualifying widow(er), enter $45,575.60
   - Married filing separately, enter $36,708.85 .... **1.** _____
2. Enter your taxable income from line 5 of the Form 1040-ES worksheet ...... **2.** _____
3. If your filing status is:
   - Single, enter $97,620
   - Head of household, enter $134,930
   - Married filing jointly or Qualifying widow(er), enter $162,770
   - Married filing separately, enter $123,570 .... **3.** _____
4. Subtract line 3 from line 2. Enter the result. (If the result is zero or less, use the schedule above for your filing status to figure your tax. DO NOT use this worksheet.) .... **4.** _____
5. Multiply the amount on line 4 by 28% (.28). Enter the result ...... **5.** _____
6. Multiply the amount on line 4 by 5% (.05). Enter the result ...... **6.** _____
7. Multiply $574 by the number of exemptions claimed. (If married filing separately, see **Note** below.) Enter the result .... **7.** _____
8. Compare the amounts on lines 6 and 7. Enter the **smaller** of the two amounts here . ... **8.** _____
9. **Tax.** Add lines 1, 5, and 8. Enter the total here and on line 6 of the Form 1040-ES worksheet ...... **9.** _____

Note: *If married filing separately and you did **not** claim an exemption for your spouse, multiply $574 by the number of exemptions claimed. Add $574 to the result and enter the total on line 7 above.*

Figure 8.1. The 1990 federal tax schedules.

you don't have to worry about the tables for head of household, joint returns, and married taxpayers who file separately. (It's not often that married taxpayers would want to file separately if even their lawyers are still talking.) You don't need a lookup table at all if you know in advance what tax bracket your taxable income will fall in.

Only Form 1040 and Schedule A are included here. You can make additional calculations—adding up medical expenses, for example—in a separate part of the worksheet, and then incorporate the totals in the main forms as cell references. In Releases 2.2 and 3, you can also make the secondary calculations in separate worksheets and then build the results into your main worksheet by linking files. Consult your manual for details.

Setting Up the Tax Forms with 1-2-3

The basic forms of the model hardly require an explanation. Form 1040 is shown in Figure 8.2, Schedule A in Figure 8.3. Just copy the relevant lines from the federal forms onto your worksheet. (We'll explain the formulas shortly.) In the figures, the width of column B is 50 to accommodate the text from the forms, but you can enter shorter labels and set the column width narrower. Some lines have been omitted in the figures to make the examples simpler; add any you need. As you set up the worksheet, just enter zeroes as space markers (some entries go in column C and some in column D).

The worksheets are shown already completed. Note, however, that the formulas include a number of range names, such as TAX, OWE, AGI, and DEDUCT. This makes the formulas easier to understand, and also easier to write without having to move the cursor point to cells all over the worksheet. But only Release 3 of 1-2-3 allows you to refer to a range name in a formula before you have defined the range with /Range Name Create. Thus, with earlier releases, you cannot simply copy the model. (Even with Release 3, formulas that include undefined range names return ERR messages until you define the ranges.)

This is not a serious problem. Just copy the forms, entering 0's as place markers for the formulas and values in columns C and D, and then go back and use /Range Name Create to define the ranges you will be using in the formulas. The range names are shown in Table 8.1. Once the range names are defined, you can proceed fill in the formulas, as explained in the next section.

Table 8.1. Range names used in the tax worksheets.

Location	Range Name
Filing Status (C5)	STATUS
Standard Deduction (C6)	STANDARD
Amount per exemption (C7)	EXEMPT
Exemptions (C3)	EX#
Adjusted gross income (D31)	AGI
Taxable income (D39)	INC
Enter tax (D40)	TAX
Total payments (D45)	PAY
Refund or amount you owe (D47)	OWE
Total itemized deductions (D96)	DEDUCT

The first seven rows of Figure 8.2 do not match Form 1040 exactly. When you finish the worksheet, the first two lines will become titles, constantly displaying your tax liability and the amount you owe as you work on the forms. Rows 5-8 are useful for writing formulas. They also allow you to update the standard deduction and exemption amount later without having to make other changes in the worksheet.

Understanding the Formulas

Most tax calculations are simple arithmetic. The next step is to set up the basic formulas on each form. For now, bypass actual tax calculation in D40. The rest of the calculations require only very basic formula writing. For example, the formula for Total income (line 23, Form 1040) is @SUM(D11..D18). The calculation for Total Itemized Deductions (line 26, Schedule A) is @SUM(D56..D93), the total of the column D entries for Schedule A. Your ranges in the @SUM calculations may vary, depending on which lines from the federal forms you include in the worksheet.

Some calculations require only addition, subtraction, or multiplication. AGI, for example, is simply Total income less Total adjustments, here +D19-D28. (Again, your cell references may vary, depending on the lines you include.) Some calculations involve range names as cell references.

	A	B	C	D
1				
2	1040	Tax +TAX		
3		Amount you owe +OWE		
4	Filing Status		Joint	
5	Standard Deduction		5,450	
6	Amount per exemption		2,050	
7	Exemptions		3	
8				
9				
10	INCOME			
11	7 Wages, salaries, tips, etc.			0
12	8a Taxable interest income			0
13	9 Dividend income			0
14	10 Taxable refunds of state and local taxes			0
15	11 Alimony received			0
16	12 Business income or loss			0
17	13 Capital gain or (loss)			0
18	14 Capital gain distributions not reported on line 13			0
19	23 Total income			@SUM(D11..D18)
20				
21	ADJUSTMENTS TO INCOME			
22	24 Your IRA deduction			0
23	25 Spouse's IRA deduction			0
24	26 Self-employment health insurance deduction			0
25	27 Keogh retirement plan and self-employed SEP			0
26	28 Penalty on early withdrawal of savings			0
27	29 Alimony paid			0
28	30 Total adjustments			@SUM(C22..C27)
29				
30	ADJUSTED GROSS INCOME			
31	31 Subtract line 30 from line 23			+D19-D28
32				
33	TAX CALCULATION			
34				
35	32 Amount from line 31 (adjusted gross income)			+AGI
36	34 Enter larger of standardized or itemized deduction			@IF(DEDUCT>STANDARD,DEDUCT,STANDARD)
37	35 Subtract line 34 from line 32			+D35-D36
38	36 Multiply $2,050 by total exemptions on 6e			+EXEMPT*EX#
39	37 Taxable income			+D37-D38
40	38 Enter tax			TO COME LATER
41				
42	PAYMENTS			
43	54 Federal income tax withheld		0	
44	55 1990 estimated tax payments		0	
45	61 Total payments			@SUM(C43..C44)
46				
47	REFUND OR AMOUNT YOU OWE			+TAX-PAY

Figure 8.2. Formulas for Form 1040 (1989 version).

	A	B	C	D
48				
49				
50	SCHEDULE A			
51	MEDICAL AND DENTAL EXPENSES			
52	1a Prescription medicines, doctors, dentists, etc.		0	
53	1b Other		0	
54	2 Total		+C52+C53	@IF(C54>C55,C54-C55,0)
55	3 7.5% AGI		0.075*AGI	
56	4 Subtract			
57				
58	TAXES YOU PAID			
59	5 State and local income taxes		0	
60	6 Real estate taxes		0	
61	7 Other taxes		0	
62	8 Add lines 5 through 7			@SUM(C59..C61)
63				
64	INTEREST YOU PAID			
65	9a Deductible home mortgage to institutions		0	
66	9b Other deductible home mortgage interest		0	
67	10 Deductible points		0	
68	11 Deductible investment interest		0	
69	12a Personal interest you paid		0	
70	12b Multiply line 12a by 10%		0.1*C69	
71	13 Add lines 11 through 12b			@SUM(C65..C68)+C70
72				
73	GIFTS TO CHARITY			
74	14 Contributions by cash or check		0	
75	15 Other than cash or check		0	
76	16 Carryover from prior year		0	
77	17 Add amounts on lines 14 through 16			@SUM(C74..C76)
78				
79	CASUALTY AND THEFT LOSSES			
80	18 Casualty and theft losses			0
81				
82	MOVING EXPENSES			
83	19 Moving expenses			0
84				
85	JOB EXPENSES AND MOST OTHER MISC. DEDUCTIONS			
86	20 Unreimbursed employee expenses		0	
87	21 Other expenses		0	
88	22 Add amounts on line 20 and 21		0	
89	23 Multiply AGI by 2%		0.02*AGI	
90	24 Subtract line 23 from line 22			@IF(C88>C89,C88-C89,0)
91				
92	OTHER MISCELLANEOUS DEDUCTIONS			
93	25 Other miscellaneous deductions			0
94				
95	TOTAL ITEMIZED DEDUCTIONS			
96	26 Add amounts on 4, 8, 13, 17, 18, 19, 24, and 25			@SUM(D56..D93)

Figure 8.3. Formulas for Schedule A (1989).

On line 36, for example, total exemptions is +EXEMPT*EX#. This is the amount per exemption from C7 times exemptions in C8. The formula +C7*C8 yields the same result.

Note: Remember that personal interest is no longer deductible after the 1990 tax year, so you will need to delete lines 12a and 12b from Schedule A for later years. At this writing, it is not known how the lines on Schedule A will be renumbered.

There are three @IF formulas in the model. @IF, remember, takes an argument in the form of (*condition,x,y*). If the condition argument is true, @IF returns *x*; if it is false, the formula returns *y*. For example, the calculation of the deduction in D36 is @IF(DEDUCT>STANDARD,DEDUCT,STANDARD). If total deductions on Schedule A (the cell D96, named DEDUCT) is greater than the standard deduction (entered and named in C6), the total of itemized deductions is entered. If not, the formula returns the standard deduction. Similarly, the @IF calculation in D56 returns total medical expenses less 7.5% of adjusted gross income if the result is positive, 0 if the answer is negative. The same method is applied in D90 to the 2% AGI exclusion for miscellaneous deductions.

You can replace the @IF calculations with simpler mathematical formulas *if* you are certain of the outcome. For example, if you know that your itemized deductions will exceed the standard deduction, you can simply enter +DEDUCT in D36. On the other hand, if you know that your medical expenses will not be more than the 7.5% AGI exclusion, there is no point in making any calculation at all. (Fairly large uninsured medical expenses are required to meet the test—$3,750 if your AGI is $50,000, for example.)

Still, the model is designed for flexibility. And you will get inaccurate totals if you omit the @IF calculations and the values that feed into them cross the threshold in either direction. Including the logical functions at the outset saves you from having to double-check your work every time you make a change.

It is not possible to suggest every calculation that might come up in the course of filling out a tax return, so we're going to leave you to your own devices for the rest of the simple arithmetic. In any case, you should be comfortable with such 1-2-3 basics as @SUM, cell references, and mathematical operators before attempting tax calculations.

Filling In the Values

At this point, your worksheet will calculate your taxable income. You can enter values—wages and salaries, for example—directly into the model. You can also make calculations elsewhere on the worksheet and incorporate the results in the model as cell references. The model is even more useful, however, if you fill in the tax calculation first. Then you can see how your entries actually affect your tax liability.

Calculating the Tax

The model is now complete except for the actual tax calculation. This is line 38, Enter tax, on Form 1040 and D40 in Figure 8.2. Tax is based on Taxable income. To make your tax calculation, you need to understand the basic IRS schedules. Here, the 1990 schedules are used. For later years, all you have to do is to look up the comparable numbers on the current schedules.

There are, in effect, four tax brackets for each filing status. The first two brackets are simple. A single taxpayer pays 15% on the first increment, $19,450 in 1990. For the next increment, up to $47,050, the rate is 28%. Only the bracket thresholds vary for other filers. The next two brackets actually represent 5% surcharges. The first bracket, from $47,050 to $97,620 for singles in 1990, effectively eliminates the 15% tax bracket. Thus, a single taxpayer with exactly $97,620 in taxable income will pay 28% on the entire amount. Now the 15%-bracket surcharge comes off, but another 5% surcharge is added until the tax benefit of exemptions is eliminated. The upper limit of this bracket depends on the number of exemptions. Finally, the rate drops back to 28% for all additional income.

In short, the rate is 15% for the first increment, 28% for the next increment, then 33% until the 15% bracket and exemptions are eliminated, and 28% thereafter.

Calculations based on the federal tax schedules are relatively easy to make. (The IRS has a tendency to make things look more complicated than they are.) If your taxable income is less than $50,000, however, you should be aware that your actual tax must be determined by the tax tables that come with Form 1040. Because of rounding, there will be a slight difference between the table amount and the amount calculated using Schedules X, Y, and Z. You can compensate for this by duplicating the calculation the IRS uses in the tables, as explained in the next section.

Figure 8.4 shows the tax calculations for 1990 for joint filers with taxable incomes of $30,000, $60,000, $90,000, and $180,000 (with three exemptions), one for each tax bracket. (Remember that the brackets will change each year, so you'll need a current tax schedule.) You can make

	P	Q	R	S	T
1					
2					
3	Taxable income	$30,000.00	Taxable income	$60,000.00	
4	x 15%	0.15	Less base	$32,450.00	
5		==========		============	
6		$4,500.00	Taxable margin	$27,550.00	
7			x 28%	$7,714.00	
8			+ Base tax	$4,867.50	
9				============	
10			Total	$12,581.50	
11					
12					
13	Taxable income	$90,000.00	Base tax		$45,575.60
14	Less base	$78,400.00	Taxable income	$180,000.00	
15		==========	Less base	$162,770.00	
16	Taxable margin	$11,600.00		============	
17	x 33%	$3,828.00	Taxable margin	$17,230.00	
18	+ Base tax	$17,733.50	x 28%		$4,824.40
19		==========	Margin x 5%	$861.50	
20	Total	$21,561.50	Exemptions x $574	$1,722.00	
21			Lesser of two		861.50
22					==========
23			Total		$51,261.50

Figure 8.4. Calculating tax with Schedules X, Y, and Z.

the tax calculation on a separate part of your worksheet, then incorporate the result in your Form 1040 calculations as a cell reference. You can also condense the tax calculation into a single formula in the TAX cell.

The calculation for the couple with $30,000 in income is simple multiplication. Back on Form 1040, remember, we named the Taxable income cell INC. So the formula in Q6 is simply +INC*0.15.

The couple with taxable income of $60,000 can see from the schedules that they fall in the 28% tax bracket, because their taxable income is more than $32,450 and less than $78,400. So their tax is $4,867.50 (referred to here as base tax) plus 28% of their taxable income above $32,450 (referred to in the figure as base). You can enter the calculation in a single cell this way:

```
0.28*(INC-32450)+4867.5
```

The computation for the $90,000 couple follows the same form. Their tax $17,733.50 plus 33% of their taxable income above $78,400. The single-cell calculation looks like this:

```
0.33*(INC-78400)+17733.5
```

The worksheet for the upper income couple follows the IRS worksheet shown in Figure 8.1. The purpose of this tax bracket, remember, is gradually to eliminate the tax benefit of exemptions. A 5% surtax is added to the base rate of 28% for income above $162,770 until the benefit of the exemptions is eliminated. Then the rate reverts to the basic rate of 28%.

What makes the calculation seem complicated is that the upper limit of the surtax bracket depends on how many exemptions you claim. In 1990, each exemption is worth $574. So the marginal tax rate is 28% plus the 5% surtax (effectively 33%) until you have paid a surtax of $574 for each exemption. Once you cross that threshold, the tax calculation is:

```
Base tax + 28% Taxable margin + (Exemptions   X   $574)
```

The IRS worksheet in Figure 8.1 calculates both the 5% surtax on the taxable margin and the maximum surtax (the number of exemptions multiplied by $574), and then taking the lesser of the two. Remember that on Form 1040 we named Taxable income INC and Exemptions EX#. This helps in a single-cell formula, but it's still a cellful using the IRS method:

```
45575.6+0.28*(INC-162770)+@MIN(0.05*(INC-162770),574*EX#)
```

The @MIN function finds the lowest value in a range: @MIN(*range*). Here, the range is two values, the 5% surcharge on the taxable margin and the full surcharge calculated by multiplying $574 by the number of exemptions.

You can simplify the formula, because the first two elements are redundant. The base tax, $45,575.60, is simply 28% of the base taxable income at which the surcharge kicks in. Thus, this formula yields the same result:

```
0.28*INC+@MIN(0.05*(INC-162770),574*EX#)
```

If you know in advance whether your taxable income is high enough to exhaust the exemption surcharge, you can simplify the formula further. In the case of very high incomes, this will be obvious, and it's easy to calculate the cutoff point for the exemption surcharge.

For taxable incomes that exceed the 15% bracket, the tax benefit of each exemption is 28% of the amount of each exemption. For 1990, the calculation is 0.28*2050 = 574. The surcharge is 5%, so the income interval required to eliminate the tax benefit of one exemption is 574/0.05 = $11,480. To find the threshold at which the surcharge is removed, multiply the number of exemptions by that number and add it to the base taxable income at which the surcharge kicks in. In 1990, that figure is $162,770 for joint filers. If you claim three exemptions, the calculation looks like this:

Base	$162,770
3 x $11,480	34,440
	=======
Total	$197,210

Thus, the exemption surcharge applies to taxable income above $162,770 but less than $197,210. If our hypothetical taxpayer's income is higher than the latter figure, the tax calculation becomes very simple:

```
0.28*INC+3*574
```

Or, more generally:

```
(Tax rate  X   Taxable income) + (Exemptions  X  Exemption value)
```

In fact, if your income is above the surtax threshold, you can make the tax calculation even easier by eliminating exemptions from your calculations on Form 1040. (You'll still have to include them on your actual return, but you don't have to in your calculations.) Just enter 0 in the Tax Calculation section, where the form asks you to multiply the number of exemptions by the amount of each exemption. Now the tax calculation is really simple: 0.28*INC. After all, the two surtaxes first eliminate the 15% bracket, and then the tax benefit of exemptions, so this is all that's left.

If your taxable income falls within the exemption surtax range, the calculation is still easy:

```
0.28*INC+0.05*(INC-162770)
```

Or, again, more generally:

```
(Tax rate  X  Taxable income) + (Surcharge X  (Taxable income - Base))
```

When you calculate your own taxes, you will have to adapt these calculations to your own situation and the variables that apply to the current tax year. Once you understand the general principles, however, the calculations are not at all difficult. On Form 1040, as shown in Figure 8.2, you can enter one of the formulas suggested here for line 38, Enter tax. In the figure, the entry in this cell, D40, is TO COME LATER.

Next, we'll look at a more precise tax calculation for taxable incomes under $50,000, then a model that makes your worksheet more flexible and easier to update.

Making Precise Calculations for Taxable Income under $50,000

If your taxable income is less than $50,000, your tax is determined by the tax tables that come with Form 1040. For planning and paying estimated taxes, the calculations just described will be adequate. Almost certainly, however, the result will be slightly off your actual tax. The IRS tables use a rounding method that is fairly easy to duplicate with 1-2-3.

The IRS tables divide taxable income into $50 increments. The tax is calculated at the midpoint of each increment, using the formulas from Schedules X, Y, and Z. If your income is at least $30,000 but less than $30,050, for example, the computation is based on a taxable income of $30,025. This will cost you a few dollars if your taxable income is near the bottom of the range, or save you a few if it's near the top. If you're in the 28% bracket, you will save $14 if you can find one extra deduction that lowers your taxable income from $30,001 to $29,999. The next $49 in deductions won't matter, but you save another $14 if you find a deduction that drops your taxable income to less than $29,950.

The IRS tables also round the tax to the nearest dollar. So, to determine your precise tax you must first round your taxable income to the midpoint of its $50 range, calculate your tax, and then round the tax to the nearest dollar.

Rounding Taxable Income

To duplicate the IRS tables for taxable income under $50,000, you first need to round your taxable income to the midpoint of its $50 range. This is not a simple rounding calculation, but it's not difficult. Here's what to do.

Taxable income, remember, is named INC in the model. To find the midpoint of the $50 range in which your taxable income falls, enter this formula:

```
50*@INT(INC/50)+25
```

Let's break down the formula:

- INC/50 divides your taxable income by 50. If your taxable income is $30,037, for example, the result will be 600.74. A number not useful by itself.

- The @INT function finds the integer of the previous calculation. That is, it strips away the numbers to the right of the decimal, which constitute the remainder or mantissa of the division. So the value of @INT(INC/50) is an even 600.

- Next, we multiply the result of the @INT calculation by 50 to find the lower end of the $50 range for taxable income. Here, 50*600 = $30,000.

- Finally, because the tax calculation is based on the midpoint of the $50 range, we add 25. So the final result of the calculation is $30,025, and you can use the schedules to calculate your tax on that number.

Well, you could have seen the outcome if you already knew that your taxable income was $30,037. The advantage of making this calculation is that it still works if you make a change on your tax forms that bumps you into another $50 range.

By the way, *do not* enter the result of this calculation as your taxable income on your actual tax return. In the example, the actual taxable income is $30,037, so $30,025 might look like a mathematical error, even though the tax is the same. So put the @INT calculation elsewhere on your worksheet and base your tax calculation on the result.

If you are not sure whether your income will cross the $50,000 threshold, you can use @IF to refine the formula a step further:

```
@IF(INC<50000,50*@INT(INC/50)+25,INC)
```

This formula will find the midpoint of your $50 range if your taxable income (INC) is less than $50,000, or leave it as it is if INC is $50,000 or more. This way, your tax calculation should be correct for any taxable income. Just round the tax to the nearest dollar if your taxable income is less than $50,000. If your tax is more than $50,000, you can round the tax if you also round all of the other values on your return to the nearest dollar. (See *Note About Rounding* below.) If you don't round the other values, don't round the tax calculation, either.

Calculating the Tax

Once you have determined your adjusted taxable income, as just explained, you can use the methods described earlier to calculate your tax. Again, the IRS tables round the tax to the nearest dollar.

For a joint filer with a taxable income of $30,037, the tax is based on $30,025, as we have just seen. That falls in the 15% tax bracket for 1990, and will stay there, barring a major change in the tax law. Thus, the basic tax calculation is simply:

```
0.15*30025 = $4,503.75
```

That obviously rounds out to $4,504. You can use @ROUND to round automatically. In this case, the calculation is:

```
@ROUND(0.15*30025,0) = $4,504
```

This formula rounds the calculation to 0 decimal places, exactly as the IRS rules require. You can adapt @ROUND to any of the other tax calculations discussed earlier. You can also further automate your tax worksheet, as explained below.

Using @VLOOKUP to Calculate Your Tax

The tax calculation formulas described above work fine if you know your tax bracket in advance. If you slip from one bracket to another, however, you have to rewrite the formula (or formulas)—and you could make a dangerous mistake by failing to notice you have crossed a bracket threshold. In addition, you will have to rewrite the formulas every year to compensate for the indexing of the tax brackets.

Using @VLOOKUP can solve all of these problems. The calculations below automatically accommodate shifts from one tax bracket to the next. You will still have to update the bracket ranges, of course, but you can do that with simple cell entries; the basic formulas will remain intact unless Congress changes the tax tables in a more fundamental way.

@VLOOKUP, remember, looks up a value in a table exactly the way you look up your tax calculation on Schedules X, Y, and Z. It takes this form: @VLOOKUP(*x,range,column offset*). *X* is a value (here taxable income). *Range* is the lookup table. *Column offset* tells 1-2-3 how many columns to the right to look for the result. The left column of the lookup table must contain values in ascending order. @VLOOKUP goes down the list, comparing each value to *x* until it finds *x* or the largest value that is not greater than *x*. Then it takes the value the number of columns to the right specified by the offset.

> **Note:** *x* must be greater or equal to the first number in the left column of the lookup table. For this reason, it is recommended that you enter some number in D11, Wages, salaries, tips, etc., even if you haven't made the calculations yet. Otherwise, you will get ERR messages in some cells and negative numbers in others.

Setting Up the Lookup Table

The first step is to set up a lookup table based on the current tax schedules, so you can use @VLOOKUP to calculate your tax. You can also modify the lookup table slightly so you can use it alone to estimate taxes if you know your approximate taxable income. All you have to do before you start is to enter your estimated taxable income, using whatever calculations you want, and assign it the range name INC. You will also need to enter values and assign range names in several other cells to use the formulas as shown here.

You should already have filled in your filing status, standard deduction, amount per exemption, and number of exemptions, as shown in Figure 8.2. These entries should be assigned the range names STATUS, STANDARD, EXEMPT, and EX#. You will need all but the standard deduction to set up the table. You should also enter some value in the Income section of Form 1040, so that line 23, Total income, has a positive value. This makes it easier to make sure the lookup table works properly.

Now go to an area of your worksheet below and to the right of your tax forms to set up the lookup table. (This will allow you to insert and delete columns and rows and to change column widths in either part of your worksheet without affecting the other.) The calculations shown in Figure 8.5 simply reproduce the calculations in the IRS schedules shown in Figure 8.1. In the example, Total income, named INC, is $90,000. Adj

	F	G	H	I	J	K
98	TAX CALCULATION					
99						
100	Exemption Value		574			
101	Adj Taxable Income		78400			
102	Tax		17733.5			
103						
104	SINGLE			HEAD OF HOUSEHOLD		
105	Income	Base Tax	Tax	Income	Base Tax	Tax
106	0		11760	0		11760
107	19450	2917.5	19423.5	26050	3907.5	18565.5
108	47050	10645.5	20991	67200	15429.5	19125.5
109	97620	27333.6	20991	134930	37780.4	19125.5
110	5% Surtax		20991	5% Surtax		19125.5
111	Full Surtax		23674	Full Surtax		23674
112						
113	JOINT RETURN			MARRIED, SEPARATE		
114	Income	Base Tax	Tax	Income	Base Tax	Tax
115	0		11760	0		3551.1
116	32450	4867.5	17733.5	16225	2433.75	19842.75
117	78400	17733.5	17733.5	39200	8866.75	21802.75
118	162770	45575.6	17733.5	123570	36708.85	21802.75
119	5% Surtax		17733.5	5% Surtax		21802.75
120	Full Surtax		23674	Full Surtax		23674

Figure 8.5. Setting up a lookup table to calculate tax.

Taxable Income is $78,400, $90,000 less the standard deduction of $5,450 for a joint filer and three exemptions of $2,050 each. The numbers have been left in the General format because you will not be looking at these values routinely.

It takes some work to complete the calculations as shown. In addition to entering the formulas, you must define the lookup table for @VLOOKUP to work. The underlying formulas are shown in Figures 8.6 and 8.7. Remember that you need to complete only the table for your own filing status unless you want a model that will work in any situation. If you're single, for example, you don't need the joint calculations, and vice versa. Note that the calculation in the Tax column for each filing status is reliable *only* for the correct tax bracket.

	F	G	H
98	TAX CALCULATION		
99			
100	Exemption Value		+EXEMPT*0.28
101	Adj Taxable Income		@IF(INC<50000,50*@INT(INC/50)+25,INC)
102	Tax		@VLOOKUP(ADJ,@@(STATUS),2)
103			
104	SINGLE		
105	Income	Base Tax	Tax
106		0	0.15*ADJ
107		19450 0.15*F107	+G107+0.28*(ADJ-F107)
108		47050 +G107+0.28*(F108-F107)	+G108+0.33*(ADJ-F108)
109		97620 0.28*F109	@MIN(H110..H111)
110	5% Surtax		+G109+0.33*(ADJ-F109)
111	Full Surtax		0.28*ADJ+EX#*EXVAL
112			
113	JOINT RETURN		
114	Income	Base Tax	Tax
115		0	0.15*ADJ
116		32450 0.15*F116	+G116+0.28*(ADJ-F116)
117		78400 +G116+0.28*(F117-F116)	+G117+0.33*(ADJ-F117)
118		162770 0.28*F118	@MIN(H119..H120)
119	5% Surtax		+G118+0.33*(ADJ-F118)
120	Full Surtax		0.28*ADJ+EX#*EXVAL

Figure 8.6. Formulas for tax calculations and lookup tables for single and joint filers.

These calculations are easier than they look, and they work the same way for all four lookup tables. You must enter the formulas for Exemption

	I	J	K
104	HEAD OF HOUSEHOLD		
105	Income	Base Tax	Tax
106	0		0.15*ADJ
107	26050	0.15*I107	+J107+0.28*(ADJ-I107)
108	67200	+J107+0.28*(I108-I107)	+J108+0.33*(ADJ-I108)
109	134930	0.28*I109	@MIN(K110..K111)
110	5% Surtax		+J109+0.33*(ADJ-I109)
111	Full Surtax		0.28*ADJ+EX#*EXVAL
112			
113	MARRIED, SEPARATE		
114	Income	Base Tax	Tax
115	0		0.15*K111
116	16225	0.15*I116	+J116+0.28*(ADJ-I116)
117	39200	+J116+0.28*(I117-I116)	+J117+0.33*(ADJ-I117)
118	123570	+J117+0.33*(I118-I117)	@MIN(K119..K120)
119	5% Surtax		+J118+0.33*(ADJ-I118)
120	Full Surtax		0.28*ADJ+EX#*EXVAL

Figure 8.7. Lookup table formulas for heads of household and couples filing separately.

Value and Adj(usted) Taxable Income first because these values are used in the lookup tables. You must also complete the lookup table(s) before you can make the Tax calculation. We'll offer some possible shortcuts along the way.

Dealing with Exemptions in the 33% Bracket

Exemption Value is simply the amount of tax you save for each exemption. In 1990, the amount of each exemption is $2,050, so the exemption value is $2,050 × 28%, or $574. We've already entered Amount per exemption in C7 and assigned it the range name EXEMPT, so the formula is +EXEMPT*0.28. In later years, you can simply enter the new value for EXEMPT in C7 without changing the formula here.

This calculation is relevant only if you reach the top tax bracket on Schedules X, Y, and Z, when the exemption surtax kicks in. If you are certain that your taxable income will fall below the top bracket, you can skip this calculation.

Assign this calculation the range name EXVAL. You will use it in the lookup tables.

Calculating Adj(usted) Taxable Income

Adj(usted) taxable income makes a difference only if your taxable income is less than $50,000. As explained earlier, when your taxable income is below that figure, your actual tax is determined by the tax tables that come with Form 1040. The tables divide income into $50 increments and calculate the tax on the midpoint.

Here, the formula is:

```
@IF(INC<50000,50*@INT(INC/50)+25,INC)
```

If your taxable income is less than $50,000, this formula finds the amount used to calculate the IRS tables. If taxable income is $50,000 or more, the formula leaves INC as it is. For a full explanation, see *Making Precise Calculations for Taxable Income under $50,000*, above.

If you are sure your taxable income is over $50,000, you can skip this formula. Just enter +INC to retrieve your taxable income from Form 1040.

Either way, assign the calculation the range name ADJ, for adjusted taxable income. This, too, will make the lookup table calculations easier.

Entering the Lookup Tables

Skipping the actual tax calculation for the moment, you can now set up the lookup table(s). Let's take a slightly different look at the lookup table for joint filers, shown in Figure 8.8. The calculations are the same for all four tax schedules; only the cell references differ.

Look again at the IRS schedules in Figure 8.1. For 1990, joint filers pay 15% on the first $32,450 in taxable income. In the next bracket (to $78,400), they pay 15% on the first $32,450 ($4,867.50), plus 28% of the

	F	G	H
113	JOINT RETURN		
114	Income	Base Tax	Tax
115	0		0.15*ADJ
116	32450	0.15*F116	+G116+0.28*(ADJ-F116)
117	78400	+G116+0.28*(F117-F116)	+G117+0.33*(ADJ-F117)
118	162770	0.28*F118	@MIN(H119..H120)
119	5% Surtax		+G118+0.33*(ADJ-F118)
120	Full Surtax		0.28*ADJ+EX#*EXVAL

Figure 8.8. The lookup table formulas for a joint return.

excess. Above that, they pay 15% on the first bracket, 28% on the second, and 33% on the excess. It gets just a bit trickier in the last bracket, over $162,770. More on that shortly.

Now look at Figure 8.8. In the first four rows under Income, the tax bracket amounts are simply copied from the IRS schedules. The formulas under Base Tax and Tax calculate your tax using the rules described in the last paragraph. A joint filer with taxable income of less than $32,450 pays a straight 15% tax (0.15*ADJ). The maximum tax for the 15% bracket is 15% of $32,450. This calculation appears under Base Tax in G116, as the formula 0.15*F116. In the next bracket, a joint filer pays that amount (+G116), plus 28% on the excess—0.28*(ADJ-F116). And so on.

By the beginning of the top bracket (starting at $162,770), the effect of the 15% bracket has been eliminated by the surtax, so the base tax is 28% of $162,770. The formula in G118, 0.28*F118, makes this calculation. Now, the 5% exemption surcharge begins. You pay 28% on the first $162,770, calculated in G118, plus 33% of the excess (ADJ-F118). Thus, the tax calculation in H119 is:

```
+G118+0.33*(ADJ-F118)
```

However, you cannot be surcharged more than the value of your exemptions. This is EXVAL, already calculated in H100, times the number of exemptions (EX#). After the exemptions are paid off, tax is calculated with this formula, as shown in H120:

```
0.28*ADJ+EX#*EXVAL
```

The tax you actually pay is the smaller of the two, so for the actual tax calculation in H118, the formula is @MIN(H119..H120). @MIN simply finds the smaller of the values in the range.

The lookup table is now finished, but there is more to do before you make your actual tax calculation.

Defining the Lookup Tables

For joint returns, the lookup table consists of the first four rows in the Income, Base Tax, and Tax columns, indicated by boldface type in Figure 8.9. The range is comparable for the other tables.

	F	G	H
113	JOINT RETURN		
114	Income	Base Tax	Tax
115	0		11760
116	32450	4867.5	17733.5
117	78400	17733.5	17733.5
118	162770	45575.6	17733.5
119	5% Surtax		17733.5
120	Full Surtax		23674

Figure 8.9. Defining the lookup table.

You could enter the lookup formula this way: @VLOOKUP(ADJ,F115..H118,2). However, its cleaner to assign a range name to the table. Besides, the model is set up so that you can switch filing status without changing the lookup formula, and this *requires* a range name. Here, we've used /**R**ange **N**ame **C**reate to name the lookup tables SINGLE, JOINT, HEAD, and SEPARATE. You can use any names you like.

Calculating Your Tax

Finally, we come to the actual tax calculation in H102. @VLOOKUP will go down the left column of the lookup table until it finds the largest value that is less than Adj(usted) Taxable Income, then look two columns across to retrieve the tax value.

In H102, the tax formula is @VLOOKUP(ADJ,@@(STATUS),2). ADJ is the adjusted taxable income, and 2 is the column offset, telling 1-2-3 to look two columns to the right when it finds the appropriate tax bracket. @@(STATUS) requires a little more explanation.

Remember that back in C5, we entered Joint for Filing Status, and assigned that cell the range name STATUS. @@ is an indirect cell pointer. The @@ function is a little difficult to explain but easy to use. Here, Joint is the contents of the cell named STATUS, so the *range* named JOINT defined as the lookup table, and the formula calculates the tax for a joint return. If you change the STATUS entry to Single, the formula will go to the SINGLE lookup table, and so on. Using this method allows you to change tax status without revising the lookup tables.

For a joint return, you can get the same result by entering @VLOOKUP(ADJ,JOINT,2). This may be simpler. However, if you want to change your filing status, you will have to make a change in the tax formula rather than simply changing the entry for Filing status.

> **Note:** The manual and most 1-2-3 books seem to imply that, when you use @@(cell), the contents of the cell referred to must be the range name or address of a single cell. However, within an argument where a range is called for, you can use @@(cell) to identify a cell that identifies a *multicell range.* For example, @@(STATUS) by itself simply returns the value 0. But @SUM(@@(STATUS)) returns the total of the values in the range named JOINT, when JOINT is centered in the cell named STATUS. Further, note that @@ was first included in Release 2. For earlier releases of 1-2-3, you will have to use the second method to define the range in the @VLOOKUP formula.

Including the Tax Calculation on Form 1040

Now, you need to include the tax calculation in your tax forms. You may also want to round your tax to the nearest dollar if your taxable income is less than $50,000 or if you elect to round all the entries on your tax forms, as the IRS allows you to do.

The easiest way to transfer your tax calculation to Form 1040 is to assign a range name to it. We've already assigned the name TAX to line 38, Enter tax (D40). So use another, such as TAXCALC. Now go to D40 (or whatever cell your actual tax occupies) and enter +TAXCALC.

This will complete the form unless you need to round your tax. If you're sure you want to round to the nearest dollar, you can enter this formula in D40:

```
@ROUND(TAXCALC,0)
```

This would be appropriate if you're sure your taxable income will be less than $50,000, or if you've rounded *all* of the values on your tax returns. See the note about rounding below in the latter case.

If you're not sure about the $50,000 threshold—or if you just want a more flexible model—you can use this formula in D40:

```
@IF(INC<50000,@ROUND(TAXCALC,0),TAXCALC)
```

This will return your tax to the nearest dollar if your taxable income (INC) is less than $50,000, but leave the tax calculation unrounded if INC is higher.

Adding Titles to Show the Status of Your Work

The model is now essentially complete. However, as you fill in the values on your tax forms and schedules, you may want to know how changes affect your tax and the amount you owe. How much does it help when you find an additional deduction? How much does it cost when you add the interest, previously overlooked, from your money market account? You can use titles to display this information at the top of your screen whenever you are working on the forms.

You have already calculated your tax (TAX, in D40) and the amount you owe (OWE, in D47). But these cells will not be on the screen when, say, you are working on Schedule A. The solution is to enter these calculations at the top of your worksheet as titles.

This is already done in Figure 8.2. In B1, the entry is "Tax and in B2 the entry is "Amount you owe. The double quotation mark (") makes the label flush right. In C1, enter +TAX. This is your total tax liability. In C2, enter +OWE. This is your total tax less the amount you've already paid. Underneath, you might want to enter a double line (use \=, and then copy to columns to the right) to separate the titles from the rest of your worksheet.

To designate these rows as titles, place the cursor in the row *beneath* the bottom row of your titles. (This will be row 3 if you do not include the double line, row 4 if you do.) Now enter /Worksheet Titles Horizontal. From now on, Tax and Amount you owe will always be displayed at the top of the screen when you are working at the left side of the worksheet. (Note that you have also frozen the top two or three rows for sections of the worksheet in columns to the right, a factor to consider in setting up other parts of the model.)

Suppose, for example, that you are about to enter your state and local income tax deduction. The top half of Figure 8.10 shows your Tax and Amount you owe before you enter the deduction. The bottom half of the figure shows the result of entering $5,130 for state and local taxes. The amounts are also automatically adjusted on Form 1040.

Updating the Model

Under the current tax law, the tax brackets, standard deductions, and amount per exemption are indexed to inflation. This guarantees that your tax calculations will change each year, even if there is no change in the tax law. The model is easy to update.

For the standard deduction and amount per exemption, all you have to do is to change the values for those entries (C6 and C7 of the model.) The worksheet will make the necessary adjustments automatically.

The procedure for updating the tax brackets depends on how you set up your actual tax calculation. If you did not set up lookup tables, you

	A	B	C
1		Tax	17,734
2		Amount you owe	2,176
3	==
58	TAXES YOU PAID		
59	5 State and local income taxes		0
60	6 Real estate taxes		0
61	7 Other taxes		0

	A	B	C
1		Tax	16,054
2		Amount you owe	496
3	==
58	TAXES YOU PAID		
59	5 State and local income taxes		5,130
60	6 Real estate taxes		0
61	7 Other taxes		0

Figure 8.10. Adding titles to the top of the worksheet allows you to see the tax effect of changes immediately.

will have to revise the tax computation according to the new schedules. As long as the tax rates don't change, you should be able to do this by editing rather than starting over. If you do use lookup tables, all you have to do is to change the values in the Income column of the tables to match the new schedules. The model will make all of the necessary adjustments.

There almost certainly be other changes in the actual forms, and you will have to revise the forms and schedules accordingly. Absent a change in the basic calculations, however, the basic structure of the model should hold up.

A Note about Rounding

If your taxable income is less than $50,000, you will need to round your actual tax, as explained earlier, to get precisely the amount shown in the tax tables that come with Form 1040. This should pose no problem.

The IRS also allows you to round *all* of the entries on your tax forms, and this can be tricky in 1-2-3 if you format the values on your worksheets to 0 decimal places. When you do that, 1-2-3 rounds *each entry* correctly, but the program continues to use the unrounded values in calculations. For example, if you enter 2.40 in one cell and 2.25 in another, the value 2 will be displayed in both cells. However, if you add these two cells, it will appear that 2 + 2 = 5. Only the display is rounded, not the values themselves.

You can overcome this problem by using @ROUND in the appropriate places. To make sure you catch all of the extra pennies, you can format your forms to display 2 decimals, then round any value that is not even. On the whole, however, it's probably easier not to elect the rounding option for calculating taxes with 1-2-3.

These are the IRS instructions about rounding:

"You may round off cents to the nearest whole dollar on your return and schedules. To do so, drop amounts under 50 cents and increase amounts from 50 to 99 cents to the next dollar. For example, $1.39 becomes $1 and $2.50 becomes $3.

"If you do round off, do so for all amounts. However, if you have to add two or more amounts to figure the amount to enter on a line, include cents when adding and only round off the total. **Example.** You received two W-2 forms, one showing wages of $5,000.55 and one showing wages of $18,500.73. On Form 1040, line 7, you would enter $23,501 ($5,000.55 + $18,500.73 = $23,501.28)."

(Note that you would get $23,502 if you rounded first.)

There are at least two situations in which rounding can create problems on your 1-2-3 tax worksheet. The first is when you make secondary calculations on the worksheet. In the IRS example, you could add the amounts from your W-2 forms in D10. The display would be correct, but you could run into a problem when you use @SUM to calculate Total income in D19. You encounter the same potential difficulty if you add the W-2 form amounts somewhere else in the worksheet, and then incorporate the result in Form 1040 as a cell reference.

The second risky situation is where the forms and schedules require you to multiply a value by a percentage. Examples include the income exclusions for medical and miscellaneous deductions, the calculation of self-employment tax, and (for 1990 only) the personal interest deduction.

These calculations are not likely to result in round numbers, and you can run into trouble when you add them up.

Again, you can compensate with @ROUND. However, the main benefit of rounding is to make the arithmetic easier, and 1-2-3 does that for you, so rounding may be more trouble than it's worth.

A Note about Ranges in @Function Arguments

The tax model is designed so that you can add or delete rows in the forms and schedules without making major changes in formulas. However, it is important to understand how ranges work to avoid unexpected results in @Function calculations. Some of the same problems apply to simple cell references.

A range is a rectangle defined by the cells at its diagonally opposite corners, usually top left and bottom right. A range may occupy a single column. For example, Total income in the Figure 8.2 is @SUM(D11..D18). D11 is top left, and D18 is bottom right, even though both are in the same column. If the range were D11..H11, the same would apply, even though both cells are in the same row.

You can freely delete and insert rows and columns *within* a range, but not at its edges. Simply put, if you delete any corner of a range with the /Worksheet Delete command, you destroy the range definition. ERR messages will appear in any calculation that refers to the range. You will also get ERR messages in any formulas that contain references to cells in the deleted area.

In Figure 8.2, for example, you can delete row 15, which contains Alimony received. The worksheet will recalculate correctly. However, deleting row 11 (Wages, salaries, tips, etc.) or row 18 (Capital gain distributions) will disrupt the @SUM calculation and any other calculations that contain a cell reference to Total income.

Note: The /Range /Erase command does not carry the same risk. It blanks out a range, but does not disrupt range definitions.

Inserting at the edge of a range can be even riskier because you may get incorrect calculations but not ERR messages. If you make this mistake without realizing it, the only way to spot it is to notice the incorrect result. That can be very difficult if, for example, you are using @SUM to total a long column of numbers. It might be next to impossible in a more complicated calculation, such as one using @DSUM or a formula that includes multiple calculations.

Suppose you want to add line 18, Rents and royalties, on Form 1040, below Capital gains distributions in the model. It's easily done. Just execute /Worksheet Insert Row with the cursor in row 19 and enter the new information. However, your rents and royalties will not be included in the Total income calculation. If you check the formula in what is now D20, you will find that it is still @SUM(D11..D18), which does not include the new value in D19.

You can solve the problem by editing the range formulas. This is best done in advance when deleting rows because you can simply edit the end of the range you're eliminating. For example, if you want to delete line 14, Capital gain distributions, change the formula in D19 to @SUM(D11..D17). If you delete first, the formula changes to @SUM(ERR), and you have to redefine the whole range. When you insert, you may have to edit the range after the insertion.

When using @SUM, you can protect yourself against this problem by including blank cells at the corners of the range. In the Total income calculation, for example, you could insert a blank row 19 and change the formula in what is now D20 to @DSUM(D10..D19). You can even enter a double line (with \=) in the blank cells to mark the margins of the range. Now, you can insert and delete at will within the @SUM range. The calculation will not be affected because 1-2-3 treats blank cells and labels (including \=) as having values of 0.

> **Note:** Do not use this method for ranges referred to in other @Function formulas. Zeroes do not affect addition, but in some other formulas—@AVG, for example—they will become part of the calculation and are likely to wreak havoc with the results.

Conclusion

As noted at the outset, the worksheets described in this chapter are by far the largest in this book. Most people, however, will not need all of the features in the full-blown worksheet. Just take the ones you need. That is, after all, one of 1-2-3's greatest advantages over programs designed for a specific purpose. With 1-2-3, you can incorporate your own assumptions and your own requirements to produce what is, in effect, a custom program that does exactly what you want it to do—no more, no less. Once you have set up a tax model that meets your needs, you should be able to use it, with relatively minor revisions, for years to come.

9

A Guide to @Functions

Next to mathematical operators, such as +, -, *, and /, @Functions are perhaps the most basic key to 1-2-3 calculations. From the beginning, 1-2-3 has provided functions that allow you to add or average columns (or rows), to make annuity calculations, to perform basic statistical calculations, to work with logarithms, and so on. Functions that condense extended calculations into a single step remain the core of 1-2-3's @Function repertory, and they have been expanded with each major release.

This chapter is a basic guide to the 1-2-3 @Functions. The 1-2-3 release in which a function first appeared is indicated in the heading for each function. Where no release is shown, the function is available in all releases. The functions are divided into the standard categories used in the 1-2-3 manual. Within each category, functions that make similar calculations are grouped together. Otherwise, they are listed alphabetically.

The @Functions fall into these categories:

- Financial functions, including compound interest, annuities, internal rate of return and net present value, and depreciation.

- Math functions, including basic math, logarithms, and trigonometric functions.

- Statistical functions, including basic statistical functions, as well as standard deviation and variance.

- Database statistical functions, which allow you to make statistical calculations on records from a database that meet certain criteria.

- Date and time functions, which allow you to make a variety of date and time calculations, such as the interval between two dates or times.

- Logic functions, which calculate the results of conditional (or logical) formulas.

- String functions (all new with Release 2.0), which allow you to perform various operations on "strings," which are labels or other strings of characters that are not values.

- Special functions, which, in early releases of 1-2-3, simply allowed you to look up data in a table and to set a warning flag when data were not available or a calculation yielded an error. Beginning with Release 2.0, special functions are expanded to perform a variety of other tasks. These are used mostly to determine various conditions in logic formulas and macros.

With these tools, you can expand the examples we have discussed so far to perform almost any calculation you might need to manage a business or your personal finances.

Financial Functions

All of 1-2-3's financial @Functions involve the time value of money, and all involve at least three of these variables: present value (or principal, in the case of a loan), future value, interest rate, term, and payments. The interest rate and term must always be expressed in the same periods. For example, if interest is compounded monthly, the term must be expressed in months; if the term is expressed in years, you must use an effective annual interest rate. Reconciling periods is discussed in Chapters 1 and 2. For depreciation, the rate varies from year to year, except in the case of straight-line depreciation.

The financial @Functions fall into four categories:

1. Compound interest functions make calculations involving a lump sum at a fixed interest rate. These functions are discussed in detail in Chapter 1.

2. Annuity functions involve a regular series of payments (an annuity) at a fixed interest rate. All of these functions are designed for ordinary annuities, with payments at the end of each period. However, they can be adapted easily for annuities due, with payments at the beginning of each period. Annuities are explained in detail in Chapter 2. Further variations, including combining lump-sum and annuity calculations, are covered in Chapter 6.

3. @IRR and @NPV calculate the internal rate of return and net present value of an uneven series of cash flows. While the cash

may vary, periods and interest rate must be consistent. @IRR and @NPV are covered in Chapter 4.

4. 1-2-3 provides @Functions for calculating depreciation using double-declining balance, the sum of the years' digits, and straight-line depreciation. Release 3 adds a function for variable declining balance, which can be adapted to the Modified Accelerated Cost Recovery System (MACRS) method used in the current tax law. These functions, along with MACRS, are discussed in Chapter 5.

Compound Interest

1-2-3 provides two @Functions for making calculations involving compound interest on a lump sum. @CTERM calculates the term required to reach a future value, given present value and periodic interest rate. @RATE computes the rate required to reach a future value, given present value and term. For additional compound interest calculations, see Chapter 1.

@CTERM (Release 2.0)

@CTERM(*interest,future value,present value*) calculates the number of compounding periods required for a present value to reach a future value at a constant interest rate. The term and the compounding period must be expressed in the same periods. For example, if interest is compounded monthly, you must find the *monthly* interest rate, and the term will be calculated in months.

Example: You have deposited $10,000 at an Annual Percentage Rate of 12%, compounded monthly. How long will it take to accumulate $20,000?

Answer: @CTERM(0.01,20000,10000) = 69.66 months. Because interest is compounded monthly, the periodic interest rate is .12/12 = .01 (or 12%/12 = 1%).

@CTERM, APR, and calculating periodic interest rates are discussed in detail in Chapter 1.

The underlying formula for @CTERM is

$$\frac{\ln\ (FV/PV)}{\ln\ (1+i)}$$

where ln is the natural logarithm; FV is the future value; PV is the present value; and i is the periodic interest rate.

@RATE (Release 2.0)

@RATE(*future value,present value,term*) calculates the rate required to reach a future value, given the present value and term.

Example: If you deposit $10,000, what monthly interest rate is required for your investment to grow to $20,000 in seven years?

Answer: @RATE(20000,10000,7*12) = 0.0082859 = 0.82859%. This is the monthly percentage rate. The advertised annual percentage rate (see Chapter 1) should be 12*0.08259% = 9.94%.

Note: The 1-2-3 manual offers an example of a bond purchased for $10,000 with a maturity value of $18,000. This example is realistic only in the case of a zero coupon bond, where no periodic interest payments are made. Most bonds pay semiannual interest, and you would need to include these interest payments in a calculation of the bond's rate of return. See Chapter 7.

The formula use by @RATE is

$$\left(\frac{FV}{PV}\right)^{1/n} - 1$$

This is the nth root of (FV/PV) minus 1, where FV is the future value, PV is the present value, and n is the term.

Annuities

Annuities are an even series of payments at a fixed interest rate over a given term. Again, all 1-2-3 @Functions assume that payments come at the end of each period (ordinary annuities), as with loans. Formulas are provided here for adapting the functions to payments that come at the beginning of each period (annuties due). See also Chapters 2 and 6.

@FV

@FV(*payment,interest,term*) calculates the future value of an ordinary annuity (end-of-period payments, as with a loan). Interest must be expressed in the same periods as the term. To convert to an annuity due (beginning-of-period payments, as with a lease), multiply by (1+*interest*):

```
@FV(payment, interest, term) * (1+interest)
```

Example: You plan to deposit $10,000 a year at an effective annual rate of 10% for 10 years. How much will you have if you make the deposits at the end of each year? How much if you make the deposits at the beginning?

Answers: @FV(10000,0.1,10) = $159,374.25 and @FV(10000,0.1,10)* (1+0.1) = $175,311.67.

The formula used by @FV is:

$$pmt * \frac{(1+i)^n - 1}{i}$$

where *pmt* is the periodic payment; *i* is the periodic interest rate; and *n* is the number of periods.

Calculating periodic interest rates is explained in detail in Chapter 1. Annuities are covered in Chapters 2 and 6.

@PMT

@PMT(*principal,interest,term*) calculates the payment of an ordinary annuity (payments at the end of each period, as with a loan). As with all annuity calculations, the interest and term must be expressed in the same period. (See Chapters 1 and 2.) To convert the function for an annuity due (payments at the beginning of each period, as with a lease), divide by (1+*interest*): @PMT(*principal,interest,term*)/(1+*interest*).

Example: You have a choice of purchasing a $10,000 piece of equipment and leasing it. In either case, payments will be monthly for five years, calculated at 15% APR. Assuming no salvage value, how do the payments compare?

Answers: In both cases, you must convert APR to monthly interest (0.15/12) and the term to months (5*12). For a loan the answer is @PMT(10000,0.15/12,5*12) = $237.90. For a lease the answer is @PMT(10000,0.15/12,5*12)/(1+0.15/12) = $234.96.

This is the formula:

$$prin * \frac{(i)}{1-(i+1)^{-n}}$$

where *prin* is the principal; *i* is the periodic interest rate; and *n* is the term.

@PV

@PV(*payment,interest,term*) calculates the present value of an even series of payments at the end of each period. By definition, the present value of a loan is the principal. To convert the calculation to an annuity due, with payments at the beginning of each period, multiply by (1+*interest*):

```
@PV(payment,interest,term)*(1+interest)
```

Example: You have a choice of purchasing a $10,000 piece of equipment and leasing it. If you take out a loan, the monthly payments will be $238 for five years. If you lease, the monthly payments will be $235 for five years. If your cost of capital is 15%, how do the payments compare, assuming no salvage value?

Answers: In both cases you must convert APR to monthly interest (0.15/12) and the term to months (5*12). For a loan the answer is @PV(238,0.15/12,5*12) = $10,004.23. For a lease the answer is @PV(235,0.15/12,5*12)*(1+0.15/12) = $10,001.60. The difference is insignificant because the loan and lease have been calculated on the same terms. In fact, rounding the payments to the nearest dollar is the only reason the present values differ at all.

@PV uses this formula:

$$pmt \quad * \quad \frac{1-(1+i)^{-n}}{i}$$

where *pmt* is the periodic payment; *i* is the periodic interest rate; and *n* is the number of periods.

@TERM (Release 2.0)

@TERM(*payment,interest,future value*) calculates the time required to reach a future value, given regular payments at the end of each period (ordinary annuity) and a periodic interest rate. To convert to beginning-of-period payments (annuity due), divide by (1+*interest*):

```
@TERM(payment,interest,future value)/(1+interest)
```

Example: You can save $1,000 a year. The effective annual percentage rate (see Chapter 1) is 8.75%. How long will it take you to accumulate $10,000 if you make your deposits at the end of the year? How long if you make your deposits at the beginning of the year?

Answers: For end-of-year payments the answer is @TERM(1000,0.0875,10000) = 7.49 years. For beginning-of-year payments the answer is @TERM(1000,.0875,10000) = 6.9 years.

It will take a few months less to accumulate $10,000 if you make your deposits at the beginning of the year instead of at the end.

@TERM uses this formula:

$$\frac{\ln\ (1\ +\ (FV\ *\ i\ /\ pmt))}{\ln\ (1+i)}$$

where ln is the natural logarithm; *FV* is the future value; *i* is the periodic interest rate; and *pmt* is the periodic payment.

Internal Rate of Return and Net Present Value

Internal rate of return and net present value are used to evaluate uneven cash flows. Although the amount of the cash flow may vary, the periods must be regular. If some cash flows occur on a monthly basis, for example, then cash flows (even if 0) must be entered for every month. @IRR calculates the internal rate of return for a series of payments, given an initial outlay. @NPV calculates the net present value of a series of payments, given a specified interest rate. @IRR and @NPV are discussed in detail in Chapter 5.

@IRR

@IRR(*guess,range*) calculates the internal rate of return for an uneven series of cash flows, including an initial outlay, expressed as a negative value. The cash flows may vary, but they must be for the same periods. For example, you will need to use monthly cash flows if there are cash flows after 1 month, after 6 months, and after 10 months. (The values for the intervening months will be 0.) The IRR will be for the same period.

Guess is your estimate of what the IRR might be. In most cases, a guess of 10% (0.01) will work. Range is the range containing the cash flows.

Example: You purchase 100 shares of stock at $100 a share. You receive dividends of $3.25 a share the first year, $2.00 the second, $4.50 the third, $4.00 the fourth, and $5.00 the fifth. At the end of the fifth year, you sell at $140 a share, so the total inflow for the year is $145 per share. What is the internal rate of return?

Answer: As shown in Figure 9.1, @IRR(0.1,B2..B7) = 10.17%.

	A	B	C
1			
2	Cost	(10,000)	
3	Year 1	325	
4	Year 2	200	
5	Year 3	450	
6	Year 4	400	
7	Year 5	14,500	
8			
9	IRR	10.17%	@IRR(0.1,B2..B7)

Figure 9.1. Calculating internal rate of return.

Note: @IRR assumes that cash flows occur at the end of each period. If the first inflow comes at the same time as the initial outflow, subtract it from initial cost.

@IRR calculates internal rate of return by trial and error. You will see an ERR message if it cannot calculate the answer within 0.0000001 after 30 iterations. If this occurs, try changing your guess.

@IRR is explained in detail in Chapter 4. For more information about using @IRR to analyze stocks and bonds, see Chapter 7.

@NPV

@NPV(*range,interest*) returns the value of a series of uneven cash flows at a given interest rate, sometimes called a hurdle rate. The cash flows must be at even intervals, and the period for the interest must match the intervals of the cash flows. That is, if cash flows are monthly, then you must calculate the monthly interest rate, as explained in Chapters 1 and 2.

Like @IRR, @NPV assumes that all cash flows come at the end of each period. If the first cash flow occurs immediately, you must add it to the @NPV of the remaining cash flows, since it is not discounted at all. Unlike @IRR, @NPV does not require you to include the initial outlay. If you do not, the return on the investment exceeds the hurdle rate if the result of the @NPV calculation is greater than the initial outlay. If you do include the initial outlay, the return is more than the hurdle rate if the result of the calculation is greater than zero.

Example: Your daughter Becky is going to college in four years. (She starts at the beginning of the fourth year.) You expect the cost to be $11,000 the first year, $12,000 the second, $13,500 the third, and $14,500 the fourth. How much must you set aside now to cover the cost if you can earn 8% per year?

Answer: As shown in Figure 9.2, the Total cost is $51,000, but you can cover the expense by setting aside $33,220 now.

	A	B	C
1			
2	Becky's College Plan		
3			
4	Year 1	0	
5	Year 2	0	
6	Year 3	0	
7	Year 4	11,000	
8	Year 5	12,000	
9	Year 6	13,500	
10	Year 7	14,500	
11		========	
12	Total	51,000	
13	@NPV	33,220	@NPV(0.08,G3..G9)

Figure 9.2. Calculating the net present value of an uneven series of cash flows.

The formula for @NPV is

$$\sum_{i=1}^{n} \frac{v_1}{(1+int)^i}$$

where $v_1...v_n$ is a series of cash flows; *int* is the interest rate; *n* is the number of cash flows; and *i* is the current iteration (1 through *n*).

@NPV is discussed in detail in Chapter 4. It is also used in analyzing investments in Chapter 7.

Depreciation

1-2-3 includes depreciation @Functions using the following methods: double-declining balance, straight-line, and sum-of-the-year's digits. Release 3 adds a variable declining balance function (@VDB), which can be adapted to the current tax system. With the exception of @VDB, the depreciation functions may require some adaptation to the tax law and business practice. Depreciation is discussed in Chapter 5.

DDB (Release 2.0)

DDB(*cost,salvage,life,period*) calculates the depreciation of an asset using the double-declining balance method. DDB is a method of calculating accelerated depreciation commonly used before 1981, but is now of limited use because of changes in the tax laws. Frequently, businesses switched to the straight-line method at the point it yielded a higher depreciation allowance.

> *Example*: A piece of equipment cost $10,000, has a life of five years, and should have a salvage value of $1,000 when it is fully depreciated. What is the DDB depreciation schedule?
>
> Year 1: @DDB(10000,1000,5,1) = $4,000
> Year 2: @DDB(10000,1000,5,2) = $2,400
> Year 3: @DDB(10000,1000,5,3) = $1,440
> Year 4: @DDB(10000,1000,5,4) = $ 864
> Year 5: @DDB(10000,1000,5,5) = $ 296
>
> Total $9,000
> Salvage Value $1,000
> ======
> $10,000

The formula for @DDB is

$$\frac{BV * 2}{n}$$

where BV is the book value at the beginning of the period; and n is the nth period. See Chapter 5 for a discussion of depreciation.

@SLN (Release 2.0)

@SLN(*cost,salvage,life*) computes annual straight-line depreciation for an asset, where cost is the original cost of the item, salvage is the salvage value at the end of the period, and life is the item's useful life.

Many businesses use straight-line depreciation for internal accounting and reports to shareholders. You can also use straight-line depreciation under the current tax law, but salvage value is not counted. That option may be attractive for businesses that expect low earnings or losses in their early years.

Investment real estate must be depreciated by the straight-line method under the current tax law, but, again, salvage value is not taken into account. Only the structure may be depreciated, not the land on which it stands. The tax law specifies the life for various types of property. @SLN does not prorate depreciation for the first and last years, as required by the law. Depreciation is discussed in Chapter 5.

Example: A piece of equipment costs $10,000 and should have a salvage value of $2,000 at the end of five years. What is the annual depreciation?

Answer: @SLN(10000,2000,5) = $1,600.

SLN uses this formula:

$$\frac{(c - s)}{n}$$

where c is the cost of the property; s is the salvage value at the end of the property's useful life; and n is the useful life of the property in years.

@SYD (Release 2.0)

The sum-of-the-year's digits method of calculating accelerated depreciation for tax purposes was used mainly before 1981. Although the method is now seldom used, 1-2-3 can make the calculation. Depreciation is discussed in Chapter 5.

@SYD(*cost,salvage,life,period*) calculates the depreciation for a given year, using the sum-of-the-year's digits method.

Example: A piece of equipment costs $10,000 and should have a salvage value of $2,000 at the end of five years. What is the depreciation for the second year?

Answer: @SYD(10000,2000,5,2) = $2,133.33.

@SYD uses a complicated-looking formula to calculate depreciation:

$$\frac{(c - s) * (n - p + 1)}{n * (n + 1) / 2}$$

where c is the cost; s is the salvage value; n is the life of the property; and p is the period for which depreciation is being calculated.

This is a complicated way of expressing a simpler idea. The denominator is simply the sum-of-the-year's digits. For an asset with a life of five years, for example, the denominator is

```
1+2+3+4+5 = 15
```

The numerator is the basis in the property (cost − salvage) multiplied by its life. The life is reduced by one for each succeeding year. Thus, for the asset in the example, @SYD(10000,2000,5,1) = $2,666.67 is the calculation for the first year. Or, (10000-2000)*5/15 = $2,666.67, and so on.

@VDB (Release 3)

@VDB, Release 3's variable declining balance function, is the only @Function capable of calculating depreciation under the Modified Accelerated Cost Recovery System (MACRS), the method currently required for tax calculations. You can also use @VDB to calculate accelerated depreciation by other methods. See Chapter 5 for a fuller discussion of MACRS, including methods of making the calculations with earlier releases of 1-2-3.

@VDB provides three critical options, all necessary to calculate depreciation under MACRS:

1. It allows you to prorate depreciation for the first and last periods, as required under MACRS. Under the rules, equipment is depreciated for a half year in its first and last years unless you bought more than 40% of the depreciable assets placed in service during the year during the fourth quarter. In the latter case, you begin depreciating all equipment at the midpoint of the quarter in which it was placed in service. Again, see Chapter 5 for details.

2. You can specify the double-declining balance factor (200%) used by MACRS.

3. Although it does not require you to do so, @VDB allows you to switch to the straight-line method of depreciation at the point in an asset's life where straight-line depreciation yields a higher depreciation allowance than the double-declining balance method. This, too, is the method used by MACRS.

@VDB takes a rather elaborate argument:

```
@VDB(cost,salvage,life,start period,end period,
     [depreciation factor],[switch])
```

This is not as complicated as it might at first appear. In fact, the function is quite naturally suited to MACRS calculations. Cost is simply the original cost of a depreciable asset. Salvage value is not taken into account under MACRS, so that value will be 0. Life is also determined by the MACRS rules. Cars, light trucks, computers, typewriters, and other office equipment are depreciated over five years. Furnishings, such as desks, files, and refrigerators, are depreciated over seven. Only real estate and a few special categories of assets fall into different categories.

Start period and *end period* refer to the asset's age at the beginning and end of the fiscal period being analyzed. Under the midyear rule, the first year's *start period* is 0, and the *end period* is 0.5. Under the midquarter rule, the *start period* is also 0 the first year. The *end period* depends on the quarter the property was placed in service. You can enter it as either a fraction or as a decimal:

First Quarter	7/8 or	0.875
Second Quarter	5/8 or	0.625
Third Quarter	3/8 or	0.375
Fourth Quarter	1/8 or	0.125

For the next year, the *start period* is the previous year's *end period*; the *end period* is that value plus 1, and so on. Under the midyear convention, for example, the first year's *start period* is 0, and the *end period* is 0.5. For the second year, the *start period* is 0.5, and the *end period* is 1.5. And so on.

The last two elements of the argument are optional, and not required for MACRS calculations. [*Depreciation factor*] can be any value greater than 0, but the default is 2, or 200%, which is the double-declining balance factor used under MACRS. [*Switch*] can be either 0 or 1. If it is 0, @VDB switches to straight-line depreciation when it yields a higher depreciation allowance than double-declining balance depreciation. If [*Switch*] is 1, @VDB does not switch to straight-line depreciation. Since MACRS does make the switch, you can omit the switch and accept the default.

Figure 9.3 shows the annual depreciation under the MACRS midyear rule for a $10,000 asset with a life of five years. Note that only a half-year's depreciation is calculated in the first and last years.

For an explanation of how the MACRS calculation works, see Chapter 5.

Math Functions

The math @Functions help with a variety of basic calculations. Here, they are divided into three groups: Basic Math, Logarithms, and Trigonometry. For the most part, these functions are fairly self-explanatory if you understand the basic math. A few basic mathematical concepts are provided along the way.

	A	B	C
1	Equipment Depreciation under MACRS		
2			
3	Cost	10000	
4	Life	5	
5	First year	0.5	
6			
7			
8	Year 1	2000	
9	@VDB(B3,0,0.5,B5)		
10	Year 2	3200	
11	@VDB(B3,0.5,1.5,B5)		
12	Year 3	1920	
13	@VDB(B3,1.5,2.5,B5)		
14	Year 4	1152	
15	@VDB(B3,2.5,3.5,B5)		
16	Year 5	1152	
17	@VDB(B3,3.5,4.5,B5)		
18	Year 6	576	
19	@VDB(B3,4.5,5,B5)		
20		========	
21	Total	10000	

Figure 9.3. Calculating MACRS depreciation with @VDB.

Basic Math

The basic math functions perform basic mathematical tasks, such as finding absolute value, calculating a square root, rounding, and providing the value of *pi* to 10 decimal places. They are generally quite straightforward. Applications are suggested in the examples below.

@ABS

@ABS(x) calculates the absolute, or positive, value of x. @ABS(–10), for example, is 10. @ABS is used to reverse the sign in some annuity calculations and to calculate deviations from the mean in some statistical calculations in Chapter 7.

@INT

@INT(x) returns the integer value of x. For example, @INT(10.7) = 10, and 10*@INT(10.7) = 100. This is in contrast to formatting a cell as Fixed, with 0 decimal places. In that case, the display will be 11, but if you multiply that value by 10, the result will be 107. @ROUND(10.7) will also display 11, but 10*@ROUND(10.7) = 110.

For a practical application of @INT, see the discussion of precise tax calculations for taxable incomes under $50,000 in Chapter 8.

@MOD

@MOD(x,y) calculates the modulus, or remainder, of the division x/y. For example, @MOD(10,3) = 1, because 10/3 = 3 with a remainder of 1.

@MOD can be used with @DATE to calculate the day of the week. If you divide a date number by 7 and get a remainder of 1, the date falls on Sunday; 2 is Monday, 3 is Tuesday and so on. Saturday is 0.

Example: @MOD(@DATE(95,7,4),7) = 3. July 4, 1995, falls on a Tuesday.

@PI

@PI returns the value pi, about 3.141593. For example, the area of a circle with radius r is $pi*r^2$. Thus, the area of a circle with a radius of 3 meters is @PI*3^2 = 28.274334 square meters (rounded). You can also use @PI to convert angle measurements between degrees and radians. (See the trig functions in this chapter.)

@RAND

@RAND generates a random number between 0 and 1. You can copy it into a range of cells. You can use @RAND in combination with other functions and operators to generate numbers in any range. For example, @RAND*1000 generates random numbers between 1 and 1,000.

@RAND recalculates every time the worksheet recalculates. In many models, you will want to freeze the original random numbers. You can do this with the /Range Value command. If you copy your @RAND calculations onto themselves, the values in the range are permanently frozen. If you copy the values to a new range, the new range will be frozen, but the original values will continue to recalculate.

@ROUND

@ROUND(x,n) rounds x to n decimal places. For example, @ROUND(@PI,2) rounds pi to two decimal places: 3.14.

x can be any value; n can be any value between 15 and -15. If n is positive, x is rounded to n decimal places. If n is negative, x is rounded to the positive nth power of 10. For example, @ROUND(x,-2) rounds to the nearest 100 (10^2). Thus, @ROUND(2333,-2) = 2,300; @ROUND(-2333,-2) = -2,300.

Note that @ROUND functions differently from decimal formats and @INT. @ROUND actually rounds the underlying value, not simply the display. Decimal formats, by contrast, round the display, but not the underlying values; other calculations are not affected. @INT actually doesn't round; it simply lops off the numbers to the right of the decimal.

@SQRT

@SQRT(x) finds the square root of x. For example, @SQRT(2) = 1.414214 (rounded). Of course, @SQRT(4) = 2 (exactly). In Chapter 7, @SQRT is used to determine Economic Order Quantity to optimize inventory management.

> **Note:** You can also use a fractional exponent to find the nth root of a number: the nth root of $x = x^\wedge(1/n)$. Thus, the square root of 2 = @SQRT(2) = 2^(1/2) = 1.414214 (rounded). The cube root of 8 = 8^(1/3) = 2 (exactly). The 4th root of 16 = 16^(1/4) = 2 (exactly).

Logarithms

Logarithms are a variation on exponential calculations. If $x = y^n$, then n is the logarithm of x to the base y, and x is the antilogarithm of n. In principle, y could be any value. In practice, only two values are used: base 10 and the theoretically derived constant e, which is approximately 2.718282. Logarithms to the base 10 are called common logarithms; those to the base e are called natural logarithms.

Many logarithmic calculations can be derived from three simple equations:

```
log (x*y) = log (x) + log (y)

log (x/y) = log (x) - log (y)

log (xⁿ) = n * log (x)
```

Logs are not necessary for ordinary multiplication and division in 1-2-3 because the program automatically makes those calculations anyway. However, they are sometimes useful in solving exponential equations. To calculate the term for a lump sum to reach a future value, for example, @CTERM uses this equation, where i is the interest rate:

$$\frac{\ln\ (FV\ /\ PV)}{\ln\ (1\ +\ i)}$$

In Chapters 1 and 2, natural logs are used to solve problems involving continuous compounding. Natural logs are also used in Chapter 6 to solve for the term of an annuity.

@EXP

@EXP(x) is the inverse of the natural logarithm function, @LN(x). That is, it converts a natural log back into an ordinary number. If @LN(x) = y, then @EXP(*y*) = *x*. (The calculation is subject to slight rounding errors if you enter the values directly, rather than making the first calculation on your worksheet, and then using a cell reference in the second.) You can also use @EXP to calculate the natural logarithm constant e: @EXP(1) = 2.718282 (rounded).

Example: Find the cube root of 110,592, given that @LN(x^n) = n*@LN(x).

Answer: You can perform this calculation in three steps as follows. First, @LN(110592) = 3*@LN(x). Then, dividing both sides of the equation by three, you get @LN(110592)/3 = 11.653487/3 = 3.871201 = @LN(x). Finally, use @EXP to determine the value of x: @EXP(3.871201) = 47.999999 = x.

Actually, this is a very slight rounding error. If you make the above calculations using cell references, the result is 48 (exactly). Calculation check: 48^3 = 110,592.

There is an easier way to do this particular calculation: 110592^(1/3) = 48 (exactly). Still, the illustration makes the point. Many logarithmic calculations resolve without using @EXP. However, some mathematical equations use the value e directly. Chapters 1 and 2, for instance, provide examples of using @EXP to solve problems involving continuous compounding.

@LN

@LN(x) finds the natural logarithm of x (that is the log to the base e, the natural logarithm constant). The constant e is approximately 2.718282 (see @EXP). For example, @LN(2) = 0.693147 (rounded). That means that e^0.693147=2 (approximately).

@LN is used in Chapter 6 to solve for term of an annuity with a beginning balance. See @EXP above for an additional example.

@LOG

@LOG(x) calculates the common logarithm of x, or the log to the base 10. For example, @LOG(100) = 2 (exactly), because $100 = 10^2$. Other than the base, @LOG functions much like @LN.

To convert a common log to an ordinary number (the antilogarithm), simply invert the calculation: @LOG(100) = 2; 10^2 = 100. This is the equivalent of the @EXP function for natural logarithms.

Example: Find the cube root of 110,592.

Answer: @LOG(110592)/3 = 1.681241 (rounded) or 10^1.681241 = 47.999974. As with the same example under @EXP, this a slight rounding error. If you use a cell reference in the second calculation (or do the entire calculation in one cell), the answer is exactly 48.

Trigonometric Functions

Trigonometric functions are based on right triangles, but can be applied to any triangle. The three basic ratios used by 1-2-3's trig functions are based on an acute angle of a right triangle:

```
sine (angle) = opposite side/hypotenuse

cosine (angle) = adjacent side/hypotenuse

tangent (angle) = opposite side/adjacent side
```

There are no @Functions for the other three basic trigonometric ratios:

```
cotangent (angle) = adjacent side/opposite side

secant (angle) = hypotenuse/adjacent side

cosecant (angle) = hypotenuse/opposite side
```

These omissions are easily remedied with the following simple ratios:

```
cotangent = 1/tangent

secant = 1/cosine

cosecant = 1/sine
```

1-2-3's trig @Functions measure angles in radians. To convert from radians to degrees, multiply by 180/@PI. To convert from degrees to radians, multiply by @PI/180.

Example: 45(degrees)*@PI/180 = 0.785398 radians. 0.785398(radians)*180/@PI = 44.99999 degrees. The reason the latter calculation does not equal 45 degrees exactly is that the measurement in radians is rounded to six decimal places.

The examples given here all involve right triangles because the purpose is to explain 1-2-3's @Functions rather than to provide a text on trigonometry. As a point of reference, however, it may be useful to provide the Law of Sines and the Law of Cosines. With these two laws, 1-2-3's trig @Functions, some basic algebra, and the certainty that the angles in a triangle always add up to 180 degrees, you can find all of the angles and sides of any triangle if you know either two sides and an angle or two angles and a side.

In these laws, each angle of a triangle is assigned a small letter, and the opposite side is assigned the corresponding capital letter, as shown in Figure 9.4.

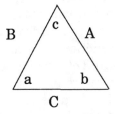

Figure 9.4. Standard labeling for the angles and sides of a triangle.

The Law of Sines states (using 1-2-3 format):

`@SIN(a)/A = @SIN(b)/B = @SIN(c)/C`

The Law of Cosines is easier to follow in standard mathematical notation:

$$A^2 = B^2 + C^2 - 2BC(\cos\ a)$$

$$B^2 = A^2 + C^2 - 2AC(\cos\ b)$$

$$C^2 = A^2 + B^2 - 2AB(\cos\ a)$$

Thus, for example, if you know sides A and B and angle a, you can easily use the Law of Sines to calculate angle b.

According to the Law of Sines:

`@SIN(a)/A = @SIN(b)/B`

Since a, A, and B are known, you can calculate the sine of b by multiplying both sides of the equation by B:

`B*@SIN(a)/A = @SIN(b)`

And, since the arcsine of x is the angle whose sine is x, you can complete the calculation:

`@ASIN(B*@SIN(a)/A) = b`

In less conveniently arranged examples, the algebra can get a little curlier, but it doesn't go past high school Algebra 1. If you are measuring angles in degrees, be sure to make the conversions to and from radians when using 1-2-3's trig functions. 1-2-3's trig functions are also easily adaptable to three-dimensional trig calculations and other more complex trig applications. That, however, is beyond the range of this reference section. If you don't already use trigonometry, the chances are you don't need to, but the equations in any basic trig text should be adaptable to 1-2-3.

@ACOS

@ACOS(x) calculates the arccosine of x. This is the angle whose cosine is x, measured in radians. To convert to degrees, multiply by 180/@PI. The cosine of an acute angle in a right triangle is adjacent side/hypotenuse. Thus, when you know the lengths of the hypotenuse and another side, you can use @ACOS to find the angle in between.

Example: As an airplane takes off, it traverses 1,000 yards on the ground, but actually has traveled 1,100 yards through the air. What is its angle of ascent?

Answers: @ACOS(1000/1100) = 0.429600 radians. @ACOS(1000/1100)*180/@PI = 24.61997 degrees.

@ASIN

@ASIN(x) calculates the arcsine of x. This is the angle, measured in radians, whose sine is x. To convert to degrees, multiply by 180/@PI. The sine of an acute angle in a right triangle is opposite side/hypotenuse. If you know the hypotenuse and the opposite side, you can use @ASIN to find the angle.

Example: The airplane has now traveled 2,000 feet through the air and has reached an altitude of 1,000 feet. What is its average angle of ascent?

Answers: @ASIN(1000/2000) = 0.523599 radians. @ASIN(1000/2000)* 180/@PI = 30 degrees (exactly).

@ATAN

@ATAN(x) figures the arctangent of x. The result is the angle, measured in radians, whose tangent is x. To convert to degrees, multiply by 180/@PI. The tangent of an acute angle in a right triangle is opposite side/adjacent side. If you know these values, you can use @ATAN to determine the angle.

Example: An airplane is at an altitude of 1,000 feet and has traveled 1,750 feet in ground distance. What is its angle of ascent?

Answers: @ATAN(1000,1750) = 0.519146 radians. @ATAN(1000,1750)* 180/@PI = 29.744881 degrees.

@ATAN2

@TAN2(x,y) calculates the four-quadrant arctangent of the angle defined by x and y. This is the angle, measured in radians, of the angle whose tangent is y/x. To convert to degrees, multiply by 180/@PI.

x and y can be any values. If y is 0, @TAN2 returns 0. If both x and y are 0, the function returns an ERR message.

Example: Think of a circle divided in quadrants. The angle bisecting the upper right quadrant is 45 degrees and can be defined by the coordinates 2,2 (or any equal positive coordinates). Moving clockwise, the angle bisecting the next quadrant is -45 degrees, defined by -2,2. The next quadrant is bisected by an angle of -135 degrees, defined by -2,-2. The final quadrant, the upper left, is bisected by a 135 degree angle, defined by 2,-2. The @ATAN2 calculations for these angles are shown in Table 9.1.

Table 9.1. Using @ATAN2 to calculate four-quadrant angles measured in radians and degrees.

Formulas		Radians	*180/@PI		Degrees
@ATAN2(2,2)	=	0.785398	*180/@PI	=	45
@ATAN2(2,-2)	=	-0.785398	*180/@PI	=	-45
@ATAN2(-2,-2)	=	-2.356194	*180/@PI	=	-135
@ATAN2(-2.2)	=	2.356194	*180/@PI	=	135

@COS

@COS(x) finds the cosine of angle x, measured in radians. To convert from degrees to radians, multiply by @PI/180. For example, the cosine of a 30-degree angle is @COS(30*@PI/180) = 0.866025.

The cosine of an acute angle in a right triangle is adjacent side/hypotenuse. If you know the angle and one of these values, you can calculate the other.

Example: An airplane is climbing at a 30-degree angle and has traveled 1,500 feet through the air. How much ground distance has it covered?

Answer: First, convert degrees to radians and calculate the angle's cosine: @COS(30*@PI/180) = 0.866025. Then, calculate the distance travelled using the cosine: x/1500 = 0.866025. Thus, x = 1500*0.866025 = 1299.38016. (The airplane has traveled about 1,300 feet, measured on the ground.)

@SIN

@SIN(x) calculates the sine of x, where x is an angle measured in radians. To convert degrees to radians, multiply degrees by @PI/180. For example, the sine of a 30-degree angle is @SIN(30*@PI/180) = 0.5.

The sine of an acute angle in a right triangle is opposite side/hypotenuse. Thus, if you can measure an angle in degrees or radians and the length of the opposite side or the hypotenuse, you can calculate the third value.

Example: You are installing a television antenna on a flat roof. The instructions say that the guy wires should be installed at a 35-degree angle to a flat surface (the angle opposite the antenna). If the antenna is 20 feet tall, how long are the guy wires?

Answer: First, convert degrees to radians and calculate the angle's sine: @SIN(35*@PI/180) = 0.573576. Then, use the sine value to calculate how long the wires are: 20 feet/x = 0.573576. Thus, x = 20/0.573576 = 34.868936. The guy wires are about 35 feet long, so if you want to install three, you will need at least 105 feet of wire.

@TAN

@TAN(x) computes the tangent of angle x measured in radians. To convert degrees to radians, multiply by @PI/180. For example, the tangent of a 30-degree angle is @TAN(30*@PI/180) = 0.577350.

The tangent of an acute angle in a right triangle is opposite side/adjacent side. If you know the angle and one of these values, you can compute length of the other side.

Example: You are installing a 20-foot television antenna on a flat roof. The instructions say that the guy wires should be at a 55-degree angle to the antenna. How far away from the base of the antenna should you fasten the guy wires?

Answer: Convert degrees to radians and calculate the tangent of the angle: @TAN(55*@PI/180) = 1.428148. Then, use the tangent to find out how far away the guy wires should be fastened: x/20 = 1.428148. This gives x = 20*1.428148 = 28.562960. (The guy wires should be attached about 28.5 feet from the base of the antenna.)

Statistical Functions

The statistical functions perform a variety of ordinary mathematical tasks, such as finding the average (mean) or sum of the values in a range. In most cases, the argument is a range of values, such as monthly sales figures or test scores for students in a class. The range can be identified as a range address (e.g., A1..A20) or as a range name you have assigned using /Range Name Create. Applications are generally straightforward.

Blank cells within ranges are ignored, but it is important to note that labels and 0's evaluate to 0, which counts as an entry. This can cause unwanted results with any of the statistical functions except @SUM. (@SUM simply adds up the values in a range, so 0's don't matter.) If the range contains a NA or ERR message, any of the statistical functions will yield the same result.

This section is divided into two parts. The first covers the basic statistical functions. The second covers standard deviation and variance, which are somewhat more technical.

Basic Statistical Functions

The basic statistical functions include such commonplace calculations as average (mean), the maximum and minimum values in a range, and counting the number of entries in a range. The applications are largely self-explanatory.

@AVG

@AVG(*range*) finds the average, or mean, of the values in a range or list. For example, @AVG(12,19,11,20) = 11.5. You would get the same answer with @AVG(A1..A4) if those values occupied the range. In a range, @AVG ignores blank cells, but labels evaluate to 0, thus altering the calculation.

@COUNT

@COUNT(*range*) counts the number of entries in a range or list. Labels and 0's count, but blank cells do not. For example, @COUNT(1,2,3,4) = 4. In Figure 9.5, @COUNT(A1..B4) = 4, because the double line counts as well as the numbers and labels.

```
            A                        B
1 Hammers                           10
2 Mallets                           26
3                            ============
4 Total                             36
5
6 @COUNT(A1..B4) = 4
```

Figure 9.5. @COUNT(range) calculates the nonblank spaces in a range.

@MAX

@MAX(*range*) returns the highest value in a range or list. Labels count as 0, but blanks are ignored. See the example under @MIN.

@MIN

@MIN(*range*) returns the least value in a range. As with @MAX, labels count as 0, but blanks are ignored. In Figure 9.6, @MAX(B1..B4) = 36. @MIN(B1..B4) = 0, because the double line evaluates to 0. However, @MIN(E1..E4) = 10, because the blank cell E3 doesn't count.

```
          A          B          C          D          E
1 Hammers            10              Hammers            10
2 Mallets            26              Mallets            26
3              ==========
4 Total              36              Total              36
5
6 @MAX(B1..B4)                  36
7 @MIN(B1..B4)                   0
8 @MIN(E1..E4)                  10
```

Figure 9.6. Finding maximum and minimum values in a range with @MAX and @MIN.

@SUM

@SUM(*range*) finds the total of values in a range or list. Blanks and labels count as 0. For example @SUM(1,2,3,4) = 10. In Figure 9.6, above, @SUM(A1..B4) and @SUM(E1..E4) both evaluate to 72 (10 + 26 + 36), because blanks are ignored and labels count as 0.

@SUMPRODUCT (Release 3)

@SUMPRODUCT(*range1,range2,range3*...) multiplies the corresponding values in each range, and then totals the results. The ranges must be the same size and shape; otherwise @SUMPRODUCT returns an ERR message. This function is available only in Release 3.

In Figure 9.7, the values in column A are multiplied by the values in column B. @SUMPRODUCT does not return the values in column C, which are provided to illustrate how the function works. Here, the result is equal to 10*50+20*60+30*70+40*80. The @SUM version of the calculation solves the problem a step at a time; the @SUMPRODUCT formula makes the calculation in a single step.

	A	B	C	D
1			AxB	
2	10	50	500	
3	20	60	1,200	
4	30	70	2,100	
5	40	80	3,200	
6			===========	
7	@SUM(C2..C5)			7,000
8	@SUMPRODUCT(A2..A5,B2..B5)			7,000

Figure 9.7. In Release 3, @SUMPRODUCT multiplies the values in two or more ranges, and then totals the results.

Standard Deviation and Variance

Two statistical calculations, standard deviation and variance, require special attention. Both are measures of the variation of the data being analyzed from the average for a group. The higher the standard deviation or variance, the more widely values for the group vary around the group average.

In statistics, it is important to distinguish between an entire population and a sample of a population for these calculations. The Census Bureau, for example, would survey the entire population of a county, while a pollster would survey a random sample. Statisticians have found that sampling tends to create a downward bias in calculating the degree to which values vary. Thus, they use slightly different formulas for populations, as opposed to samples. If you use the same values, sample standard deviation and sample variance will be somewhat larger than comparable calculations for a population census. However, the difference is small when the size of the sample is greater than 30.

In all releases, @STD and @VAR calculate *population* standard deviation and variance. Release 3 adds @STDS and @VARS for calculating sample variance and sample standard deviation. For earlier releases, formulas are provided below for converting @STD and @VAR to calculations for population samples. Standard deviation and variance are discussed in further detail in Chapter 7.

The next sections give a brief overview of 1-2-3's @Functions for calculations standard deviation and variance, based on the records from Porky's Pig Farm.

The Mathematics of Standard Deviation and Variance

Suppose Porky's Pig Farm wants to analyze the variation in the weights of its pigs. Figure 9.8 shows calculations of population variance, population variance, standard deviation, and sample standard deviation, using the mathematical formulas, rather than @Functions. Standard deviation is the square root of the variance, so it is simplest to explain variance first.

Here is the formula for calculating population variance:

$$\frac{\sum (v_1 - avg)^2}{n}$$

where v_1 is the ith item on the list; avg is the average for the list; and n is the number of items in the list.

The idea is quite a bit simpler than the equation looks. First, find the average for the group (in this case, the pigs' weights). This is 385.3, computed with @AVG in B21. Next, subtract the average from each pig's weight and square the difference. This is done in column C. (The average difference between individuals and the group average is 0 by definition. Although the calculation has more elaborate theoretical underpinnings, squaring the difference yields all positive values.) Finally, add up the sum of the squares and divide by the number of individuals in the population to determine the variance. This calculation appears in C24, using this formula:

```
@SUM(C4..C19)/@COUNT(C4..C19)
```

The population variance is 3,443.07, a number that makes direct sense only if you are comparing it to the variance of another pig population or using it for further calculations.

Population standard deviation is simply the square root of the variance. The mathematical formula for population standard deviation is

$$\sqrt{\frac{\sum (v_1 - avg)^2}{n}}$$

In C27, Porky's makes this calculation using this formula:

```
@SQRT(@SUM(C4..C19)/@COUNT(C4..C19))
```

	A	B	C
1	Porky's Pig Farm		
2			
3		Weight	(B-avg)^2
4	Alberta	404.9	384.16
5	Alfreda	441.9	3203.56
6	Catbaby	375.2	102.01
7	Dusseldorf	366.9	338.56
8	Elvira	478.1	8611.84
9	Elvis	374.7	112.36
10	Emmanuel	422.0	1346.89
11	Fred	312.2	5343.61
12	Grunt	303.1	6756.84
13	Leon	321.0	4134.49
14	Madigan	316.7	4705.96
15	Napoleon	449.9	4173.16
16	Sam	308.7	5867.56
17	Smitty	411.5	686.44
18	Watanabe	397.3	144
19	Zapolski	481.1	9177.64
20			=========================
21	Average	385.3	
22	@AVG(B4..B19)		
23			
24	Population Variance		3,443.07
25	@SUM(C4..C19)/@COUNT(C4..C19)		
26			
27	Population Standard Deviation		58.68
28	@SQRT(@SUM(C4..C19)/@COUNT(C4..C19))		
29			
30	Sample Variance		3,672.61
31	@SUM(C4..C19)/(@COUNT(C4..C19)-1)		
32			
33	Sample Standard Deviation		60.60
34	@SQRT(@SUM(C4..C19)/(@COUNT(C4..C19)-1))		

Figure 9.8. Calculating population standard deviation and variance without @Functions.

If data shown in Figure 9.8 represents the entire population of Porky's Pig Farm, the standard deviation is 58.68 pounds. As a rule of thumb for a population with a normal distribution, about two-thirds of the population will fall within one standard deviation of the average, 95% within two standard deviations, and nearly all will fall within three standard deviations.

If the data in the example are merely a sample of the pigs on Porky's farm, Porky might want to calculate the sample variance and sample standard deviation of the pigs' weights. The mathematical equations are very similar to those for the calculations for a population. To compensate for the downward bias, $n-1$ is substituted for n in the denominator.

$$\textit{Sample variance} = \frac{\sum(v_1 - avg)^2}{n - 1}$$

In C30, this calculation is made with the formula @SUM(C4..C19)/(@COUNT(C4..C19)-1). The result is 3,672.61, somewhat more than the population variance, as expected.

$$\textit{Sample standard deviation} = \sqrt{\frac{\sum(v_1 - avg)^2}{n - 1}}$$

In C33, this calculation is made using the formula @SQRT(@SUM(C4..C19)/(@COUNT(C4..C19)-1)). The result is 60.60, again somewhat higher than the population standard deviation.

Standard Deviation and Variance @Functions

With 1-2-3's @Functions, you can calculate standard deviation and variance without making the sum-of-the-squares calculation in solutions just described. Release 3 provides functions for calculating sample standard deviation and sample variance. With earlier versions, you have to use a more complicated formula, but you can still bypass the sum of the squares. The functions are listed here in alphabetical order.

@STD

@STD(*range*) returns the population standard deviation of the values in the range. Again, it is important to distinguish between population standard deviation and sample standard deviation.

Example: Using the data in Figure 9.8 (without the calculations in column C), Porky's Pig Farm can calculate the population standard deviation of the pigs' weights as shown in Figure 9.9. The answer is 58.68—the same, of course, as the result of making the calculation the long way.

	A	B	C
35	@STD (range)		
36			
37	Population standard deviation		
38	@STD (B4..B19)		58.68

Figure 9.9. Calculating population standard deviation with @STD.

@STDS (Release 3)

In Release 3, @STDS(range) calculates the sample standard deviation in a range of values. Statisticians have found that there is a downward bias in a sample of a population as opposed to a complete census of the population. Thus, a sample standard deviation will be somewhat higher than a population standard deviation, using the same values.

If you have an earlier version of 1-2-3, you can substitute this formula:

@STD (*range*) *@SQRT (@COUNT (*range*) / (@COUNT (*range*) -1))

Example: Suppose that the pig weights shown in Figure 9.8 represent a random sample of the pigs at Porky's Pig Farm. In Figure 9.10, Porky's has calculated the sample standard deviation both ways. In the first, in C41, Porky's uses Release 3's @STDS function. In C44, the calculation is made using the formula given above. The answers, of course, are the same.

	A	B	C
39	@STDS(range) (Release 3.0)		
40			
41	Sample Standard Deviation		60.60
42	@STDS(B4..B19)		
43			
44	Sample Standard Deviation		60.60
45	@STD(B4..B19)*SQRT(@COUNT(B4..B19)/(@COUNT(B4..B19)-1))		

Figure 9.10. Calculating sample standard deviation with Release 3's @STDS function and with a formula that can be used with earlier releases.

@VAR

@VAR(*range*) calculates the population variance of the values in a range. It is often important to distinguish between population variance and sample variance. Sample variance will be somewhat larger than population variance, but the difference is small when the sample is larger than 30.

Example: Suppose that the values for Porky's Pig Farm shown in Figure 9.8 represent the entire population of pigs at the farm. Porky's has already calculated the variance for weights using the mathematical formula. The farm can make the calculation more simply using @VAR, as shown in Figure 9.11. The answer, 3,443.07, of course, is the same.

	A	B	C
46	@VAR(range)		
47			
48	Population Variance		3.443.07
49	@VAR(B4..B19)		

Figure 9.11. Calculating variance with @VAR.

@VARS (Release 3)

In Release 3, @VARS(*range*) computes the sample variance for the values in the range. The outcome of the sample variance calculation will be somewhat higher than the result of a population variance calculation, but the difference is small when the sample is more than 30.

If you do not have Release 3, you can substitute this formula:

```
@VAR(range)*@SQRT(@COUNT(range)/(@COUNT(range)-1))
```

Example: Suppose the pig weights for Porky's Pig Farm, shown in Figure 9.8, represent a random sample of the pigs at the farm, rather than a census of the population. Porky's has already calculated the sample variance mathematically. Figure 9.12 shows the same calculation using @Functions. The calculation in C52 uses Release 3's @VARS function. The calculation in C55 uses the formula above. The 1/100th of a pound difference in the latter calculation is a result of rounding.

	A	B	C
50	@VARS(range) (Release 3.0)		
51			
52	Sample Variance		3,672.61
53	@VARS(B4..B19)		
54			
55	Sample Variance		3,672.61
56	@VAR(B4..B19)*(@COUNT(B4..B19)/(@COUNT(B4..B19)-1))		

Figure 9.12. Calculating sample variance with Release 3's @VARS function and with a formula that can be used with earlier releases.

Database Statistical Functions

A 1-2-3 database is simply a range in which each row includes information about an individual item or person. This is called a record. Specific information about each item or person is entered across the columns of the database. The column entry for each record is called a field. For the database functions to work correctly, each column must be labeled with a heading.

The database statistical functions are similar to the statistical functions described above, except that they allow you to analyze information that meets certain criteria.

Example: Esmerelda's Weight Boutique wants to analyze the results for its patients in September. Each record includes fields recording the patient's name, sex, starting weight, ending weight, and loss, as shown in Figure 9.13. Although you can set up more elaborate criteria, Esmerelda simply wants to distinguish between males and females, as indicated by *m* and *f* in the Sex column.

	A	B	C	D	E
1					
2		Esmerelda's Weight Boutique			
3		September Group			
4					
5	Patient	Sex	Start	End	Loss
6	Aaron, J.	f	178	173	5
7	Black, Q.	m	297	278	19
8	Bronstadt, D.	m	190	172	18
9	Dover, P.	m	240	203	37
10	Harpole, M.	f	145	124	21
11	James, R.	f	151	150	1
12	Kazutsky, B.	f	142	131	11
13	Kramer, A.	f	163	143	20
14	May, A.	m	265	243	22
15	Meltzer, R.	m	203	187	16
16	Ringwalt, F.	m	311	307	4
17	Rogers, L.	f	150	139	11
18	Vaden, R.	m	283	269	14
19	Willis, S.	f	132	122	10

Figure 9.13. A database for Esmerelda's patients in September.

Using this database, Esmerelda can use all of 1-2-3's statistical functions to analyze her patients' progress for the month.

Database @Function Arguments

All database functions (except Release 3's @DQUERY function) require the same argument: (*input,offset,criterion*). Let's look at the components.

The input range is the range that defines the database, including column headings. In Esmerelda's case, this is A5..E19. You can refer to the input range by its address, or you can assign it a name, using the **/Range Name Create** command. In the examples that follow, Esmerelda has assigned the name SEPTEMBER to the range A5..E19.

The offset is the column offset for the data you want to analyze. The left column of the database is 0. For the examples based on Figure 9.13 that follow, Esmerelda will use an offset of 4, indicating the Loss column.

The criterion component of the argument is very flexible. You can use criterion to restrict the analysis to database records that meet one or more specifications. At a minimum, the criterion consists of a column heading in one cell, with a value, label, or formula entered in the cell below. (See Using Database @Functions in Chapter 6 for a full explanation of criteria.)

The criterion range consists of at least two cells. In an argument, you can refer to the range by its address or by its range name. In the examples here, Esmerelda uses two criterion ranges:

> Sex
> m

and

> Sex
> f

The first, in D24..D25, identifies records with *m*, for male, in the Sex field. Esmerelda has assigned this range the name MEN. The second, in D27..D28, identifies records with *f*, for female, in the Sex field. This is named WOMEN in the examples below. Figure 9.14 shows the criteria entries on the worksheet.

	A	B	C	D	E
22	Criteria				
23					
24	Men			Sex	
25				m	
26					
27	Women			Sex	
28				f	

Figure 9.14. Setting criteria for database @Functions.

In summary, most of Esmerelda's database calculations will use the argument (SEPTEMBER,4,MEN) or (SEPTEMBER,4,WOMEN). For example, @DAVG(SEPTEMBER,4,MEN) yields the average weight loss for men enrolled in the program during September.

@DAVG

@DAVG(*input,offset,criterion*) finds the average value in a certain column (offset) of the entries in a database that meet the specifications in the criterion range.

Example: Esmerelda's Weight boutique wants to know the average weight loss of its patients for September, broken down by gender. Esmerelda can make the calculation as shown in Figure 9.15.

	A	B	C	D
30	@DAVG(input,offset,criterion)			
31				
32	Average loss, men			18.57
33	@DAVG(SEPTEMBER,4,MEN)			
34				
35	Average loss, women			11.29
36	@DAVG(SEPTEMBER,4,WOMEN)			

Figure 9.15. Calculating database averages for records that meet criteria.

Men lost an average of 18.7 pounds in September. Women lost an average of 11.29 pounds.

@DCOUNT

@DCOUNT(*input,offset,criterion*) counts the nonblank entries in a certain column (offset) of a database that meet certain criteria.

Example: Esmerelda's Weight boutique has already calculated the average weight loss for men and women. In Figure 9.16, Esmerelda counts the number of men and women in the program in September. The column offset doesn't really matter in this case, since there are no blank cells in the database, but Esmerelda selects 4, the column designating each patient's weight loss. There were seven men and seven women in the program in September.

	A	B	C	D
38	@DCOUNT(input,offset,criterion)			
39				
40	Number of men			7
41	@DCOUNT(SEPTEMBER,4,MEN)			
42				
43	Number of women			7
44	@DCOUNT(SEPTEMBER,4,WOMEN)			

Figure 9.16. Counting the records in a database that meet criteria.

@DGET (Release 3)

@DGET(*input,offset,criterion*) returns a value or label from a database record that meets certain criteria. If there is more than one record that meets the criteria, @DGET returns an ERR message. @DGET is available only in Release 3.

Example: Andrew May, a former patient at Esmerelda's Weight boutique, inquires how much weight he lost in September. Esmerelda uses the same database shown in Figure 9.13 to look up the information. The input range is A5..E19, which is assigned the range name SEPTEMBER. The offset is 4, where each patient's weight loss is listed. She enters this criterion range to find May's record, and assigns the name range PATIENT:

Patient
May, A.

Now she can find May's record by entering @DGET(SEPTEMBER,4,PATIENT), as shown in Figure 9.17. May lost 22 pounds in September. To find the record for another patient, Esmerelda can simply change the second line of the criterion range.

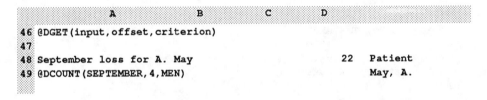

	A	B	C	D	
46	@DGET(input,offset,criterion)				
47					
48	September loss for A. May			22	Patient
49	@DCOUNT(SEPTEMBER,4,MEN)				May, A.

Figure 9.17. Finding a value for a specific record with @DGET.

@DMAX

@DMAX(*input,offset,criterion*) returns the largest value in the offset column of a database that meets the criteria.

Example: See @DMIN.

@DMIN

@DMIN(*input,offset,criterion*) returns the smallest value in the offset column of a database that meets the criteria.

Example: Esmerelda's Weight Boutique wants to find the maximum and minimum weight losses for men and women during September. Esmerelda can use @DMAX and @DMIN to extract the information from her database, as shown in Figure 9.18.

	A	B	C	D
51	@DMAX(input,offset,criterion)			
52	@DMIN(input,offset,criterion)			
53				
54	Maximum loss, men			37
55	@DMAX(SEPTEMBER,4,MEN)			
56				
57	Minimum loss, men			4
58	@DMIN(SEPTEMBER,4,MEN)			
59				
60	Maximum loss, women			21
61	@DMAX(SEPTEMBER,4,WOMEN)			
62				
63	Minimum loss, women			1
64	@DMIN(SEPTEMBER,4,WOMEN)			

Figure 9.18. Using @DMAX and @DMIN with a database.

In September, the men in the program lost 4 to 37 pounds; the women lost 1 to 21.

@DQUERY (Release 3)

@DQUERY(*function,ext-arguments*) is used with /Data External commands to send a command to an external database. These commands are available only in Release 3. @DQUERY is used in a criterion range to retrieve records from an external data base.

The function argument is the name of a command in the external database. It can be a literal string, enclosed in quotation marks, a reference to a cell that contains a label, or a formula that evaluates to a string. The name of the external command will appear in the cell where @DQUERY is entered. For example, if you enter @DQUERY("IN-VOICES",[ext-arguments]) in B2, INVOICES appears in that cell.

The extension arguments are the arguments required by the external database command.

> **Note:** @DQUERY recalculates only when you use /Data Query Del; /Data Query Extract; /Data Query Modify Extract; or /Data Query Unique.

@DSTD

@DSTD(*input,offset,criterion*) calculates the population standard deviation of a group that meets the criteria. Standard deviation is a measure of the degree to which individuals in a population vary from the average (mean) for the population. @DSTD treats the subgroup that meets the criteria as a population; the calculation is based on the average for the subgroup, *not on the average of the population as a whole*. For example, if you use @STD to segregate males from females in a population, @DSTD measures the degree to which individual males differ from the average for males and the degree to which individual females differ from the average for females.

Example: Esmerelda's Weight Boutique wants to compare the variation weight loss for men with that for women. Using the same worksheet shown in Figure 9.13, Esmerelda makes the calculations shown in Figure 9.19. Since the standard deviation for men is higher than the standard deviation for women, Esmerelda concludes that there is more variation for men than for women when weight loss is measured in pounds. (Actually, if you make an additional calculation to determine weight loss as a percentage of starting weight, standard deviation of the percentages for men and women turns out to be about

	A	B	C	D	E
66	@DSTD(input,offset,criterion)				
67					
68	Standard deviation, men			9.194053	
69	@DSTD(SEPTEMBER,4,MEN)				
70					
71	Standard deviation, women			6.734013	
72	@DSTD(SEPTEMBER,4,WOMEN)				

Figure 9.19. Using @DSTD to calculate the standard deviation of groups within a population.

the same.)

@STDS (Release 3)

@STDS(*input,offset,criterion*) calculates the sample standard deviation for a population sample that meets the criteria specified in the argument. As with @DSTD, the calculation is based on the average for the group within the sample that meets the criteria, not the average for the entire sample.

@STDS is available only with Release 3 of 1-2-3. For earlier versions, substitute this formula to get the same result:

```
SQRT(@DCOUNT(argument)/(@DCOUNT(argument)-1))
```

Example: Suppose that the data shown in Figure 9.13 is a random sample of patients at Esmerelda's Weight Boutique, rather than a summary of patients' progress for September. Esmerelda has labeled the database SAMPLE. This allows her to make more general conclusions about her patients. To determine the sample standard devia-

	A	B	C	D	E
74	@DSTDS(input,offset,criterion)			(Release 3.0)	
75					
76	Sample standard deviation, men			9.930712	
77	@DSTDS(SAMPLE,4,MEN)				
78					
79	Sample standard deviation, women			7.273565	
80	@DSTDS(SAMPLE,4,WOMEN)				

Figure 9.20. Calculating sample standard deviation with Release 3.0 (see text for Release 2.2 and earlier).

Note: The sample standard deviation is slightly higher than the standard deviation for both men and women.

tion for men and women, Esmerelda makes the calculations shown in Figure 9.20, using 1-2-3 Release 3.

For earlier releases, use these formulas: @DSTD(SAM-PLE,4,MEN)*@SQRT(@DCOUNT(SAMPLE,4,MEN)/(@DCOUNT(SAMPLE,4,MEN)-1)) and @DSTD(SAMPLE,4,WOMEN)*@SQRT(@DCOUNT(SAMPLE,4,WOMEN)/(@DCOUNT(SAMPLE,4,WOMEN)-1))

@DSUM

@DSUM(*input,offset,criterion*) totals the values in the offset column for records in the database that meet the criteria.

Example: Esmerelda's Weight Boutique wants to know the total lost by men and the total by women in September. Using the database shown in Figure 9.13, Esmerelda makes the calculations shown in

	A	B	C	D	E
86	@DSUM(input,offset,criterion)				
87					
88	In September, 7 men lost			130	
89	@DSUM(SEPTEMBER,4,MEN)				
90					
91	In September, 7 women lost			79	
92	@DSUM(SEPTEMBER,4,WOMEN)				

Figure 9.21. Using @DSUM to figure subtotals for a group.

Figure 9.21. During the month, seven men lost a total of 130 pounds, and seven women lost a total of 79.

@DVAR

@DVAR(*input,offset,criterion*) calculates the variance of the values in the offset column for the records in the database that meet the criteria. This is the subgroup's variance from the average of the subgroup, not from the average for the entire database.

	A	B	C	D	E
92	@DVAR(input,offset,criterion)				
93					
94	Variance, men			84.53061	
95	@DVAR(SEPTEMBER,4,MEN)				
96					
97	Variance, women			45.34693	
98	@DVAR(SEPTEMBER,4,WOMEN)				

Figure 9.22. Calculating variance for database records that meet certain criteria.

Example: Esmerelda's Weight Boutique wants to determine the variance of weight loss for men and women during September. Using the database shown in Figure 9.13, Esmerelda makes the calculations shown in Figure 9.22.

As expected, the variance for men is higher than for women. This means that there was more variation in the number of pounds lost for men than for women.

@DVARS (Release 3)

In Release 3, @DVARS(*input,offset,criterion*) calculates the sample variance of the values in the offset column for the records in a database that meet the criteria. Sample variance is a measure of the variation of a subset of a total population, as compared for the average for the subset that meets the criterion.

For releases before 3.0, you can use this formula to calculate sample variance:

```
@DVAR(argument)*@DCOUNT(argument)/(@DCOUNT(argument)-1)
```

Example: Suppose Esmerelda's Weight Boutique database, shown in Figure 9.13, represents a random sampling of patients, rather than a

	A	B	C	D	E
100	@DVARS(input,offset,criterion)			(Release 3.0)	
101					
102	Sample variance, men			91.30349	
103	@DVARS(SAMPLE,4,MEN)				
104					
105	Sample variance, women			52.90476	
106	@DVARS(SAMPLE,4,WOMEN)				

(See text for Release 2.2 and earlier)

Figure 9.23. Determining sample variance with Release 3's @DVARS function.

population census for September, and that Esmerelda has assigned the range name SAMPLE to the database. Using @VARS with Release 3, Esmerelda can calculate the sample variances for men and women as shown in Figure 9.23. For earlier releases, these formulas— @DVAR(SAMPLE,4,MEN)*@DCOUNT(SAMPLE,4,MEN)/(@DCOUNT (SAMPLE,4,MEN)-1)) and @DVAR(SAMPLE,4,WOMEN) *@DCOUNT (SAMPLE,4,WOMEN)/(@DCOUNT(SAMPLE,4,WOMEN)-1)) —yield the same results.

As expected, the sample variance for both groups is slightly higher than the variances calculated with @DVAR.

Date and Time Functions

1-2-3 assigns a serial date number between 1 (January 1, 1900) and 73050 (December 31, 2099) to every date in the 20th and 21st centuries. Beginning with Release 2.0, the program also assigns a time value between 0.000000 (midnight) and 0.999988 (11:59:59 p.m.). The time value is a decimal fraction of a day. Thus, 1:03.15 p.m., April 7, 1990 = 32970.543924, because 32970 is the serial number for the date and 0.543924 is the serial number for the time.

Date and time @Functions allow you to manipulate these serial numbers for a variety of useful purposes. The most common application is probably calculating the interval between two dates or times. You could use a date function, for example, to calculate when an invoice is due, given today's date and due date of 30 days. With a time function, you can determine the interval between two times. Before Release 2.0, 1-2-3 offered date functions, but not time functions.

Date and time serial numbers do not make much sense by themselves, but the display is easily converted into a more intelligible form with /Range Format Date and /Range Format Date Time commands. The options are illustrated in Table 9.2. (The same options are available with /Worksheet Global Format command.) In all cases, the date/time serial number is 32970.543924, representing 1:03.15 p.m., April 7, 1990.

Table 9.2. Date and time formats.

Format	Example
Date 1 (DD-mm-YY)	07-Apr-90
Date 2 (DD-MM)	07-Apr
Date 3 (MMM-YY)	Apr-90
Date 4 (Long Intn'l)	04/07/90
Date 5 (Short Intn'l)	04/07
Time 1 (HH:MM:SS AM/PM)	01:03:15 PM
Time 2 (HH:MM AM/PM)	01:03 PM
Time 3 (Long Intn'l)	13:03:15
Time 4 (Short Intn'l)	13:03

Four date formats and four time formats are offered. With Time 1 and Time 2, time is calculated on a 12-hour clock. For the international time options, a 24-hour clock is used. To format a cell to display 07-Apr-90, for example, you would enter /Range Format Date 1 (DD-MM-YY). To format for Time 4, enter /Range Format Date Time 4 (Short Intn'l).

The following explanation of the time and date @Functions suggests practical applications.

@DATE

@DATE(*yy,mm,dd*) returns the serial value of the date indicated by the argument. If the cell is not assigned a date format, the date will appear as a serial number. If the cell is formatted, the result will appear in the date format selected, such as 17-Jan-91.

The argument must meet these specifications:

- *yy* can be any integer between 0 (1900) and 199 (2099).

- *mm* can be any integer between 1 and 12.

- *dd* can be any integer between 1 and 31. However, @DATE returns an ERR message if you enter an invalid date, such as February 31.

Examples: @DATE(91,1,10) = 33248 = 10-Jan-91 shows how @DATE works. @DATE is often used to calculate the interval between two dates. For example, if you issue an invoice on January 10, due in 30 days, you can calculate the due date this way: @DATE(91,1,10)+30 = 33278 = 09-Feb-91. You can use a similar technique to calculate the number of days between July 4 and Christmas: @DATE(91,12,25)-@DATE(91,7,4) = 174 days.

You can also use @DATE in conjunction with @MOD to calculate the day of the week a certain date falls on. When you divide the serial date number by 7, the remainder (or modulus) will be 0 if the date falls on Saturday, 1 for Sunday, and so on up to 6 for Friday. For example, @MOD(@DATE(91,2,9),7) = 0. February 9, 1991, falls on a Saturday, so you might give your customer in the earlier example until February 11 to pay the invoice.

@DATEVALUE (Release 2.0)

@DATEVALUE(*string*) returns the serial date value of a label that looks like a date. The label can be a literal string or a formula that evaluates to a string. It must be in one of the date formats listed in Table 9.4. @DATEVALUE can be used with information imported from another program, such as a word processor, as well as with 1-2-3 data.

Example: Suppose you have entered '25-Dec-91 in A1 and '4-Jul-91 in B1. (Note the apostrophes designating labels.) To determine the number of days between July 4 and Christmas, you can enter @DATEVALUE(A1)-@DATEVALUE(B1) = 174 days.

@DAY

@DAY(*date number*) converts a serial date number to the day of the month, an integer between 1 and 31.

Examples: Here are three ways @DAY can be used: @DAY(32963) = 31, because 32963 is March 31, 1990; @DAY(@DATEVALUE("25-Dec-91")) = 25; @DAY(@NOW) = 4 if entered on July 4.

@D360 (Release 3)

In Release 3, @D360(*start date,end date*) converts date calculations to a 360-day calendar (12 months of 30 days each). The 360-day calendar is used by some banks and other businesses for calculating interest, determining when payments are due, and so on. The start and end dates must be in a proper 1-2-3 date format. If the start date comes after the end date, @D360 returns a negative number.

Examples: You deposit $10,000 on September 15. If the bank pays 12% interest, compounded daily on a 360-day basis, how much will be in the account on November 1? First, determine the number of days your money earns interest: @D360(@DATE(91,9,15),@DATE(91,11,1) = 46 days. Then, determine the daily interest rate: Daily interest rate = 0.10/360 = 0.033333%. Finally, calculate how much you will have: Future value = 10000*(1+0.033333%)^46 = $10,154.49.

You can also use @D360 to determine whether invoices are overdue, based on a 360-day calendar. Suppose, for example, you have used @DATE to enter invoice dates in column A. The entry in A5 is @DATE(91,10,11). You can use this formula to determine whether the invoice has been outstanding for more than 30 days: IF(@D360(A5,@TODAY)=30,"Overdue",""). If the invoice has been outstanding for more than 30 days, the formula returns Overdue. If not, it returns a blank.

@HOUR (Release 2.0)

@HOUR(*time number*) converts a serial time number to an hour, based on a 24-hour clock. A serial time number can be any value between 0.000000 (midnight) and 0.999988 (11:59:59 p.m.). Usually, the time number is supplied by another time @Function, such as @TIME or @NOW. @HOUR ignores numbers to the left of the decimal, which are reserved for date serial numbers.

@HOUR might be useful, for example, to calculate the frequency of transactions by hour. If a bank has a record of the times of transactions, for example, it might want to break the results down by hour to determine how many tellers to have on hand during various periods of the day.

Examples: @HOUR(@TIME(15,33,22)) = 15, because 15,33,22 represents 3:33:22 p.m., which falls in the 15th hour on a 24-hour clock. @HOUR(0.648171) also returns 15, because the decimal in the argument is the time serial number for 3:33:22 p.m. @HOUR(@NOW) returns the current hour.

@MINUTE (Release 2.0)

@MINUTE(*time number*) extracts the minute after the hour from a time serial number. Usually, the time number is supplied by another time @Function.

Examples: @MINUTE(@TIME(15,33,22)) = 33, because 15,33,22 represents 3:33:22 p.m. @MINUTE(0.648171) also returns 33, because the decimal in the argument is the time serial number for 3:33:22 p.m. @MINUTE(@NOW) returns the current minute.

@MONTH

@MONTH(*date number*) calculates the month from a date serial number, which is usually supplied by another Date @Function. The result can be any integer from 1 (January) to 12 (December).

> *Examples*: @MONTH(32963) = 3, because 32963 is March 31, 1990. @MONTH(@DATEVALUE("25-Dec-91")) = 12. @MONTH(@NOW) = 7 if entered anytime in July.

@NOW (Release 2.0)

@NOW, which uses no argument, returns the current date and time serial number from your computer's clock. You can display the result in any of the date and time formats. @NOW is often used in conjunction with other date and time functions. In Release 2.0, @NOW replaces the @TODAY function in earlier releases, which provided only a date stamp. (Note that @TODAY still works in Releases 2.0 and 2.2, even though it is not mentioned in the manual. @TODAY works slightly differently in Release 3, although the result is the same. See the entry on @TODAY for details.)

It is important to remember that @NOW recalculates every time you recalculate your worksheet. If you have set calculation on Automatic, @NOW recalculates every time you enter a new value. In some situations, obviously, this will wreak havoc with your worksheet. You can use the /Range Value command to convert @NOW to a pure value and end the recalculations. If you want to @NOW to continue recalculating, copy the values to a new range. If you want to freeze @NOW where it is permanently, copy the value range onto itself. You should do this *immediately* after entering a formula containing @NOW. Otherwise, @NOW may continue to recalculate when you don't intend for it to, and you may not be able to recover the original result.

> *Example*: At 11:45:40 a.m. on March 30, 1990, you entered @NOW and froze the value with /Range Value. The display depends on the cell

format. Examples are provided in Table 9.3. Regardless of the format, however, 1-2-3 continues to make calculations based on the full date and time serial number.

Table 9.3. Sample displays for the display of @NOW.

Format	Result
General	32963.490046
Time 1 (HH:MM:SS AM/PM)	11:45:40 AM
Date 1 (DD-MMM-YY)	31-Mar-90

@SECOND (Release 2.0)

@SECOND(*time number*) returns an integer from 0 to 59, indicating the seconds portion of a date-time number. The time number is usually provided by another time and date function.

Examples: @SECOND(@TIME(11,45,40)) = 40, because 40 is the seconds portion of the time argument 11,45,40. @SECOND(0.6455) = 31, because 0.6455 is the time number for 2:29:31 p.m.

@TIME (Release 2.0)

@TIME(*hour,minutes,seconds*) returns the time number, based on a 24-hour clock, indicated by the argument. This function is often used to calculate elapsed time. Hours can be any integer between 0 (midnight) and 23 (11 p.m.). Minutes and seconds can be any integer between 0 and 59.

If the cell containing the formula is assigned the general format, the result will be a decimal between 0.000000 (midnight) and 0.999988 (11:59:59 p.m.). Note that these values represent a decimal fraction of a day. Thus, to convert elapsed time to hours, you must multiply by 24. With the /Range Format Date Time command, you can display the result in a more intelligible format, such as 11:45:40 AM.

Example: An attorney works on a case from 9:30 a.m. to 11:45 a.m. How much is the bill if he or she charges $100 an hour?

Answer: To solve this problem, you must subtract the starting time number from the ending time number, multiply by 24 (to convert the time number to hours), and then multiply by $100 to determine the total bill: @TIME(11,45,0)-@TIME(9,30,0))*24*100 = $225.

If you simply want to display the elapsed time, however, the multiplication is not necessary: @TIME(11,45,0)-@TIME(9,30,0) = 0.1783.

This seemingly unintelligible number is actually a fraction of a 24-hour day. You can use the /Range Format Date Time 3 (Long Intn'l) command to convert it to a much more readable form: 02:15:00. However, the underlying value is still expressed as a fraction of a day, not as 2 hours and 15 minutes or 2.25 hours. Thus, further calculations can yield unexpected results if you do not fully understand the date and time functions.

@TIMEVALUE (Release 2.0)

@TIMEVALUE(*string*) converts a label that looks like a time in one of 1-2-3's time formats into a time number. The string can be a literal string enclosed in quotation marks, a reference to a cell that contains a label, or a formula that evaluates to a string.

Example: @TIMEVALUE("11:45:00 AM") = 0.48958 in General format. In Time format, however, the formula returns 11:45:00 AM. See the discussion at the end of the last section for an explanation of making calculations using time numbers.

@TODAY (Varies by Release)

@TODAY returns the date number for the current date in all releases of 1-2-3, but it generates the number slightly differently in Releases 2.0, 2.1, and 2.2. (It is not included in the manuals for these releases, but it still works.)

In earlier releases, @TODAY simply generates the date number. In the releases beginning with 2.0, time functions were added to the program, and the @TODAY function changed slightly. If you enter @TODAY in these releases, the display in the control panel will be @INT(@NOW). This makes no practical difference. The function still returns the date number. In Release 3, @TODAY and @NOW function independently. Thus, when you enter @TODAY, that is what appears in the control panel, but you still get the same result.

In all cases, @TODAY returns the date number. In a format assigned a General format, it will be a number between 1 (January 1, 1900) and 73050 (December 31, 2099). If you have assigned a Date format to the cell, the result will be displayed in a more familiar format, such as 31-Mar-90.

@YEAR (Release 2.0)

@YEAR(*date number*) returns a two- or three-digit number representing the year indicated by a date number. (To convert an @YEAR calculation to a four-digit year, add 1900.) For example, a date number that falls in 1991 returns the value 91. A date number that falls in 2025, returns 125. The date number is usually supplied by another date function.

Examples: @YEAR(33597) = 91, because 33597 is the date number for December 25, 1991. @YEAR(@DATE(91,12,25)) = 91, because the @DATE function also returns the date number for December 25, 1991. @YEAR(@TODAY) or @YEAR(@NOW) = the current year. To convert an @YEAR calculation, add 1990: @YEAR(33597)+1900 = 1991 and @YEAR(@DATE(125,12,25))+1900 = 2025.

Logic Functions

Logic @Functions allow you to write conditional formulas and macros. By far, the most powerful is @IF. This function allows you to make one calculation if a condition is true and another if it is false. @IF is used extensively throughout this book. Most of the other logic functions basically test for certain conditions and are useful mainly in macros and complex formulas.

@FALSE

@FALSE returns the logical value 0 when a logic formula is false. @FALSE can be used in any logic calculation, but it is most often used in macros. @FALSE takes no argument.

Example: The formula @IF(E15>1000,@TRUE,@FALSE) returns a 1 if the value in E15 is greater than 1,000, a 0 if it is not. You would get the same result if you entered @IF(E15>1000,1,0), but @TRUE and @FALSE make it clearer what the calculation means.

@IF

@IF(*condition,x,y*) returns x if the condition evaluates to true, y if it evaluates to false. You can use any of 1-2-3's logic operators with @IF: =, <, >, <=, >=, <>, #AND#, #OR#, and #NOT#.

Examples: @IF(A5>10000,A5,0) returns the value in A5 if it is greater than 10,000; the formula returns 0 if the value in A5 is less than or equal to 10,000.

@IF(A5>10000#AND#B5<=5,A5*B5,@ERR) returns +A5*B5 if the value in A5 is greater than 10,000 *and* the value in B5 is less than or equal to 5. If *either* of the conditions is false, the formula returns an ERR message.

Within the argument for @IF, *x* and *y* can also be conditions. This is called nesting. Suppose, for example, that you are grading students' papers. Scores above 90 rate an A, scores above 80 rate a B, and scores above 70 rate a C. If a student's score is assigned the range name SCORE, you can use this formula to determine the grade: @IF(SCORE>=90,"A",@IF(SCORE>=80,"B",@IF(SCORE>=70,"C", "Needs Work"))).

This formula returns A if SCORE is greater than or equal to 90, B if SCORE is less than 90 but greater than or equal to 80, C if SCORE is greater less than 80 but greater than or equal to 70, and Needs Work if SCORE is less than 70. This formula is not hard to understand if you break it down into its components:

1. First the formula determines whether SCORE is greater than or equal to 90. If it is, it returns A. If not, it evaluates the next condition.

2. If SCORE is greater than or equal to 80, the formula returns B. If not, it moves to the next condition.

3. If SCORE is greater than 70, the formula returns C. If not, it returns Needs Work.

You can build quite elaborate formulas this way. However, it is often easier to break down conditional calculations into separate cells. Figure 9.24 shows the same calculation. The result is the same, but the formulas are easier to follow.

@IF is used in Chapter 5 to calculate depreciation under the Modified Accelerated Cost Recovery System (without Release 3's @VDB function).

	A	**B**	**C**
1	Score	Grade	Calculations
2	85	+C2	@IF(SCORE>=90,"A",C3)
3			@IF(SCORE>=80,"B",C4)
4			@IF(SCORE>=70,"C","Needs Work")

Figure 9.24. Breaking an @IF formula into its components.

It is also used to clean up loan amortization schedules in Chapter 6, and for precise income tax calculations in Chapter 8.

@ISAFF (Release 2.0)

@ISAFF(*function name*) tests whether an add-in @Function is available. The function returns 1 (true) if the function is available, or a 0 (false) if it is not. @ISAFF is used in macros to branch to an error message or to a command to attach an add-in program if the function is not available.

The function name can be a literal string, enclosed in quotation marks, a reference to a cell that contains a label, or a formula that evaluates to a string. Do *not* include the @ sign in the function name. For example, if you have an tax add-in program that includes the function @MRATE to calculate your marginal tax rate, you would enter @ISAFF("MRATE"), not @ISAFF("@MRATE").

> **Note:** @ISAFF returns a 0 (false) if you ask for a regular @Function such as @SUM, because the 1-2-3 functions are not add-ins.

@ISAPP (Release 2.0)

@ISAPP(*name*) is used in macros to determine whether the named add-in program is attached. If it is not, you can branch to an error message or to an attach command. @ISAPP returns 1 (true) if the named add-in is attached, or 0 (false) if it is not.

The *name* in the argument is the file name of the add-in program, without the .ADN extension. The name can be a literal string, enclosed in quotation marks, a reference to a cell that contains a label, or a formula that evaluates to a string. For example, to test whether Allways is attached, you would enter @ISAPP("ALLWAYS").

> **Note:** @ISAPP can identify only add-ins that can be invoked with /Add-in Invoke. It cannot recognize add-ins that contain only @Functions. In addition, some add-ins contain several files that have different names than the add-in itself. For example, an add-in called Finance might actually consist of files called LEASES.ADN and LOANS.ADN. In that case, you would have to test for LEASES and LOANS separately.

@ISERR

When a calculation returns an ERR message, the result ripples through the worksheet, so that all cells that are dependent on the original calculation also return ERR messages. You can use @ISERR to block this ripple effect or to set a condition for a branch command in a macro.

@ISERR(*x*) returns 1 (true) if *x* is the value ERR; otherwise it returns 0 (false). It is often used to eliminate ERR messages resulting from division by 0.

Example: You want to divide the value in E5 by the value in E6, then use the result in further calculations. If the value in E6 is 0, +E5/E6 returns an ERR message. However, @IF(ISERR(E5/E6),0,E5/E6) returns 0 if E6 is 0, or the result of the division if E6 is any other value. You will no longer get ERR messages from any other formulas that depend on this calculation.

@ISNA

Like ERR messages, the effect of NA (not available) messages ripples through your worksheet. Any formula or cell reference that refers to a cell that returns NA also returns NA. However, ERR messages can crop up for many reasons; NA will not appear unless you have entered @NA or a formula that evaluates to @NA. Thus, NA messages are less likely than ERR messages to turn up in unexpected places.

Nevertheless, if you need to test for NA messages, in either a formula or a macro, you must use @ISNA. @ISNA(x) returns 1 (true) if x is an NA message; otherwise, it returns 0 (false). A simple logical condition, such as E10=@NA will always evaluate to 0 (false).

Example: @IF(@INSA(E5),0,E5) returns 0 if E5 contains NA, or the contents of E5 if it does not.

@ISNUMBER

@ISNUMBER(x) determines whether x is a value. If x is a number or a blank, @ISNUMBER returns 1 (true). If x is a label or other string, the function returns 0 (false). @ISNUMBER is primarily used in macros to ensure that data referred to by a formula are of the appropriate type, but it can be used in any logic function.

Example: In A36, you enter @IF(@ISNUMBER(A35),A35,@ERR). If A35 contains a value, the formula returns that value. If A35 is blank, the formula returns 0. If A35 contains a label or other string, the formula returns ERR.

@ISRANGE (Release 3)

If you enter a formula that contains an invalid range address or range name, 1-2-3 returns an ERR message. In Release 3, @ISRANGE provides an error check against this error. The function tests to determine whether the argument range is a valid range name or address. If it is, the function returns 1 (true); if not, it returns 0 (false). @ISRANGE is most naturally used in a logic formula, such as one using @IF function.

Examples: @ISRANGE(ZZ1..ZZ10) returns a 0, because ZZ is not a valid column address. @ISRANGE(TAX) returns a 1 if you have assigned the range name TAX to a range on your worksheet; otherwise it returns 0.

If you are making a reference to a different worksheet, an @ISRANGE function might look like this: @ISRANGE(<<TAXES_90.WK3>>TAX). This formula will return a 1 if the worksheet named TAXES_90.WK3 includes a range named TAX; otherwise, it returns 0.

@IF(@ISRANGE(TAX),@SUM(TAX),"Calculate") returns the total for the range named TAX if that is a valid range; otherwise, it returns Calculate, advising you that you must calculate your taxes by another method.

@ISSTRING (Release 2.0)

@ISSTRING(x) determines whether x is a label or other string. If x is a number or a blank @ISSTRING returns 0 (false). If x is a label or other string, the function returns 1 (true). @ISSTRING is usually used in macros to ensure that data referred to by a formula are of the right kind, but it can be used in any logic formula.

Example: In A36, you enter @IF(@ISSTRING(A35),A35,@ERR). If the entry in A35 is a label or other string, the formula returns that string. If A35 contains a value or is blank, the formula returns ERR.

@TRUE

@TRUE the logical 1 (true). @TRUE can be used in any logic formula, but it is most often used in macros.

Example: The formula @IF(E15>1000,@TRUE,@FALSE) returns a 1 if the value in E15 is greater than 1,000, a 0 if it is not. You would get the same result if you entered @IF(E151000,1,0), but @TRUE and @FALSE make it clearer what the calculation means.

String Functions

String functions allow you to manipulate strings within your worksheet. Generally, a string is a label; that is, any entry that is not a value. A string can be any text, including letters, numbers, punctuation marks, and special characters. If used directly in a formula or macro, the string must be enclosed in quotation marks. A string can also be a reference to a cell that contains a label, or a formula or @Function that evaluates to a string.

@CHAR (Release 2.0)

@CHAR(x) generates the character numbered x in the Lotus International Character Set (LICS). x can be any integer between 1 and 255. Values outside of the range result in ERR messages. The LICS codes are listed in the appendix of your manual.

Examples: The English pound sign (£) is character 163, so you can generate this character by entering @CHAR(163).

You can also generate extended strings. To get £100, for example, you would enter @CHAR(163)&"100". Note that the string must be enclosed in quotation marks. In addition, the @CHAR function must be in the form of a formula. Thus, to use @CHAR to create a string that begins with a label, you must make the entry in this format: +"label"@CHAR(*x*).

@CLEAN (Release 2.0)

@CLEAN(*string*) strips unprintable characters from a string, including ASCII codes 1-32, attribute characters, and the merge character. This is most often used to remove characters imported from another program or another source. The string may be a literal string (enclosed in quotation marks) or the range name or address of a cell containing a label. It can also be a formula or an @Function that evaluates to a string.

@CODE (Release 2.0)

@CODE(*string*) returns the LICS code for the first character of a string. The string can be a literal string, enclosed in quotation marks, or the range name or address of a cell containing a label. It can also be a formula or an @Function that evaluates to a string.

Examples: @CODE("d") returns 100, the code for lowercase d. @CODE("Lotus 1-2-3") returns 76, the code for an uppercase L.

See the appendix of your manual for more information on the Lotus International Character Set.

@FIND (Release 2.0)

@FIND(*search string,string,start number*) finds the position of the search string in a string. This function is most useful when used in conjunction with @LEFT, @MID, @REPLACE, or @RIGHT.

The search string and the string can be a literal string, enclosed in quotation marks, a reference to a cell that contains a label, or a formula that evaluates to a string. @FIND is case sensitive, which means that uppercase and lowercase letters are not interchangeable. If you ask @FIND to search for an "f", it will bypass "F".

The start number is the offset at which you want @FIND to begin counting. It is important to note that the offset for the first character in a string is 0. In the string William Faulkner, for example, W is start number 0, i is 1, the first l is 2, and so on.

Examples: @FIND("F","William Faulkner",0) = 8 because F occupies the 8th position in the string, starting with W as position 0. @FIND("f","William Faulkner",0) = ERR, however, because there are no lowercase f's in William Faulkner.

If you have entered William Faulkner in A1, you can use @MID and @FIND to extract the author's last name with this formula: @MID(A1,@FIND(" ",A1,0)+1,100) = Faulkner. This formula locates the space (" ") at offset 7, adds 1, taking you to the F in Faulkner, then returns the remainder of the string. See the entry under @MID for details.

@LEFT (Release 2.0)

@LEFT(*string,n*) extracts the left n characters from a string. The string can be a literal string (enclosed in quotation marks), the range name or address of a cell that contains a label, or a formula that evaluates to a string.

Example: @LEFT("ANTIDISESTABLISHMENTARIANISM",4) = ANTI.

@LEFT is most useful in combination with formulas or other functions. The example in the manual, for instance, suggests combining the first three letters of a customer's last name with a Zip code to create an account number. If the entry in A4 is Abrams, Ann and the entry in D4 is the Zip code '019156, then @LEFT(A4,3)&D4 returns Abr09156. (The manual does not mention that the Zip code must be entered as a label.)

Other examples of uses for @LEFT include functions such as @VLOOKUP and criteria ranges for database statistical functions.

@LENGTH (Release 2.0)

@LENGTH(*string*) calculates the number of characters in a string, including spaces and punctuation.

    Example: @LENGTH("ANTIDISESTABLISHMENTARIANISM") = 31.

@LOWER (Release 2.0)

@LOWER(*string*) converts a string to lowercase letters. Punctuation and numbers are not affected.

    Example: @LOWER("Joe's Bar & Grill #2") = joe's bar & grill #2.

@MID (Release 2.0)

@MID(*string,start number,n*) returns *n* characters in a string, beginning with the start number. The string can be a literal string, enclosed in quotation marks; a reference to a cell that contains a label; or a formula that evaluates to a string.

The start number is the number of characters to the right occupied by the first character you want @MID to return. It is important to note that the first character in the string is 0, rather than 1. For example in the string TEST, T is position 0, E is 1, and S is 2.

If you want to extract the end of a string but don't know exactly how many characters follow the start number, use a large number for *n*. @MID will return the remainder of the string. If you enter 0 for *n*, @MID returns an empty string.

Examples: @MID("Joe's Bar & Grill",6,3) = Bar. @MID("Joe's Bar & Grill",6,100) = Bar & Grill.

@MID can be used with @FIND to locate part of a string to the right of a particular character. Suppose, for example, that the cell A1 contains the string William Faulkner. You can use this formula to return the author's last name: @MID(A1,@FIND(" ",A1,0)+1,100), where A1 identifies the cell containing the string William Faulkner; @FIND sets up the function to find the first occurrence of a search string; " " tells @FIND to locate the first blank space in the string; +1 adds 1 to the result to move to the first character of the last name; 0 instructs @FIND to begin counting at offset 0 (i.e., the W in William); and 100 is a large number, so that @MID will return Faulkner's entire last name.

See @FIND for further explanation of that function.

@N (Release 2.0)

@N(*range*) returns the first value in a range. If the first cell in the range contains a value, @N returns that value. @N returns a 0 if the first cell in the range contains a label, a blank or a 0. If the first-cell entry is @NA or @ERR, @N returns NA or ERR, respectively. @N is used primarily for error trapping in macros, to ensure that the range contains the appropriate type of data.

Example: The range D2..E2 contains the entries Smith and 100. @N(D2..E2) returns 0.

@PROPER (Release 2.0)

@PROPER(*string*) converts the first letter of each word in a string to uppercase and all others to lower case. Numbers and punctuation marks are not affected, although punctuation can yield unexpected results. The string can be any literal string (enclosed in quotation marks). It can also be the range name or address of a cell that contains a label, or a formula, or an @Function that evaluates to a string.

Example: @PROPER("joe's bar & grill") yields Joe'S Bar & Grill. The S in Joe's is capitalized because @PROPER takes it to be the beginning of a new word.

@REPEAT (Release 2.0)

@REPEAT(*string,n*) duplicates a string *n* times. The string can be a literal string (in quotation marks). It can also be a cell that contains a label, or a formula, or an @Function that evaluates to a string. *n* can be any positive integer.

Examples: @REPEAT("Test ",5) yields Test Test Test Test Test. (Be sure to include the space within the quotation marks, or you will get TestTestTestTestTest.) REPEAT("=",10) yields ==========.

Note: @REPEAT differs from the backslash (\) repeat command. The backslash repeats a character or string until the current cell is filled. @REPEAT generates the specified number of repetitions, regardless of column width.

@REPLACE (Release 2.0)

@REPLACE(*old string,start,n,new string*) removes *n* characters from the old string, beginning at start, and replaces them with a new string.

Old string can be a literal string, enclosed in quotation marks; a reference to a cell that contains a label; or a formula that evaluates to a string. The start number is the offset at which you wish to remove *n* characters. The left character of a string is offset 0. The new string is the string you want to insert.

Example: @REPLACE("William Faulkner",8,8,"Shakespeare") yields William Shakespeare. The replacement begins with offset 8, occupied by the F in Faulkner, and the eight characters in Faulkner are removed. The string Shakespeare is substituted in their place.

Note: You can use @FIND to locate the start character.

@RIGHT (Release 2.0)

@RIGHT(*string,n*) returns the last *n* characters in the string.

Example: @RIGHT("University of Texas",5) = Texas.

@S (Release 2.0)

@S(*range*) returns the label in the first cell of a range. If the first cell in the range is blank or contains a value, @S returns an empty string. If the first cell in the range contains @NA or @ERR, @S returns NA or ERR, respectively. @S is used primarily for error trapping in macros, to make sure that a range contains the appropriate type of data.

Example: If the range D4..D5 contains the values 1 and 2, @S(D4..D5) returns a blank. If D4 contains the label Texas, @S returns Texas.

@STRING (Release 2.0)

@STRING(x,n) converts a value to a string with n decimal places, converting the value into a label.

Example: @STRING(987.654789,2) = 987.65. 2+(@STRING,2) = 2 because the value of a string is 0.

@STRING truncates the decimal places rather than rounding them. Thus, @STRING(1.11999999,2) = 1.11.

@TRIM (Release 2.0)

@TRIM(*string*) removes extraneous spaces from a string. These include leading, trailing, and double spaces.

Example: @TRIM(" Joe's Bar & Grill ") = Joe's Bar & Grill.

@UPPER (Release 2.0)

@UPPER(*string*) converts all letters in a string to uppercase. Punctuation and numbers are unaffected.

Example: @UPPER("Joe's Bar & Grill #2") = JOE'S BAR & GRILL #2.

@VALUE (Release 2.0)

@VALUE(*string*) converts a string that looks like a value to its numerical value. You cannot include operators within the string.

Examples: @VALUE("26.75") = 26.75; @VALUE("$1.89") = 1.89; @VALUE("15%") = 0.15; 2*@VALUE("26.75") = 53.5; and @VALUE("2")+@VALUE("2") = 4. However, @VALUE("2+2") = ERR.

Special Functions

Special functions serve a variety of purposes. @HLOOKUP and @VLOOKUP are extremely useful for extracting information from a table, based on certain information. @VLOOKUP, for example, is used to look up information from depreciation tables in Chapter 5 and from tax tables in Chapter 8. @@, new with Release 2.0, also has very practical uses, as discussed in Chapters 5 and 8. Most of the other special functions are used in macros to check on various conditions.

@@ (Release 2.0)

@@(*cell reference*) is an indirect cell pointer. The argument is the address of a cell that contains a label identifying another cell or range address. This can be an address entered as a label (e.g., A1, *not* the formula +A1) or a range name. This can be useful in a formula when you want to identify a cell or range by a label in another cell. The trick here is that in formulas, references to cells that contain labels evaluate to 0. By contrast, a label referred to by @@(*cell reference*) returns the contents of the *range* identified by the cell reference.

Example: Esmerelda's Weight Boutique has run up the worksheet shown in Figure 9.25. The actual losses for women and men are shown in columns E and F. Esmerelda has assigned the range name WOMEN to E8..E14 and the range name MEN to F8..F14. These range names have also been entered as labels in B7..B10.

	A	B	C	D	E	F
1						
2		Esmerelda's Weight Boutique				
3		September Group				
4						
5	Calculation	Sex	Result		Women	Men
6	==					
7	@AVG(@@(B7))	Women	14			
8	@AVG(@@(B8))	Men	16		10	22
9	@AVG(B9)	Women	0		14	22
10	@AVG(B10)	Men	0		22	3
11					19	14
12					1	16
13					11	19
14					21	16

Figure 9.25. Using @@ within formulas.

In A7, the formula @AVG(@@(B7)) returns the correct average for the range WOMEN. In A9, however, the formula @AVG(B9) returns 0, because, without the @@ function, the label Women in B7 evaluates to 0. The same applies to MEN.

For more practical applications of @@, see the discussion of the Modified Accelerated Cost Recovery System in Chapter 5 and the tax calculations in Chapter 8.

@CELL (Release 2.0)

@CELL("*attribute*",*address*) returns information about the specified attribute of the cell or range identified by the address. You can use this in macros with other functions—usually @IF—to determine whether the target cell meets certain criteria. Table 9.4 shows the attributes @CELL accepts.

Example: {IF@CELL("type";PROFIT)="b"}{BEEP}{QUIT} causes a beep and terminates the macro if the first cell of the range named PROFIT is blank.

Table 9.4. Attribute arguments for @CELL and @CELLPOINTER.

Attribute	Result
"address"	Absolute cell address (e.g., $A$1).
"col"	Column number as a value, from 1 to 256 (e.g., 1 for column A, 5 for column E, and so on).
"color"	(Release 3) Returns 1 if the cell is formatted for color, and 0 if it is not.
"contents"	Contents of the cell.
"coord"	(Release 3) Returns absolute cell address, including worksheet letter, column letter, and row number.
"filename"	The name of the filename that includes the cell, including the path.
"format"	Returns the cell format, with 0 15 decimal places as follows:

C##	Currency
F##	Fixed
G	General
P##	Percent
S##	Scientific notation
,##	Commas
+/-	Format
D1-D9	Date formats
T	Text
H	Hidden
L	Label
A	Automatic
-	Color
()	Parentheses

Table 9.4. Continued.

Attribute	Result
"parentheses"	(Release 3) Returns 1 if the cell is formatted for parentheses, and 0 if it is not.
"prefix"	Returns the leading symbol for the following cell formats:

'	Left-aligned label
"	Right-aligned label
^	Centered label
\	Repeating label
|	Nonprinting label

No symbol if the cell is empty or contains a value.

Attribute	Result
"protect"	Returns 1 if the cell is protected, and 0 if it is not.
"row"	Returns the row number, from 1 to 8192.
"sheet"	(Release 3) Returns the worksheet letter as a number (1 for worksheet A, 2 for worksheet B, and so on).
"type"	Returns the type of data in the cell as follows:

b	blank cell
v	value
l	label

Attribute	Result
"width"	Returns the column width.

@CELLPOINTER (Release 2.0)

@CELLPOINTER("*attribute*") works exactly like @CELL, except that it returns information about the current cell instead of information about the cell at the address in the @CELL argument. "attribute" can be any of the arguments listed in Table 9.4. The argument must be enclosed in quotation marks.

Example: {IF@CELLPOINTER("type")="b"}{BEEP}{QUIT} causes a beep and terminates the macro if the current cell is blank.

@CHOOSE

@CHOOSE(*n,list*) selects the nth item in a list. The first item in the list is number 0, so the second item is 1, the third is 2, and so on. The items in the list must be separated by commas, and they can be any combination of values, strings, and range references that return a value or a string. Unlike many other @Functions, however, @CHOOSE will not accept a simple range reference as a list.

Example: Figure 9.26 shows a table of stock numbers, items, and prices. @CHOOSE(A4-1000,C3,C4,C5,C6) = 3.95. A4 is the stock number for hammers, 1001. That value minus 1000 = 1. Thus, @CHOOSE moves down one row and selects 3.95 in C5, which is the price of hammers, because C3 is offset 0, C4 is offset 1, and C5 is offset 2, and so on.

Note: Although the argument (A4,C3..C6) would work in most @functions calling for a list or range, @CHOOSE will not accept it.

```
              A            B          C
  1
  2   Stock #  Item           Price
  3      1000  Mallets          10.95
  4      1001  Widgets           3.95
  5      1002  Chisels           5.95
  6      1003  Screwdrivers      4.95
  7
  8   @CHOOSE(A4-1000,C3,C4,C5,C6) =   3.95
```

Figure 9.26. Using @CHOOSE to select an entry from a list.

@COLS (Release 2.0)

@COLS(*range*) counts the number of columns in a range. Range can be a range address or a range name. This is useful for setting printing margins.

Example: @COLS(A1..E6) returns 5. If A1..E6 is named TABLE, @COLS(TABLE) yields the same result.

@COORD (Release 3)

@COORD(*worksheet,column,row,absolute*) builds a cell address from the values in the argument. Worksheet and column can be any integers between 1 and 256; 1 represents worksheet A or column A, 2 represents B, and so on. Row can be any row number from 1 to 8,192.

The absolute argument, an integer from 1 to 8, determines which references within the argument are absolute and which are relative, as shown in Table 9.5.

Table 9.5. The effect of absolute arguments in @COORD.

Value	Worksheet	Column	Row	Example
1	Absolute	Absolute	Absolute	$A:A$1$
2	Absolute	Relative	Absolute	$A:A$1
3	Absolute	Absolute	Relative	$A:$A1
4	Absolute	Relative	Relative	$A:A1
5	Relative	Absolute	Absolute	A:$A$1
6	Relative	Relative	Absolute	A:A$1
7	Relative	Absolute	Relative	A:$A1
8	Relative	Relative	Relative	A:A1

@COORD is not very useful by itself, since it would be easier just to enter the cell address directly. However, in the argument you can use cell addresses and functions, such as @IF and @VLOOKUP, to determine the values, so that the result depends on other entries within your worksheets. The outcome can be used in conjunction with other formulas and functions, such as @@.

Examples: @COORD(3,2,10,1) = $C:$B$10 and @COORD(3,2,10,4) = $C:B10.

@ERR

@ERR is seldom used alone, but it is useful for error trapping, particularly in logic functions. For example, the formula @IF(B2>100,@ERR,B2) will return an ERR message if the value in B2 is more than 100 or the value of B2 if the value is 100 or less. The advantage is that @ERR ripples through your worksheet calculations, and an ERR message will appear in any cells that depend on the erroneous calculation.

@EXACT (Release 2.0)

@EXACT(*string1,string2*) determines whether the two strings match exactly. If the strings do not match exactly, @EXACT returns 0 (false); if the strings do match, it returns 1 (True). @EXACT is more precise than the logical operator =, because it distinguishes between uppercase and lowercase letters. It also counts leading, trailing, and double spaces, as well as accents. @EXACT is often used to compare user input strings with valid responses.

Examples: @EXACT("Joe's Bar & Grill","Joe's Bar & Grill") = 1. However, @EXACT("Joe's Bar & Grill","joe's bar & grill") = 0.

@HLOOKUP

@HLOOKUP(*criterion,range,row offset*) looks up a value in a lookup table, based on the criterion. The operation of @HLOOKUP is similar to that of @VLOOKUP, except that @HLOOKUP searches across the top row of the lookup table, while @VLOOKUP searches down the left column. A simple example is provided in the entry under @VLOOKUP. The example here is intended to suggest a more practical application.

The @HLOOKUP argument consists of three parts:

1. criterion is the lookup criterion.

2. range is the range of the table.

3. row-offset is the row from which the value will be selected.

The first row of the lookup table must be a series of values listed in ascending order. The function searches across the first row of the table until it finds the largest value not greater than the criterion, and then selects the value x rows below, as specified by the row offset. Remember that the row offset for the first row is 0. An offset of 1 returns the value one row down, and so on. If the criterion is larger than the highest number in the lookup row, @HLOOKUP returns the offset value corresponding to the highest number in the lookup row.

Example: Porky's Pig Farm can use @HLOOKUP to calculate depreciation under the Modified Accelerated Cost Recovery System (MACRS) as shown in Figure 9.27. The MACRS depreciation schedule for property depreciated under the half-year rule, provided by the IRS, is shown below the double line. MACRS divides most equipment into classes with lives of three, five, or seven years, as indicated by the entries in C12..E12. The depreciation for each class for each year is listed below. The range C12..E20 has been assigned the range name MACRS. For a full discussion of MACRS, see Chapter 5.

Above the double line, depreciable assets are listed in column A, original cost is listed in column B, MACRS class (or life) is in column

	A	B	C	D	E
1					
2	1990 MACRS Depreciation for Porky's Pig Farm				
3					
4	Item	Cost	Class	Year	Dep
5	Computer	10,000.00	5	2	3,200.00
6	Refrigerator	795.00	7	3	139.05
7	Farrowing eqpt.	32,500.00	3	2	14,446.25
8	Truck	15,250.00	5	7	0.00
9					
10	Total				7,358.55
11	===				
12		Year		3	5	7
13			1	33.33%	20.00%	14.29%
14			2	44.45%	32.00%	24.49%
15			3	14.81%	19.20%	17.49%
16			4	7.41%	11.52%	12.49%
17			5	0	11.52%	8.93%
18			6	0	5.76%	8.92%
19			7	0	0	8.93%
20			8	0	0	4.46%

Figure 9.27. Calculating MACRS depreciation with @HLOOKUP.

C, and the year for which depreciation is being calculated is listed in column D. Under MACRS, most equipment and light vehicles are classified as five-year property, so 5 is entered under Class for the computer and truck. Furnishings, including refrigerators, are depreciated over seven years, and certain equipment, including equipment used for hog breeding, is depreciated over three years. The entries for these items are made accordingly.

With this information in place, Porky's can use a simple @HLOOKUP formula to calculate the depreciation for each item. The formula in E5, depreciation for the computer, is +B5*@HLOOKUP(C5,$MACRS,D5). The formula breaks down like this:

+B5* recalls the cost of the computer, listed in B5, and sets up the multiplication by the rest of the formula

@HLOOKUP sets up the @HLOOKUP function

C5	recalls the class from column C, in this case 5, because the computer is a five-year property; this is the criterion
$MACRS	is an absolute reference to the lookup table; the absolute reference allows you to copy the formula down column E; this is the range
D5	recalls the depreciation year from column D, in this case year 2; this is the row offset

Thus, the @HLOOKUP formula looks across the top row of the lookup table (MACRS) until it finds 5 (the class), drops down two rows (year), and returns 32.00%. This value is multiplied by the cost: 10,000*32.00% = 3,200.00.

You can copy the formula in E5 down column E, because the references to class and year are relative, but the reference to the lookup table ($MACRS) is absolute. The resulting formulas are shown in Figure 9.28. The formula for the truck, now in its seventh year, returns 0, because the truck has aged out of the depreciation schedule.

	E
5	+B5*@HLOOKUP (C5, $MACRS, D5)
6	+B6*@HLOOKUP (C6, $MACRS, D6)
7	+B7*@HLOOKUP (C7, $MACRS, D7)
8	+B8*@HLOOKUP (C8, $MACRS, D8)

Figure 9.28. Formulas for calculating depreciation from Figure 9.27, using @HLOOKUP.

@INDEX

@INDEX(*range,column offset,row offset*) returns the value or label from the cell identified by the column and row offsets. The range is a range name or address that specifies of the lookup range. The column offset is the number of columns to the right from which @INDEX retrieves an entry. The row offset is the number of rows down. As usual, the left column and top row of the range are 0. A column offset of 1 returns the entry from the second column, and so on.

Sometimes databases or tables do not lend themselves to using @HLOOKUP or @VLOOKUP. The first row and/or column, for example, may not contain values in ascending order. In these cases, you can use @INDEX to specify a column and row offset independently of the values and labels in the table. You can also use formulas to determine the offsets, based on calculations that are independent of the table.

Example: Esmerelda's Weight Boutique has set up a database that ranks its women and men patients for September by the amount of weight each has lost. Now Esmerelda can use @INDEX to extract the names and weights of the top losers, as shown in Figure 9.29. She has assigned the range name WOMEN to A13..E20 and the range name MEN to A23..E30. Note that the range names include the table headings Women and Men, so that the row offset for the first row of data is 1, but the column offset for column A, which contains the names, is 0.

The formulas in B9..D9 are shown in Figure 9.30. In B8, @INDEX(WOMEN,0,1) returns the name Harpole, M., the top female weight loser, because the offset 0,1 returns the entry from column A in the first record in the range WOMEN. Similarly, @INDEX(WOMEN,4,1) returns Harpole's weight loss, because column offset 4, is column D, where her loss is recorded, and 1 is the row offset for the first record in the range. For men, the formulas in B9 and D9 return Dover, P. and 37 for the same reasons.

@INFO (Release 3)

@INFO("*attribute*") is a programmer's tool that allows you to check current system information in macros. For example, you can use @INFO to check whether there is enough RAM left to execute a macro, to check on current directory, or to check on the current recalculation mode.

In the argument, the attribute must be enclosed in quotation marks. The attributes available for @INFO are shown in Table 9.6.

	A	B	C	D	E
1					
2		Esmerelda's Weight Boutique			
3		September Group			
4					
5					
6	Top Losers				
7		Name		Loss	
8	Women	Harpole, M.		21	
9	Men	Dover, P.		37	
10					
11	Patient	Sex	Start	End	Loss
12					
13	Women				
14	Harpole, M.	f	145	124	21
15	Kramer, A.	f	163	143	20
16	Kazutsky, B.	f	142	131	11
17	Rogers, L.	f	150	139	11
18	Willis, S.	f	132	122	10
19	Aaron, J.	f	178	173	5
20	James, R.	f	151	150	1
21					
22					
23	Men				
24	Dover, P.	m	240	203	37
25	May, A.	m	265	243	22
26	Black, Q.	m	297	278	19
27	Bronstadt, D.	m	190	172	18
28	Meltzer, R.	m	203	187	16
29	Vaden, R.	m	283	269	14
30	Ringwalt, F.	m	311	307	4

Figure 9.29. Using @INDEX to extract information from a database.

	A	B	C
6	Top Losers		
7		Name	Loss
8	Women	@INDEX(WOMEN,0,1)	@INDEX(WOMEN,4,1)
9	Men	@INDEX(MEN,0,1)	@INDEX(MEN,4,1)

Figure 9.30. @INDEX formulas for extracting information from Figure 9.29.

Table 9.6. Attribute arguments for @INFO (Release 3).

Attribute	Result
"directory"	Current directory
"memavail"	Available memory
"mode"	Current mode: 0 WAIT 1 READY 2 LABEL 3 MENU 4 VALUE 5 POINT 6 EDIT 7 ERROR 8 FIND 9 FILES 10 HELP 11 STAT 13 NAMES 99 Other modes
"numfile"	Number of active files
"origin"	Cell at the top left corner of the screen, as of the most recent recalculation, as an absolute address
"osreturncode"	Value returned by the most recent /System command or {SYSTEM} advanced macro command
"osversion"	Current operation system version
"recalc"	Returns the strings "Automatic" or "Manual", depending on the current recalculation mode
"release"	Release number, upgrade level, and revision number of current 1-2-3 product
"system"	Name of the operating system
"totmem"	Total memory available (both amount currently available and amount already used)

@NA

@NA allows you to flag any calculations for which data are not available. Suppose, for example, that the range E1..E12 contains monthly sales but that sales for December are not yet available. Cell E14 contains the formula @SUM(E1..E12), to calculate sales for the year. If you enter @NA in E12 for December sales, NA will appear in E12. The @SUM calculation will also return NA, because the necessary information is not available. Like @ERR, @NA ripples through your worksheet. Any further calculations that depend on the annual total will also return NA.

You can also use @NA in logic formulas. For example, the formula @IF(B>50#OR#B5<0,B5,@NA) returns the value in B5 if B5 contains a value other than 0. The formula returns NA if B5 contains a 0, is blank, or contains a label.

@ROWS (Release 2.0)

@ROWS(*range*) counts the number of rows in a range. Range can be a range address or a range name.

Example: @ROWS(A1..A5) returns 5. If A1..A5 is named TABLE, @COLS(TABLE) yields the same result.

@SHEETS (Release 3)

In Release 3, @SHEETS(*range*) returns the number of worksheets in a given range. The range can be an address or a range name.

Release 3 introduces three-dimensional ranges, which can cover two or more consecutive worksheets in a file. The address of a three-dimensional range includes the worksheet letters of the first and last worksheets in the range, as well as the first and last cells for each worksheet. For example, A:A1..D:F20 includes the ranges A1..F20 in worksheets A, B, C, and D.

Example: @SHEETS(PAYROLL) = 4 if PAYROLL identifies the range A:A1..D:F20.

@VLOOKUP

@VLOOKUP(*criterion,range,column offset*) looks up a value in a lookup table, based on the criterion. @VLOOKUP is particularly useful for tax and depreciation tables, as explained in Chapters 8 and 5, respectively. The operation of @VLOOKUP is similar to that of @HLOOKUP, except that @VLOOKUP searches down the left column of a lookup table, while @HLOOKUP searches across the top row of the table. A simple lookup example is provided here; a more complex example is discussed under @HLOOKUP.

The argument consists of three parts:

1. criterion is the lookup criterion.

2. range is the range of the table.

3. column offset identifies the column from which the value will be selected.

The first column of the lookup table must be a series of values listed in ascending order. (Use /**D**ata **S**ort to sort the table if the left column values are not in ascending order.) The function searches down the first column of the table until it finds the largest value not greater than the criterion, and then selects the value x columns to the right, as specified by the column offset. Remember that the column offset for the first column is 0. An offset of 1 returns the value one column to the right, and so on.

Example: Figure 9.31 shows a database listing stock numbers in ascending order in column A, item labels in column B, and prices in column C. The range A3..C6 is assigned the range name STOCK. You can use @VLOOKUP to determine either the item name or price for any stock number, as shown below.

@VLOOKUP(1002,STOCK,1) = Widgets, because the function looks down column A until it finds 1,002, then returns the entry one column to the right.

@VLOOKUP(1003,STOCK,2) = 5.95, because the entry two columns to the right of 1003 is 5.95, which is the price of chisels.

	A	B	C
1			
2	Stock #	Item	Price
3	1001	Mallets	10.95
4	1002	Widgets	3.95
5	1003	Chisels	5.95
6	1004	Screwdrivers	4.95
7			
8	@VLOOKUP(1002,STOCK,1) =	Widgets	
9	@VLOOKUP(1003,STOCK,2) =		5.95

Figure 9.31. Using @VLOOKUP to retrieve entries from a lookup table.

Note: If you enter a number higher than 1004 as the criterion, @VLOOKUP will return the corresponding entry for 1004, Screwdrivers, because the function accepts the smallest number in the lookup column that is not greater than the criterion. For the same reason, a criterion of 1002.5 will return the corresponding entry for Widgets. @VLOOKUP returns an ERR message if the criterion is smaller than the lowest value in the lookup column.

Index

About the Author

Quick Guide to Financial Formulas for 1-2-3 Users is Steve Adams eighth book on computer software. Other titles include *Quicken in Business, Using Dollars and Cents, Personal Financial Planning,* and *Get Rich! Real Estate.* He has also written half a dozen software manuals and dozens of articles and software reviews for regional and national publications.

Mr. Adams is a full-time writer living in Raleigh, NC. He graduated from the University of North Carolina at Chapel Hill and did graduate work at State University New York, Stonybrook.

Inside Lotus 1-2-3 Macros
Revised and Expanded
by Richard Ridington and Scott Tucker

"Whether you're a heavy 1-2-3 user who's still trying to dig deeper into the arcane corners of Lotus macros or a casual user who's grown tired of having sand kicked in your face by the 1-2-3 guru bullies, this book's for you."

–Jim Seymour
Columnist, *PC Magazine*

The classic macro guide, now revised and expanded to cover new macro features in Lotus Release 2.2

Macros are the revolutionary hidden productivity tools of Lotus 1-2-3, the number one best-selling spreadsheet program. In Release 2.2, Lotus development Corporation has added new macro commands: unlimited macro names, a Macro Library Manager, a "macro recorder," and enhanced techniques for debugging macros.

Now, with this definitive guide, 1-2-3 users of all levels can take full advantage of Release 2, 2.01, and 2.2 macros. For novices who want to write their first macros or developers who need to know the intricacies of macro file I/O commands, this book has the information and the solutions. Topics randge from automating 1-2-3 tasks in order to save time and increase efficiency to developing full-fledged turnkey operations.

Every aspect of 1-2-3's macro facility (through Release 2.2) is covered with detailed tutorials, tips and suggestions, running margin notes, and a comprehensive index.

Book:
ISBN: 0-13-463522-1   Price: $29.95

Book/disk:
ISBN: 0-13-471434-2   Price: $49.95

The Essential Lotus Companion

1-2-3 *Spreadsheet Design* provides sound professional guidelines for creating truly valuable spreadsheets, ones that can be trusted for accuracy and revisited for easy re-use and revision.

22 practical rules for effective spreadsheet design clearly illustrate how you can create:

- Spreadsheets that are correct, free of hidden values, and that contain built-in checks that make your work more accurate

- Models that you—or someone else—can go back to weeks, months, or even years later to use and modify

- Spreadsheets that can grow large yet remain easy to understand, with detailed instructions and clarified assumptions.

Build spreadsheets that are simple, sensible, and free of error!

"A few pleasant hours with this little book made a significant improvement in my spreadsheet style."

—Michael Vitale, Assistant Professor
Business Administration, Harvard Business School
(from the previous edition)

///*BradyLine*

Insights into
tomorrow's technology from the
authors and editors of Brady

You rely on Brady's bestselling computer books for up-to-date information about high technology. Now turn to *BradyLine* for the details behind the titles.

Find out what new trends in technology spark Brady's authors and editors. Read about what they're working on, and predicting, for the future. Get to know the authors through interviews and profiles, and get to know each other through your questions and comments.

BradyLine keeps you ahead of the trends with the stories behind the latest computer developments. Informative previews of forthcoming books and excerpts from new titles keep you apprised of what's going on in the fields that interest you most.

- Peter Norton on operating systems
- Winn Rosch on hardware
- Jerry Daniels, Mary Jane Mara, Robert Eckhardt, and Cynthia Harriman on Macintosh development, productivity, and connectivity

Get the Spark. Get *BradyLine*.

Published quarterly, beginning with the Summer 1990 issue. Free exclusively to our customers. Just fill out the form below and mail it to Brady Books, 15 Columbus Circle, New York, NY 10023, Attn: J. Padlad to begin your subscription.

Name _____

Address _____

City _____ State _____ Zip _____

Name of Book Purchased _____

Date of Purchase _____

Where was this book purchased?   *(circle one)*

    Retail Store   Computer Store   Mail Order